AF270324

It's easy to become lost—in reflection, in curiosity, in wonder, in oneself—in *It's Good to Be Lost Once in a While.* Robert J. Wicks brings to each page a veritable lifetime of psychospiritual wisdom gleaned from a stunning array of disciplines, literatures, and therapeutic encounters with seekers in every corner of the globe. He permits readers to be human, to be frail and to fail, while offering a panoply of pragmatic strategies for renewed hope and healing. Lose yourself in savoring this book over time and therein find yourself encouraged and enriched.

Robert C. Dykstra, Ph.D.
Charlotte W. Newcombe Professor of Pastoral Theology
Princeton Theological Seminary
Author, *Finding Ourselves Lost: Ministry in the Age of Overwhelm*

REVIEWS OF OTHER WORKS
BY ROBERT J. WICKS

Perspective: The Calm Within the Storm

"This is the kind of book you can't put down because it is so necessary."

Alexandra Fuller
New York Times bestselling author of *Cocktail Hour
Under the Tree of Forgetfulness*

Bounce: Living the Resilient Life

"Insightful, practical, and often humorous, *Bounce* is the right tonic for the spirit we need in a stressful world."

Helen Prejean
Author of *Dead Man Walking*

Riding the Dragon

"Compassionate and wise."

Jack Kornfield
Author of *A Path with Heart*

Night Call: Embracing Compassion and Hope in a Troubled World

"*Night Call* provides an important wake-up call for those of us in healthcare. . . . This book reminds us that in order to maintain a compassionate presence with our patients and families, we must take the time to care for ourselves, maintain a healthy perspective between work and family, and identify the value of mentors throughout our careers."

M. Tish Knobf, Ph.D., R.N., FAAN,
Professor, Yale University School of Nursing

The Tao of Ordinariness

"This is a welcome recipe as many of us struggle with ambiguity, uncertainty and the pressures of modern life."

Patricia Davidson, Ph.D.
Dean, Johns Hopkins School of Nursing

"Be afraid to try new things!"

It's Good to Be Lost Once in a While

ROBERT J. WICKS

Author

Bounce

Living the Resilient Life

Letting Go and Exploring Possibility *at Different Turns in Life*

OXFORD
UNIVERSITY PRESS

OXFORD
UNIVERSITY PRESS

Oxford University Press is a department of the University of Oxford.
It furthers the University's objective of excellence in research, scholarship,
and education by publishing worldwide. Oxford is a registered trade mark of
Oxford University Press in the UK and in certain other countries.

Published in the United States of America by Oxford University Press
198 Madison Avenue, New York, NY 10016, United States of America.

© Oxford University Press 2026

Library of Congress Cataloging-in-Publication Data
Names: Wicks, Robert J. author
Title: It's good to be lost once in a while / Robert J. Wicks.
Description: New York, NY : Oxford University Press, [2026] |
Includes bibliographical references and index.
Identifiers: LCCN 2025041516 (print) | LCCN 2025041517 (ebook) |
ISBN 9780197813805 hardback | ISBN 9780197813812 epub | ISBN 9780197813836
Subjects: LCSH: Self-realization | Uncertainty |
Failure (Psychology) | Critical thinking
Classification: LCC BF637.S4 W4846 2026 (print) |
LCC BF637.S4 (ebook)
LC record available at https://lccn.loc.gov/2025041516
LC ebook record available at https://lccn.loc.gov/2025041517

DOI: 10.1093/oso/9780197813805.001.0001

Printed by Sheridan Books, Inc., United States of America

The manufacturer's authorized representative in the EU for product safety is
Oxford University Press España S.A. of Parque Empresarial San Fernando de Henares,
Avenida de Castilla, 2 – 28830 Madrid (www.oup.es/en or product.safety@oup.com).
OUP España S.A. also acts as importer into Spain of products made by the manufacturer.

I have had the privilege of writing a number of books for Oxford University Press for both professionals and for general audiences. I consider It's Good to Be Lost Once in a While *to be a capstone book for me with Oxford. All of the previous works, and now this one, have been carefully edited by my wife, Michaele. Most authors, whether they recognize it or not, are accompanied by others who offer advice and insight as well as editorial suggestions. Of all who have given me feedback on my own work, Michaele has been at center stage in the process of refining what I have done . . . and it is to her that I dedicate this work. Thank you, Michaele, for all you have done and who you are.*

"We must be willing to let go of the life we've planned, so as to have the life that is waiting for us."

—Joseph Campbell

"Where your fear is, there is your task."

—Carl Jung

"Keep some room in your heart for the unimaginable."

—Mary Oliver

Contents

Introduction: The Expert and the Novice   1

FIELD NOTES ON BEING AWAKE TO POSSIBILITY

1. Beginning Life Again . . . *Now*: The Art and Process
   of Careful Discernment   15

2. "If You Want to Go Fast, Go Alone. If You Want to
   Go Far, Go Together": Five Necessary Companions
   for the Journey   37

3. Invisible Fences: Understanding the Psychology of
   Personal Resistance to Growth and Change   63

4. Preparing Space for Possibility: Letting Go, Kenosis,
   Unlearning, Traveling Lightly . . . and the Delicate
   Role of Grieving   97

5. "Don't Just Sit There in Silence and Solitude. Do
   Nothing!": A Mini-Guide to Patience, Reflection,
   and Mindfulness   123

6. What Missing the Mark Can Teach Us: Failure,
   Faithfulness, and Epiphanies During Periods
   of Change and Uncertainty   165

7. Let's Be Clear About This: Basics in Critical
   Thinking and Developing More Accurate Ways of
   Perceiving and Understanding   193

8. Darkness and Gaining Previously Unattainable
   Wisdom: Applying the Principles of Post-Traumatic *Growth*   207

Epilogue: What Can I Do Most Beautifully with My Life?   229

Sources 251
Permissions 257
About the Author 259
Index 261

Introduction

The Expert and the Novice

"I always get to where I'm going by walking away from where I've been."

—A. A. Milne
Author, *Winnie the Pooh*

"Do not follow where the path may lead. Go instead where there is no path and leave a trail."

—Anonymous

Being concerned about the impact of what we don't already know is natural. However, an even greater danger to living a rich and meaningful life is what we think we already know, but really don't. As we move through the day and different phases of life, as well as new inner transitions and external change, we must recognize that we are simultaneously the expert and the novice. When we are willing to humbly honor this reality, we are more able to let go, unlearn, and embrace needed additional knowledge when necessary. In the process, we can also better discern our true gifts and welcome the heretofore unimaginable faces of . . . *possibility*!

Every September, I am reminded of my own daughter entering preschool almost 50 years ago. We asked her at the time how her first day of school was, and she said it was fun. We were relieved because many children cry for the first few days until they can adjust to the change. She liked it so much that we asked her once the school year was almost over if she would miss going to preschool. In response, she looked up and said, "No. I am tired of sitting in a magic circle." She was fortunate at that early age to recognize that we need to have the sense, and sometimes the courage, to change patterns that cease to be life-affirming for us.

Whether we are 5, 25, 45, or 75 years of age or older, it is important to honor when one phase of life—no matter how good it has been—is ending and another is beginning. It is time to leave the "magic circle" of the past and venture into the new place that we are now called to be. We must, in the words of French philosopher Albert Camus, respond to our "lucid invitation to live and to create."

When we ask ourselves the wrong questions or our questions are not big enough, life is never as deep or large as it might have been if we had discerned more carefully who we are and what we might do next at each stage in life. This is so, no matter how successful we might become by following the plans *others* may have had for us.

And so, in one way or another, a simple but important question I pose to myself as well my graduate students and those who come to see me for psychotherapy or mentoring, is: "How are you honoring what is new or could be different in your day and life?" I think we would all benefit from asking ourselves this question from time to time. The following brief work, on encountering inner transitions, external change, and possibility, is designed to enhance such an encouraging self-questioning and examination process, even when, *especially* when, life becomes confusing and you feel uncertain or lost. As Indian philosopher, Jiddu Krishnamurti, advises, "You have to be a light to yourself in a world that is becoming utterly dark."

Today, a sense of being or existing in the darkness is almost a psychological epidemic among the young. In addition, those who are adults often lament that life doesn't seem as secure and clear as it was when they were growing up and maturing. In response to these challenges, in many instances people don't know the correct timing to let go of the status quo, the people who are holding them back, present occupations, or the current way they are viewing the world. When this happens, there is a tendency to pull back rather than to discern what they must know in order to risk entering and making the most of a transition or place in life. When change is necessary—even after experiencing a significant loss or trauma—a crossroad presents itself to everyone: either alter one's perspective, let go, and open the door to new ways of living, or nostalgically hold on and seek to *exist* in the past rather than live fully in the present and the future that awaits them. It truly is all right to be lost once in a while. People who think they *should* always know where they are going may feel like failures in the midst of change instead of realizing that change is a constant in life and can even offer new opportunity for growth.

American novelist and nonfiction writer Anne Lamotte once shared her feelings about when she was young and trying to take care of her mother when she began showing symptoms of Alzheimer's. She cried out to the gerontology nurse that she and her brothers didn't know how to help her mother take her meds and deal with the day's tasks. To which the nurse gently replied, "How *could* you know?" Lamotte said that this obvious reality had not crossed her mind until she was asked this question. Through the awakening question by the nurse, she and her brothers could then start where they were: *not knowing.*

When people always feel they know where they are going, they also don't leave room for unexpected experiences and opportunities to see life in new ways, particularly during different turns in their day and life. They are like those who pre-schedule their holidays so efficiently that there is no space left for a surprising joy. Security and control are understandably desirable at times but can be too costly if they are the only things primarily sought. Whereas "being lost" paradoxically may not be bad, but instead be a clear invitation to become more psychologically alive in untried, creative ways. To respond to such "calls" we must be both willing and able to let go, unlearn, and meet life's invitations for us to be open so that we can both understand and meet developing situations and inner transitions in the most enriching ways possible.

Letting Go

English novelist and short story writer D. H. Lawrence once warned: "The world fears a new experience more than it fears anything. Because a new experience displaces so many old experiences." Yet, at times, true progress often involves letting go of what is preventing us from moving on—especially when we are being asked to honor a very different challenge in life.

Many years ago, I had a simple but graphic illustration of this when I was in Quantico, Virginia, training to become a U.S. Marine Corps Officer. All of the candidates, including myself, were traversing what they euphemistically referred to as "the confidence course." It included what I found to be some of the most daunting physical challenges I had encountered up to that point as a young man in civilian life. The drill instructor (DI) would demonstrate how to do it, and then all of us were ordered to follow his example. In the middle of the course, I experienced a surprise. There was a seemingly quite simple obstacle. It was a small ditch and over it was positioned a wooden A-frame with a rope hanging from it. The task was straightforward. As the DI demonstrated, you just needed to run quite quickly toward it, grab the rope, swing over to the other side of the ditch, and then keep moving forward without losing your balance.

He made it look so easy that I thought to myself, "Oh, this is a confidence builder for us after all of the previously demanding obstacles we have already encountered before we need to complete other yet even more difficult ones after it." (I was as naive back then as I am now!) However, as I continued to watch the officer candidates ahead of me attempt it, many of them failed. Some of them ran up to the obstacle, grabbed the rope, swung over, and then swung back. Others, reached for the rope, swung over, touched their feet down on the other side while still holding onto the rope, lost their balance, and fell into the ditch.

As I watched this, I wondered to myself, "What was the problem? What did I need to do to emulate the DI's approach?" Then, all of a sudden, the solution struck me. To successfully complete this task, you needed to run as fast as you could, grab the rope, swing over, and in midair . . . *let go*! If you waited until your feet were securely placed, it was too late. This is often the case at various turns in life. In such circumstances, we are called by the demands of the new situations to let go of the need for security and familiarity. Instead of relying solely on what we *already* know, we need to become more open and willing to *unlearn* in order for true change and different, richer ways of viewing life and ourselves to become possible. Otherwise, we will simply block the calls to mature and deepen in new ways.

Unlearning and Greeting Uncertainty and Change in Life . . . *and in Us*

The one constant in life is *change*. If it is not honored with a willingness to let go, open ourselves up to a new style or phase when necessary, and exhibit a sense of self marked by intrigue, acceptance, and mindfulness, we risk missing so much potential joy. When we close our "emotional and cognitive eyes" to change and fail to be alert to new possibilities, we merely exist in a psychological bubble, referred to as "the known past." The psychological price may become expensive for behaving this way. In addition, as I previously noted in my work, *The Simple Care of a Hopeful Heart*, on mentoring yourself in difficult times, hanging around waiting for the past to change, like so many people do, is also a waste of time and energy. In contrast, a spirit of unlearning and mindfulness teaches us to benefit from the moment we are in by fully exploring, embracing, and appreciating it, so we will be better able to let go of the present and change when the need arrives.

From the wisdom figures I have personally met, or from reading what they have written, I have always been impressed by their respect for uncertainty and a spirit of unlearning. It is as if the more education and experience they had, the more they realized how much they *didn't* know. Those who were so certain about their beliefs were quite different: It is as if they had walked into the corner of a psychological room early in their lives, memorized the surroundings, and spent their lives imprisoned there . . . while proclaiming loudly and repeatedly that those who would venture out to learn anew and be open were foolhardy. There was no need for a lock on their "psychological doors" . . . they didn't know they were in an interior prison (sadly of their own making). When people such as this trade love, compassion for those different than they are, and an imaginative heart for fear and familiarity it is such a shame. While they feel safe existing within a small psychological space until they die, they miss going out into "the forest of new life" where the fresh air of spiritually alive encounters can be deeply felt in their hearts.

Yet, to be open and humble enough to admit we are lost or need more help/information is easier said than done. It is so easy to unknowingly become wedded to our opinions and former successful navigations in life that being in a good position to recognize when we are merely repeating our errors can be a real challenge—no matter how much contrary information we are offered. Moreover, as is demonstrated in the following classic story by spiritual writer and psychologist Anthony DeMello, in his book *Awareness*, many of us run the risk of holding onto our views so firmly that even when there is no proof they are correct, we still refuse to budge:

A woman suddenly stops a man walking down the street and says, "Henry, I am so happy to see you after all these years! My how you have changed. I remember you as being tall, and you seem so much shorter now. You used to have a pale complexion, and it is really so ruddy now. Good grief, how you have changed in five years!"

Finally, the man gets a chance to interject, "But my name is not Henry!"

To which the persistent woman calmly responds, "Oh, so you've changed your name, too!"

Openness and a willingness to meet needed change in our lives are essential—*particularly* when we move from one phase in life to the next. Each day, a dynamic, fulfilling life relies on our willingness to welcome the new challenges and approaches that are necessary if we are to effectively navigate the different time periods. So, what might we do to prepare to accomplish this, given all that is already facing us and requiring our attention? This is the very practical question we must address given the time-consuming daily demands and tasks facing most of us today.

Psychologically Seeding Simple Changes in Ourselves

Unfortunately, in today's bustling and demanding world, few people seem to have time during the day to read and reflect for any length of time. Some realize that reading should be an essential part of a rich life. However, even in those cases, despite their best intentions, reading and reflection are often left for the weekends, and then usually only involve enjoying fiction because they understandably wish to escape, to enter and enjoy other imaginary worlds for relief. And so, given that this situation applies for many of us, the following chapters in this book have been fashioned so that no matter how harried a schedule one has, there is usually time to quickly read, or at least skim a short piece of each chapter, about a single topic.

Then, after reading several pages or a chapter, another doable task is to take only a moment or two in silence and solitude to reflect upon what you wish to take from each entry. Following this, the straightforward task is to select a "word" or "theme" to carry with you over the day or week ahead to see how it psychologically and spiritually blossoms for you. In this way, you can make the theme *yours* by letting it come to life given *your own* history, experience, personality, psychology, and philosophy or spirituality. In addition, these themes are designed to be "psychological seeds" to prepare you for undertaking little and significant changes in your life that will open the emotional doors to more fully experiencing the present or next phase in a dynamic life . . . *your* life. They are framed in a way to help you encounter, with greater awareness, the little time all of us have on this earth. When people achieve such a sense of mindfulness, it is easy to see it in both their attitude and actions. When they don't that is obvious as well. As Jamaican composer and performer Bob Marley is credited, among others, to have pointed out: "Some people feel the rain . . . others simply get wet."

All of us have the possibility to enter and experience each day and phase of our own lives more richly by retaining the wisdom that is "evergreen" and timeless while knowing when to let go of knowledge that may have been both accurate and helpful in the past, but is no longer as useful in the present or in going forward. The choice as to how we will respond to the call to move on, of course, remains in our hands. With this option in mind, the contents of the themes to follow are designed to make the journey clearer and, yes, more possible. This will be done by encouraging more intentionality through focusing on the basics of letting go, unlearning, and mindfully recognizing and embracing transitions *from a number of different angles*, including the:

- Psychological literature on overcoming resistance to change and improving clarity in our ways of reflecting, perceiving, and understanding
- Philosophical and educational writings on critical thinking
- Classic spiritual wisdom on how to enhance the process of discernment through mindfulness
- Recognition of "uncertainty" and failure as offering potential benefits rather than solely being problems to avoid or overcome
- Recent findings on post-traumatic *growth* that help us appreciate how we can deepen as persons as a result of "dark times" in ways that might not have been possible had the difficulties or trauma not happened in the first place

As noted at the beginning of this introduction, openness is a critical element for embracing the true possibilities of change—even when feeling lost. Once again:

Most people feel that it is what they don't know that will hurt them, and this is true to an extent. However, an even greater danger for all of us is what we think we already know . . . but really don't.

In essence, the probability of a new possibility being successfully welcomed increases dramatically when we are humble enough to psychologically quiet our opinions in order to see life, particularly at a new phase, differently. Remember, when we take knowledge and we add humility, we increase the chances for gaining new wisdom. Whereas, without humility, we may cognitively remain in elementary school long after we should have matured and "graduated" to a more advanced level of development in our lives.

Each day and phase of life offers a distinct *possibility* for something new. And so, if you have thrown seeds and they don't take root, maybe you need to consider different or new "soil" upon which to cast your hopes, talents, and love. Given this, the chapters to follow are meant to be psychological entryways so we don't miss the different challenges and joys each turn can offer us. However, when, why, and how we traverse these openings to understanding and embracing a new life is up to each of us. Information and good guides can help, but, in the end, it is up to us to take the time and energy to put the desire to learn anew *into action.* As the old adage goes:

> In discernment, you don't solely think your way into a new kind of action, you also need to act your way into a new kind of living.

In this regard, some thoughts offered by author and spiritual guide Christine Koellhoffer were a good awakening for me as I read them on an early sunny, warm morning. She shared in a post that *"Wait Wait . . . Don't Tell Me,* the NPR news quiz, was streaming, and it featured an interview with writer James Patterson. As the prolific author of over 60 books on the *New York Times* bestseller list, Patterson was asked what motivated him. He said that early on in his career, he heard a quote that reminded him his time was limited, and because of that, he should ask himself, 'So what can I do most beautifully?' For Patterson, that clarified what became his life's calling: telling stories."

As I watched the early sunrise and read this, a similar question came to mind for me: What talents have I been especially gifted with to share with others most beautifully . . . and, in the process, how can I help others share their talents? Yet, in asking myself this, I needed to realize that I was embracing the word "beautifully" not "successfully" because my insights may not be the ones others need. It may even cause some people to respond negatively because they upset their dark or limited view of the world caused by undesirable events and difficult people early in their own life. Sharing "beautifully" also meant my doing it while expecting nothing in return and not personalizing any cynical responses I might receive. After all, that is the beauty of a gift-giving, isn't it? A gift should be freely given to others as we also move with a spirit of openness to what gifts we are being offered today as well.

I realized further that nature offers a view of its uniqueness without any effort at all. In the case of people, it is usually a different story. Some want to be different in order to get attention, whereas there are those of us who simply want to be ourselves which happens to be different from other people. Distinguishing between the two is important in how we treat those we encounter . . . *and ourselves.* After all, isn't true ordinariness tangible wonder?

In the end, change may not only be hard, inconvenient, uncertain, and often scary at times, but these emotions, reactions, and realities can also turn out to be the most efficient gateways to experiencing new possibility. Ignoring such signs to alter our approach going forward, or waiting for it to change to our liking, is not a healthy option. The rewarding trajectory of our life for us and those in our circle of friends and family, as well as those in our work or educational setting who interact with us, depends on how we greet change and take advantage of possibility.

Careful discernment about the choices we have already made and the choices we still have before us never really ends. In the words of novelist C. S. Lewis, "You are never too old to set a new goal or dream a new dream." As long as we are alive, the chance for greater psychological and philosophical or spiritual fullness never ends as long as we value, and seek to have, an open and receptive attitude. When we have such an approach to life, we are able to see revealing information from "the corner of our psychological eye" that might be missed had we not been courageously attentive and experienced joy in the process of discovery. Adam Grant, in his book *Hidden Potential,* notes that "Progress rarely happens in a straight line; it typically unfolds in loops." This often involves departures and detours from our current intentions and goals, but—as he aptly notes as well—a digression can also prove to be a new impressive source of energy.

Knowing this helps us to see uncertainty as a new door to deeper knowledge rather than something to cause anxiety. We begin to recognize that it is even good to be lost once in a while. After all, who knows what we might experience and learn during such detours that will dramatically change us and our situation for the better? Even in interpersonal relations, isn't it important that we pay full attention to those we encounter—including those closest to us? Truly listening not only to others but to our own reflections as well is a sign of love and respect. And that is what discernment, and this book, is about: listening to ourselves more clearly and completely, and being more open to change by unlearning and letting go in order to become better at greeting . . . *possibility!*

American writer, James Baldwin, once quipped, "Not everything that is faced can be changed, but nothing can be changed until it is faced." However, the reality Baldwin addresses often overwhelms people so instead they choose to follow one of two unhelpful extremes: Either they run away, thinking that they can't make an impact, or they feel that if they do see the tough parts of reality, they believe they should be able to fix all of them or they are naive failures. Neither approach is true or helpful for them . . . or society. Instead, what is necessary for each of us to do is face life fully and do what we can. This is a simple and very needed approach, but not a popular attitude today. We must remember that discouragement (which is the last home of the ego) and inaction help no one—including *ourselves.*

Leading a Beautiful, Meaningful Life

Leading a life with meaning does not happen by accident. However, difficulties, if handled properly, can actually deepen us. As Elizabeth Kübler-Ross, known for her work on death and dying, recognizes, it isn't good fortune or an ability to succeed that is a key factor in leading a life worth living. Instead, she notes that the beautiful people she has known are ones who have suffered, experienced defeat, had great losses, and in the process found their way out of the darkness. In doing this, she said that such persons have a greater appreciation, understanding, and sensitivity for life and it can be seen in their sense of compassion, kindness, and love for others. In her own words, "Beautiful people do not just happen."

Similarly, Austrian neurologist, psychologist, philosopher, and Holocaust survivor Viktor Frankl had a deep belief that if we can say "yes" to life— no matter what our circumstances might be—we would truly be able to live with a greater sense of meaning. In this regard, he quoted German poet and dramatist Christian Hebbel, who said, "Life is not something, it is the opportunity for something." Frankl's sense was whoever had a "why" (a meaning) for life was able to live in a way that the "what" (our circumstances) were secondary. For him, meaning was something to be found and discovered and is not simply given to us.

The search for meaning also goes hand in hand with seeing, seeking, and embracing possibility. Moreover, it has been shown to have a positive impact on mental health, decreasing depressive tendencies and increasing a spirit of hope. Essentially, when we have meaning in our lives, *we feel good!*

What is fascinating is that finding meaning in our philosophical/spiritual beliefs, educational or professional pursuits, or other areas of our life is qualitatively different for each of us. The sad part is that some people are not aware of the importance and uniqueness of their own search until they become lost or lose something or someone important to them. It is at this point that post-traumatic *growth* and new psychological depth become possible. Meaning moves us. It also is something that has us interpret the world in a certain way—one that can crush us and leave us permanently lost or be the beginning of psychologically, spiritually, and philosophically spawning an even deeper, broader, more mature and compassionate outlook with respect to the world, others, and ourselves. Our perspective matters!

Buddhist monk Matthieu Ricard, who also has a Ph.D. in molecular genetics and is the author of the bestselling book *Happiness*, puts the challenge to strengthen our interior life before us well when he writes:

> We willingly spend a dozen years in school, then go on to college or professional training for several more; we work out at the gym to stay healthy; we spend a lot of time enhancing our comfort, our wealth, and our social status. We put a great deal into all this, and yet we do so little to improve the inner condition that determines the very quality of our lives.

Ricard recognizes that like birds who have lived too long in captivity, when we have the possibility before us to "fly," we merely return to the cages we have known for so long. People make decisions to convince themselves they are helpless due to past or present circumstances. Yet, a new life with greater meaning becomes available to us when our spirit is fired by a willingness to let go, unlearn, reflect, think more critically, and see the opportunity for possibility unimaginable up to this point *because of*—*not* merely in spite of—failure, tragedy, or loss.

We need to appreciate and embrace the simple sentiment of Robert Peterson in his work *The Book of Amazing Stories*: "You are always one decision away from a totally different life." *It's Good to Be Lost Once in a While* recognizes and supports this by offering information on:

- Discernment
- Discovering the five types or voices of friendship needed in our circle of friends

- Appreciating and uncovering the resistance to change that all of us encounter in some form
- Valuing kenosis (an emptying of self) and letting go
- Understanding the role of mindfulness
- Knowing how to experience failure and uncertainty so the results can deepen us, as well as enable us to appreciate the value of critical thinking—especially in resistance to a culture around us that often devalues truth and has little use for a key element of wisdom—*humility*
- Seeing how to apply the principles of post-traumatic *growth* in encountering darkness in ourselves, family, friends, and contemporary society

The subject of this book is so essential to leading a rich, meaningful, and generative life that you will find in reading it that I have intentionally done two things. First, in addition to sharing my own experiences, clinical findings, and personal discoveries, I have included the words of numerous other psychologists, known philosophers, critical thinkers, and respected spiritual sages from an array of religious traditions. As these respected wisdom figures have "walked alongside" me—especially when I felt lost—I wanted to give you the opportunity to have the same advantage. In this capstone work for me, I hope you enjoy the quotes and their wisdom.

Second, I have also compressed a good deal of information in lists at the end of each chapter under a "For Review and Reflection" heading. My goal was to minimize interrupting the flow of each chapter, while at the same time being able to include material which can provide a succinct summary and stimulus for additional consideration, as well as personal note-taking, on the topics discussed.

All this information really is a response to a central, important question all of us need to individually face *again and again*: What can I do most beautifully with my life? While the answer to it will be our own, once again, if we don't have helpful companions for the journey and ask ourselves the right questions, we will never find out who we truly are to become at each phase of our lives—even when all may seem lost. And, if we feel this is only romantic thinking, we can turn to such persons as President Nelson Mandela of South Africa who, having spent 27 years in prison, would proclaim: "The greatest glory in living lies not in never falling, but in rising every time we fall." He wanted to be proud of his future life, no matter how long it would last. We should feel the same about our lives . . . and do what we can to see that it happens. Not only we, but also others, dearly depend on it.

FIELD NOTES ON BEING AWAKE TO POSSIBILITY

1

Beginning Life Again . . . *Now*

The Art and Process of Careful Discernment

"Beautiful days do not come to you. You must walk toward them."

—Rumi

"You can't see the whole path ahead. But there is usually enough light to take the next step."

—Henri J. M. Nouwen

"Follow your heart but take your brain with you."

—Alfred Adler

Discernment is the ability to judge wisely. When it is absent from our daily lives, our life will be the lesser for it. In one of the *Harry Potter* movies, Dumbledore tells Harry, "Harry, it's not our abilities that make us who we are; it's our choices." While on the surface these may seem similar, living as a discerning person is vastly different from drifting through each day driven by possibly unexamined, lesser, or misguided values. True joy is a characteristic often found in the discerning individual—regardless of how challenging their circumstances may be.

If we are fortunate enough, appreciating this can be deeply revealing and enlightening. It may even serve as a dramatic lesson—one that marks a significant turning point in how we choose to live. With this understanding, Joseph Rudyard Kipling, an English novelist, short-story writer, poet, and journalist born in British India, warned, "Beware of overconcern for money, or position, or glory. Someday you will meet a man who cares for none of these. Then you will know how poor you are." His message: Don't miss the true point of your journey by neglecting to become a discerning person here and *now*.

Discernment includes the process of *unlearning* and letting go of what is no longer helpful for us by examining the sources of our *current* philosophy, ethics, and behavior. This process helps us determine whether the "call" to believe, think, understand, perceive, and act the way we do is clearly generative. It involves unmasking unhelpful directions such as:

- Unnecessary fears of taking steps that would actually enrich life
- Inordinate self-interest that deprives us of the personal joy that arises from compassion and reaching out to others in need
- Cultural, family, or peer pressures to move in a direction that is not in line with either our personality or interests
- An overwhelming desire to be liked, resulting in the suppression of sharing our own views or living by the ethics we prize
- The presence of significantly unreasonable self-doubt
- A failure to ask "the right" or large enough questions of ourselves
- An inordinate wish to be successful rather than being faithful to a worthy ideal inspiring a life of meaning
- A lack of respect for, and sufficient discernment of, when there is a need for greater patience on the one hand or sufficient determination in those instances when it is called for on the other
- An overpowering concern about not being increasingly financially well-off—even when, by most standards, we already have "enough"
- An extreme need to be admired or seen in a positive way by others, which drains us emotionally when the true reality is most people don't get up in the morning thinking about us
- A failure to seek and further explore our "signature strengths" and recognize under what circumstances they become our growing edges and need "psychological pruning" in some way
- An erroneous belief that if we are not able to accomplish things *totally* on our own, without the advice or assistance of others, they are not as important or reflective of our own self-worth

Falling prey to such unhelpful influences can even lead us to ask ourselves the wrong—or not large enough—questions. This poses a real danger to our ability to carefully discern what truly aligns with who we are and the gifts we possess.

Rejoicing in our authentic selves is not easy, given the powerful influences that surround us. Many people believe that being "simply yourself" is easy. In the words of the fine poet e.e. cummings, "To be nobody but yourself in a world which is doing its best, night and day, to make you everybody else—means to fight the hardest battle which any human being can fight, and never stop fighting." True ordinariness is a tangible wonder because it has become so rare today. In modern society, many people struggle to discern who they really are and the person they might grow into—especially when equipped with the right attitude, helpful influences, and supportive friends. Instead, they often allow external voices or their own unrecognized poor motivations to direct their psychological, relational, and occupational paths, guided by some of the unhelpful reasons or "voices" mentioned earlier.

Being "Extra-Ordinary"

Ordinariness is an attitude or stance that allows individuals to explore and to be genuinely intrigued by the current realities around them—and by the possibilities within themselves. It is characterized by a comfortable acceptance of oneself, which fosters appropriate transparency. Key aspects of cultivating and expressing personal ordinariness include the courage to confront unhelpful external influences—whether from those who purport to have one's best interests at heart or from other sources; genuine humility to honor one's talents while honestly and gently acknowledging personal shortcomings, without judgment; and a willingness to embrace and model a lack of egoism in interpersonal relationships—approaches that foster personal freedom in others, enabling them to become more fully themselves.

Once, when Archbishop Desmond Tutu was speaking to a group of seminarians at the General Theological Seminary, one of the seminarians nudged the dean sitting next to him and whispered, "Desmond Tutu is a holy man." Curious, the dean asked him how he knew this. Without hesitation, the seminarian replied, "I know that Desmond Tutu is holy because, when I am with him, *I* feel holy."

Most people have experienced moments with "extra-ordinary" individuals—and have also received similar feedback when they are simply being themselves. This includes the willingness to be appropriately vulnerable with others. One of the signs that you have cultivated a healthy relationship with yourself is the ability to share your failures as readily as your successes. Such openness not only relieves the need to prove that you are perfect but also creates space for others to see and embrace their own faults, defenses, failures, and psychological growth edges in the same spirit.

In my own experience, I remember delivering a presentation to a packed room of 900 people at a large conference that attracted more than 20,000 participants. Afterward, a young woman—who seemed to be in her late teens or early twenties—waited patiently at the end of a line of people, most of whom had questions about what I had shared. When it was her turn, instead of asking for clarification or elaboration, she said, "Your talk wasn't what I expected." As I began to process her comment, she added, "Somehow, given the impressive credentials that the host shared about your background, I thought you would talk down to us. Instead, you spoke candidly about your own challenges, as well as shared personal stories and ideas that were practical. You walked *with* us."

Her words touched me more deeply than those of anyone else in the room. I realized that in this moment my ordinariness and appropriate transparency, as well as my faith in those listening—rather than simply expecting them to trust me—had come across clearly. My own voice, which I tried to offer in a clear, honest, and direct way, seemed to have created a "space" that allowed at least one person to better find her own.

Robert Brooks, one of today's leading experts, speakers, and authors on resilience and motivation, has also spoken and written about the benefits of leaders revealing their failures. Rather than diminishing respect for them, such honesty tends to foster admiration—they are seen as empathic and realistic in sharing their setbacks, doubts, and mistakes, as well as how they learned and grew from those experiences. When leaders do occasionally receive negative reactions from individuals feeling they shouldn't be "putting themselves down" in front of an audience—it often reflects more about the responder than about the leaders themselves, who are simply sharing their personal mistakes, trials, detours, and challenges.

Brooks's sharing of his own insecurities and shortcomings in various situations highlights an important point he makes: "No one is a born expert. We all require hours of practice and supervision/mentoring to reach higher levels of performance and achievement." Additionally, he has found, as I have, that others can learn more readily if their defensiveness is lowered and if the atmosphere surrounding learning is one in which we aim high— acknowledging that no one is perfect. Furthermore, when personal mistakes are shared, especially by someone recognized in a particular field, it sets the stage to also discuss the steps taken to remedy the situation.

To move in this direction more often, there are some basic attitudes and tasks in seeking to find or more fully develop "our own voice." Central among them is the need to affirm that each person—including ourselves—possesses a unique style and gift worthy of being discovered and heard.

As previously mentioned, financial status or education do not necessarily determine the happiness that comes from exploring and experiencing ease with ourselves. Nor do they guarantee the freedom to accept others as they are. This is often in sharp contrast to contemporary claims about what is required for a satisfying life. Therefore, careful discernment about how we wish to live is quite important. As contemplative writer and the author of the well-known autobiography *The Seven Storey Mountain*, Thomas Merton, cautioned, "People may spend their whole lives climbing the ladder of success, only to find, once they reach the top, that the ladder is leaning against the wrong wall."

To embrace such an attitude—similar to the example of Desmond Tutu and the young woman listening to my talk—we must be willing to engage in the daily process of reflecting on and acting out of a true sense of self-awareness by:

- Affirming the belief that each person has a unique voice to be discovered through reflection, discussion with psychologically healthy and optimistic friends, and a focus on the talents and fears, or the familial or societal influences, that hold such gifts back from being fully developed
- Taking risks in exploring our "quiet gifts" . . . those we may not feel we have but which others have reflected that they see in us
- Honoring the discipline and patience that build on the courage to experiment with innovative behavior
- Expanding our tolerance for failure and looking foolish, as these experiences naturally accompany the deeper exploration of ourselves and our talents. At the same time, we must shine a brighter "psychological light" on our unnecessary fears and anxiety. (After all, metaphorically, it is silly to grimly hold onto the side of the pool when we could be swimming in it happily.)
- Knowing that being concerned about uncovering what actions we can take is good—whereas, wasting our energy on worrying, rather than using it to explore possibilities to be creative and act, is not.

An important caveat to consider is that knowing how to achieve the above is not a complete prerequisite for discovering and enjoying our true self. There will always be an element of mystery, along with deliberate and ongoing efforts to discover, value, and share our sense of self. Each phase of life presents unknown demands and new possibilities, and that is what makes these transitions so interesting!

Pat Schneider, in her book *Writing Alone and with Others*, reflects this reality in her own life. She describes her search for her unique voice by admitting, "I feel tangled as if I am on the edge of a jungle and have lost my machete." The process of exploring what it means to "simply" be our ordinary selves doesn't exclude sometimes feeling lost. Mystery is an inherent part of the search, and so is fear. The adventure of being ourselves—whether in reality or in imagination—can be quite challenging. Yet, as the well-known author and contemplative guide Thomas Merton notes in his book *A Vow of Conversation*, these tough realities need not be the final, insurmountable barriers that hold us back. He writes, "What matters is the struggle to make the right adjustment in my own life and this upsets me because there is no pattern for me to follow . . . in freedom. Hence my fear and my guilt, my indecisions, my hesitations, my back tracking, my attempts to cover myself when wrong, etc." Later, though, he adds the following: The "answers tend to be confusing and to hide the truth for which one must struggle in loneliness—but why in desperation? This is not necessary."

We who live, who have been born, and who possess a personality that can be genuinely known and honestly shared with others have a duty to encourage its growth. If we don't seek to allow it to bloom, but instead suppress or distort our talents to please others, we are essentially mocking existence and our singular place in it. Paradoxically, the community that perhaps influences us to conform will be diminished by the absence of our "ordinary presence."

To fully develop as a person requires an appreciation of our inherent worth, as well as a deeper recognition of our natural resistance to continuing on the path toward freedom and health. John Sanford, an American Jungian analyst, notes in his book *Healing and Wholeness* that even when we believe in the importance of the ongoing search for growth, the process can often feel discouraging. He cautions: "Deep inside each organism is something that knows what that organism's true nature and life goal is. It is as though there is within each person an inner center that knows what constitutes health. If our conscious personality becomes related to the inner center, the whole person may begin to emerge, though this may not bring either peace or social adaptation, but conflict and stress. . . . The movement toward health may look more like a crucifixion than adaptation or peace of mind."

The effort to help the whole person emerge requires a strong belief in the importance of facing the truth about ourselves. The relief we gain from defenses and avoiding who we are is only temporary. The cost of ignorance is too great—by not fighting the good fight to be ourselves, as e.e. cummings noted, we die a little each day, torn by anxieties and compulsions that trouble, bore, and leave us unsatisfied. In doing so, we may put others at ease by conforming to their expectations, but we will never satisfy the deep restlessness or hunger for experiencing and living the life we feel we were uniquely called to live.

The exploration of the possibilities of our ordinary selves is a never-ending journey. While a primary task of adolescence is to establish a sense of identity, that task does not conclude there. To be truly clear about who we are requires significant effort, energy, and determination. It also demands patience, perseverance, and a tolerance for failure—qualities we may not yet fully possess. However, setbacks and difficulties do not close the door to becoming stronger and more fully embracing our personal narrative. In fact, much like an experienced sea captain learning from mistakes and actively working to correct them in the present, we can deepen our understanding of ourselves and become even more adept explorers of the depth of our ordinary selves.*

Martin Seligman and others have advanced the pursuit of a more comprehensive understanding of the self through what is now called "positive psychology." This approach is not simply about sugarcoating things or ignoring negative realities; rather, it is a profound perspective that values the positive just as much as the negative. Too often, psychology and society in general have emphasized the negative, viewing the positive as superficial or trivial. A quick glance at television news reveals how society tends to prioritize sensational negative stories over positive news.

To help ourselves and others develop a stronger, more complete sense of self, we must ask questions that encourage openness and growth. Some simple yet powerful questions might include:

- What gifts do you feel you haven't explored and shared with others as fully as you would like?
- In what way have you found that your own darkness or the suffering of other people have enabled you to be more grateful for what you have in your life that is wonderful?

---

* For a more complete discussion of "ordinariness" please refer to my book *The Tao of Ordinariness: Humility and Simplicity in a Narcissistic Age* (New York, Oxford University Press, 2019).

- What are some recent experiences or ways of viewing yourself that you felt broadened your sense of self?
- In looking over your life, what events have made you value your own life differently and more deeply?
- What words would you like included in your epitaph, and how might you practice them more fully at this point than you might have been able to practice them when you were younger?
- Given your sense of self, what is the mission you have had in your life to this point—even if it hasn't been seen as this—and how would you like it to change now?

A fuller understanding of our primary talents—as well as the less-developed ones—enables our awareness to become richer, both for ourselves and for those in our family, circle of friends, and the wider network of people we encounter. Such clarity also helps us avoid becoming *novelists* of our lives, blending fiction with reality to make our sense of self seem more appealing, fascinating, or boastful in our own minds. Recognizing and fathoming more of our gifts—both small and large—allows us to accept the reality of our total self as enough. In this place, we become "extra-ordinary," appreciating the wonder of simply being, and this awareness in turn empowers us to help others explore their own sense of self with a greater sense of curiosity and awe. Additionally, we need to discern what is worth our energy and what is better left aside.

Positive Psychology . . . *A Closer Look*

One of the more contemporary movements in the behavioral sciences garnering special attention—recently mentioned—is positive psychology. This field does not seek to minimize or deny the defensive tendencies in people or the darkness present in society. Instead, it is based on the premise that if we do not also focus on individual strengths and on the positive aspects of society (such as libraries, families, and schools), we are not seeing the full picture. Therefore, an essential part of discernment is to help ourselves—and, if possible, others—to uncover and nurture personal strengths. This is important because when children, or even adults, don't know how to discover, employ, test, and develop their talents, those talents are at risk of remaining untapped, distorted, or underdeveloped. That's why searching for the best in ourselves is not merely a nicety; it is an imperative if we are to respond to the opportunities and possibilities that arise at each stage of life.

As Alan Carr emphasizes in his seminal work *Positive Psychology: The Science of Happiness and Human Strengths*, adults with a positive outlook tend to have a greater sense of curiosity and intrigue about life, and children who adopt a positive perspective learn more quickly. Consequently, with such individuals, creativity, problem-solving, and increased productivity—along with their signature strengths being more clearly recognized and effectively applied—come into play.

Accordingly, they become more aware of which activities lead to happiness and fulfillment for them. Therefore, asking ourselves relevant questions aligned with this reality is important. Some examples include:

- What rewards am I looking for both personally and professionally?
- What challenges do I find stimulating and at a level I can meet?
- What ways can I lessen worrying about my image so that I can spend more energy focusing on my own talents, gifts, and values?

By responding to such questions, we can unearth concrete, relevant information, helping us avoid stagnation or the wasted energy of going in circles. Although this was over 40 years ago, I remember a small group experience I had at Hahnemann Medical College, where a psychiatrist cautioned us that we needed to learn which fantasies to act upon and which ones to leave unfulfilled. He also pointed out that in fantasy, all the energy is spent thinking about what we wish to do or what we hope will happen to us, resulting in no real change. In contrast, with "dreaming," while most of the energy is still focused on what could be, there remains enough to act on what we truly wish to bring into reality.

The fact that we don't always get things right doesn't mean we shouldn't learn from the past so that the future can be different. That's why discernment—the ability to understand and judge wisely—is so crucial. Whether we are making decisions during the day or transitioning from one phase of life to another, several overarching questions are important to ask ourselves. These questions are straightforward and include:

- What are the mature and immature reasons for, and ways of, responding in a positive way to a call to change directions?

- If I don't wish to make a change, is this understandably prudent or am I simply afraid of or avoiding responsibility and rejecting a chance for a richer, more compassionate life in some way?
- Do I see the value of doubt as a way of opening myself up to re-evaluating my views, and understanding of past experiences so as to see self and life even more clearly?

Such questions, while fairly simple and direct, are not always easy to address. One reason for this is that throughout life, many external "helpful voices"—whether well-intentioned or even correct at one point—have influenced us from birth. These voices may have been appropriate then but are no longer relevant now. For example, in the extreme, while it makes sense for a young child not to cross the street alone, it is clearly problematic if an older person does not do so!

Therefore, as adults, we need to "look both ways" and distinguish between these different voices, deciding which are still helpful and which promptings are no longer beneficial. Their influence can be very powerful—whether these messages are direct or indirect, learned from family, peers, society, or spiritual and philosophical communities. They can also originate from within—perhaps as positive inclinations in the past—that have become exaggerated or inappropriate over time. Accordingly, an unhealthy pursuit of success, the desire for a certain image, egoism, and exaggerated self-interest may go unnoticed because they are based on what once was good or simply enjoyable.

Moreover, internal "messages" rooted in early conditioning—and reinforced by those around us—can be transmitted nonverbally, even before we could speak or comprehend their implications. Many of those who raised us did so out of their own needs, insecurities, or unfulfilled desires. While they loved us and wanted the best, they might have unknowingly conveyed messages or teachings that no longer serve us today—indeed, that no longer serve anyone well.

Recognizing these limiting "mental fences" is also facilitated by greater awareness of our feelings. Once we can tune into the pulse of our emotions, we gain insight that prompts us to examine our ways of thinking, perceiving, and understanding more clearly. In doing so, we may discover that what feels familiar and appealing—especially with those we hold close—may actually be blocking our willingness to recognize new possibilities and take appropriate action.

To reiterate, discernment involves not only reflection and attentive awareness but also action. The act of moving toward a goal or stepping into change often reveals new information that wouldn't be available if we only stayed in the realm of thought. As 13th-century Persian scholar, poet, and mystic Rumi states, "As you start on the way, the way appears." This principle applies both to daily choices and to more dramatic turns in our personal and professional lives.

At one point, I moved from clinical practice and university teaching to retirement—seeking more time for writing and sharing presentations on self-care, resilience, maintaining a healthy perspective, and preventing secondary stress (the pressures helpers and healers experience when reaching out to others). As I prepared for this transition, a young, insightful counselor who respected me asked, "Why this move, now?" I smiled at her perceptive question. It marked an important step in my life, as I wanted to remain as much of a healing presence as possible, while also recognizing that I needed a change.

I then looked directly at her and said, "As usual, you ask questions that cut to the core. You will be a benefit to so many, as you have already been, because of your clinical insight into what is the most important reason for a change. The honest answer is simpler than you might imagine. As a psychotherapist, I needed to honor the pain that people had in dealing with their lives. It didn't matter that it might not seem so big to others. It had to be significant enough for me to honor it. Then, at one point, I realized I was on the verge of letting them down. I couldn't focus on their individual challenges as sensitively as I had in the past. In my travels around the world and here in America, I had to confront terrible individual and communal tragedies—abused children, teenagers dead or traumatized for life after the bus carrying them to a competition swerved to avoid an oncoming car and went off a cliff. I also encountered widespread suffering from starvation—not only in poor countries but also here in the United States. Moreover, due to ignorant and self-interested political leaders, refugees and the impoverished were suffering simply because their skin color or language, and some so-called religious leaders made decisions that failed to honor the intrinsic value of every person. This vast landscape of pain made me realize I was not respecting—perhaps not even seeing—the personal pain of those coming to me with their "first-world problems." They deserved my respect, but I found it difficult to provide it regularly since I couldn't see them weekly. Additionally, the demands of a full-time faculty role prevented me from responding to requests from helping professionals around the world who needed my guidance on resilience during critical times. It was time for a change."

I then said to her, "We need to honor where we are at any given moment and ask ourselves whether we can be most useful to those who seek our help. Each person, regardless of circumstances, deserves our healing attention, and we should give it wholeheartedly. We must identify who we are being called to serve at different phases of our lives—and then do everything we can to respond fully to those calls. That, for me, is the essence of being a clinician." Seeing the look on her face and her slow nodding in agreement, I knew she had heard and understood me—and that she would reflect on this in her own personal and professional life.

Signature strengths such as humility and discernment, along with the steps we are called to take when making decisions, can make all the difference. When I was speaking in South Africa about resilience to those rebuilding after apartheid, a woman approached me during the break and exclaimed, "I just can't do it anymore!" I asked her, "Well, what exactly do you do?" She replied, "I'm a social worker assigned to seek justice for women who have been sexually and physically abused. They often need to take a day off work to go to court. Since they are poor and often single parents, this is difficult for them, but they want justice, so they do it. When we finally arrive at court, the judge—usually male—looks at the papers and often says, 'I haven't had time to read this yet . . . make another appointment!'" Then, almost whispering, she added, "I'm a total failure at what I do."

After a few moments, I waited for her emotion to settle, then asked, "Who was with her at that moment, besides yourself?" She replied, "No one." I followed by asking, "Would it be an exaggeration to say that you were closer to her at that moment than anyone else in the world?" She responded, "No, that wouldn't be an exaggeration." Then, softly, I said, "And you want to leave this?" As she reflected on my question, I added, "Don't you realize that those of us in helping professions are not in the 'success' business—we are in the 'faithfulness' business."

I hope my words helped her discern what truly matters in life for those she serves and how she views her work. The same applies to all of us. Recognizing the importance of needed change—and how to pursue it—is not easy, especially when we face what we might call "failure." Any effort that can help us choose the most helpful attitude or path is worthwhile. It can make all the difference—not only in our lives but also in the lives of our family, friends, colleagues, and those who reach out to us in some way.

What Questions Make Discernment Work Better?

And so, discernment about potential changes in life is facilitated by asking ourselves specific questions that deepen our consideration of the personal and situational factors involved. Carefully questioning ourselves requires time for reflection—before, during, and after decision-making. It involves identifying patterns and examples that bring to life the various options, especially those made in connection with certain people, organizations, or communities. As noted earlier, this process includes gathering as much information as possible on our own, embracing the wisdom of others, thoroughly reviewing the alternatives, and carefully considering the implications of the choices we make.

In doing so, our core values, goals, ideals, and integrity must guide us as we transition from one phase of life to another or make important daily decisions. Each of these moments presents unique challenges, limits, and possibilities. Even in the final stage of life—often characterized by society as a time of limited possibilities—we are still free to see the world in ways that were not accessible in youth or middle age. As Kurt Vonnegut's character in his novel *The Piano Player* remarks, "Out on the edge you can see all kinds of things you can't see from the center." To this, American author, writer, and activist Parker Palmer, in his book *On the Brink of Everything*, adds, "When you ask the wrong questions, you end up with the wrong answers."

The questions we ask ourselves can help us sift through unfounded fears, unhelpful or destructive habits, and modes of thinking, perceiving, understanding, and acting. They also cultivate patience to consider alternatives without confusing it with procrastination. Discernment is a delicate process that requires us to recognize when we are genuinely seeking greater self-awareness and when we are indulging in self-absorption. If we are willing to be truly honest with ourselves and to consult trusted mentors, this often becomes evident when we are feeling moody or exhibiting self-righteousness.

Additionally, discernment is a process that allows us to be *timely* in our actions and consider whether postponing certain steps is reasonable—or whether we are instead driven by misplaced self-doubt. In such cases, we can distinguish between the desire to reach our full potential—which is a healthy aspiration—and the unhealthy need for approval, success, prosperity, recognition, or self-sufficiency.

Timing is more important than most people realize as well. Many years ago, I was invited to have breakfast with Archbishop Desmond Tutu and some of his old friends in South Africa. Unfortunately, my trip was canceled, and by the time I was able to present in Johannesburg and Cape Town, he was much older and not receiving many visitors. The opportunity to meet him was lost. This experience taught me that timing is crucial—not only in the choices we make but also in how we respond to others.

Once, a brilliant young psychotherapist presented a case to me. At one point, I asked, "Why did you say that to the patient?" He responded almost indignantly, "Well, it was the right thing to say." (Very smart people sometimes respond that way—especially when they are young.) I then softly expanded my question, saying, "Ah, let me expand the question so what I am asking is clearer: Why did you say that? Why did you say that *now*? Why did you say that now *in that way*? And, *What did you expect for an answer*? Timing is crucial, doctor. It can make all the difference." He remained silent and nodded before making an additional response. Reflection on, and timing in, the changes we decide to make in our own lives, and the interventions we make with others—whether informally or professionally—can significantly influence outcomes. When facing change, especially in the face of the unknown or the "unfathomable," remembering this is more practical and important than most people realize.

Furthermore, the "lyrics" of discernment—the questions about where we are heading—are supported by the "music" of meaning-making. This is a generative attitude rooted in values that, at the end of life, will minimize sadness and disappointment over missed opportunities or regrets about how we acted. In *The Top Five Regrets of the Dying*, Bonnie Ware reflects on the common causes for upset shared by her terminally ill patients in their final days. Some of these themes are valuable to consider at any time of life in terms of making daily and life choices. They are also echoed in Robin Sharma's book *The Monk Who Sold His Ferrari*. Such overriding tenets from them, as well as other wisdom figures through the ages, include such simple, helpful advice/themes as:

- Emphasize personal growth, meaningful relationships, and what we feel would lead to joy and peace rather than only pleasure and comfort.
- Do what you can to psychologically understand your gifts and growing edges and then be true to yourself rather than simply chasing the expectations of others.

- Take care of yourself so that you can live life more fully and compassionately. (Remember that one of the greatest gifts you can share with/model for others is a sense of your own peace, a healthy perspective, inner resilience, and worthwhile values . . . *but* you can't share what you don't have!)
- Discern the difference between reasonable risk-taking and being rash.
- Be grateful so that you can both see and enjoy what is *already* in your life.
- In choosing a way of life, emphasize balance so that you don't run through life and, in the process, miss it and those around you whom you cherish.
- Seek ways to become more in touch with, and be able to share, your feelings and values in a healthy way.
- Prioritize spending some time in silence and solitude for mindfulness meditation and reflection.
- Give yourself technology-free periods (no cell phone or computer) during the day.
- Set aside time for reading and taking notes on your own journey.
- Be mindful of the simple gifts (someone's smile, a cup of tea or coffee, a chance to take a walk) of life.
- Temper your own ego so that you don't waste time on what people think of you.

Perseverance, Proper Pacing . . . and *Patience*

Finally, in addition to responding to the earlier questions, perseverance and pacing are crucial when discerning actions throughout the day—especially as we transition from one phase of life to another. To navigate this effectively, we need to become aware of and respond to the question: When is it time to push forward, and when is patience the more appropriate course? In contemplating the answers to this question, two events in my own life particularly exemplified this.

As a young man during my training many years ago to become a U.S. Marine Corps officer, I had as a platoon mate a lawyer who wanted to be part of the military judicial system. He had also been a long-distance runner in college, and I was impressed by his ability to persevere and pace himself during our long hikes. So, I asked him how he managed it—was it simply because he was in such excellent physical condition?

His response was a surprise—and a valuable lesson—for me. He said, "Bob, it's not simply about being in good shape. You are in as good, or possibly even better, physical condition than I am. It's a matter of perseverance informed by a sense of pacing. In a long-distance race, if you cross the finish line with energy still left, you probably ran too slowly. If you peak too early, you ran too fast." After a pause, he added, "On the other hand, if, as you crossed the finish line, you were ready to vomit, you persevered at just the right speed for the entire race," and we both laughed.

This point was reinforced for me through my work with older adults—especially men—who often develop avoidable physical problems later in life. When they were young, they paid close attention to their physical condition, went to the gym, increased the repetitions and demands of their workouts, and served as excellent role models in maintaining that part of their routine. However, as they aged, instead of adjusting to their new stage of life and continuing at a sustainable level, they kept pushing themselves as they did in their youth. This often resulted in stress fractures and strained muscles that could have been avoided with proper pacing.

By honoring the stage of life we're in, we are called to make different decisions about how we live in each of them. What may be admirable at one age can become foolhardy at another. Discernment respects this reality and helps us avoid unnecessary discouragement, reduce psychophysiological disorders, and face the challenges of aging with a sense of curiosity and appreciation rather than nostalgia.

Hopefully, as we age, we will develop a greater appreciation for patience, rather than valuing rushing or confusing impulsiveness with courage. Ideas often need time to psychologically germinate, and patience allows that process to unfold. Waiting also gives us the opportunity to observe more of the factors currently at play, so our judgments are based on a richer, more relevant set of information. It also helps us stay mindful and notice what might otherwise be obvious but overlooked. Regarding this, Akiko Busch, in her enchanting work *Patience: Taking Time in an Age of Acceleration*, notes:

> In the age of multitasking, cognitive psychologists have come up with the term "inattention blindness" to describe the tendency to overlook what is happening directly in front of you because you are preoccupied with something else—the call on your iPhone, the text message or music. But

expectation can be just as distracting as these electronic devices. . . . How often do we miss what is happening in front of our eyes only because we are diverted by anticipation of something else.

She also points out that patience is not a passive exercise. While we actively wait during an inner transitional phase, transformation can occur. The time between two phases serves a purpose. For example, in waiting for treatment, acceptance of an illness may develop. During the period when we are seeking something from another person—something we wish were already in our lives—we may find it within ourselves. Additionally, delaying an immediate response often allows us to frame our words or actions in a much better way when we do eventually respond.

Patience also gives us the space to more clearly decide what is most beneficial to focus on during our day . . . and our life. Winnifred Gallagher, in her book *Rapt: Attention and the Focused Life*, writes, "The focused life requires not just a robust capacity for paying attention but also the discerning choice of targets that will invite the best possible results."

Is it any wonder, then, that one of the most frequently cited passages from Rilke's *Letters to a Young Poet* connects patience to a sense of readiness and emphasizes the importance of fully honoring the questions we may still have:

> Be patient toward all that is unsolved in your heart and try to love the questions themselves, like locked rooms and like books that are now written in a very foreign tongue. Do not now seek the answers, which cannot be given you because you would not be able to live them. And the point is, to live everything. Live the questions now. Perhaps you will then gradually, without noticing it, live along some distant day into the answer.

Yes, patience is indeed a fundamental element in the process and art of discernment. Rushing to succeed or rushing to figure out *everything* involved in making a choice—whether related to a necessary inner transition or an external change—is a mistake. We must also honor the mystery of life. Just as it is good to be lost once in a while, it can also be a source of joy when we allow life to surprise us, and this requires patience and pauses when necessary.

As Adam Alter notes in *Anatomy of a Breakthrough*: "Patience makes the difference when bad timing conspires against you—and patience often steps in to salvage ideas that come too soon." In turn, patience and reflection help us realize that seeing life's possibilities more clearly also involves recognizing the importance of having healthy friends to walk alongside us—something many overlook today.

Furthermore, as we will see, discernment not only more accurately reveals true possibilities in our lives but also heightens our awareness of the "invisible fences" we have psychologically erected—barriers that blind us from noticing and taking advantage of what is right before us. Therefore, cultivating the right kind of voices within our interpersonal network and understanding our psychological resistances can elevate the discernment process, empowering us to uncover and respond to new possibilities more effectively.

Identifying who these important people might be within our current circle of friends is key. Even if we do not see them present today, the words of Swiss psychiatrist Carl Jung remind us: "An old alchemist gave the following consolation to one of his disciples: 'No matter how isolated you are and how lonely you feel, if you do your work truly and conscientiously, unknown friends will come and seek you.'"

For Review and Reflection . . .

Key Questions to Ask

Developing Your Own Process of Discernment

When we feel a call to change—despite initial concerns—do we primarily experience a sense of peace and renewed energy about the new direction, or do we still remain anxious? If so, what additional information or support could help reduce that upset and natural hesitancy?

Have we explored the alternatives (staying the same, making other choices) to responding positively to what we feel called to do?

We often take actions that in the short run may make us feel good but in the long run are not very healthy or compassionate choices. And so, what are the many mature and immature motives, benefits, and risks for making such a change?

Taking into consideration previous appropriate obligations to others is important. Given this, how does a change now fit into the lives of family, friends, and the larger community of which we are a part?

What feedback have we sought and received with respect to discerning the possibility of a different attitude and approach to something we are facing during the day that seems to demand it, as well as what we feel may be a new calling if we are approaching a different life phase?

When we envision ourselves reacting differently or in a new role, what does it look like for us?

In terms of timing, why now instead of before or later?

What factors (personal satisfaction, a sense of calling, financial rewards, obedience to others, fame, etc.) are behind our positive or negative response?

What feelings do you have regarding your response? When you lean back and reflect, what thinking, perceiving, and understanding might be causing such emotions?

How are the needs of others determining the choice(s) being anticipated or made?

Is this decision in line with current values as to what is "the right thing" to do?

In looking back on the flow of our life, will this choice lead to something different in our life or is it in harmony with the past?

In taking a step back from this choice, how would we advise a person like ourselves who came to see us for advice with the same discernment question?

Where does this decision fit in terms of both personal short-term and long-term goals?

Will we enjoy or resent responding in the way we think we should?

Do we have a time scheduled during the day or week to review our gifts, talents, and shortcomings so that we can have a period for ongoing discernment?

Are we aware of what activities and involvement provide us not simply with satisfaction and pleasure (as good as these experiences are), but also a true sense of joy and a positive sense of challenge?

Since they are already in our lives and give us strength, what people and activities in our life do we enjoy, have gratitude for, and fully appreciate ?

What is the most important personal and professional goal you have during this phase of life?

When you ask friends and family members you trust to describe your major strengths and virtues, what do they say? In line with this, what would you add to that list, and how are you balancing and pruning these gifts so that they bloom more fully?

What are the successful strategies you have to open up new possibilities and face challenges to maturing personally and developing professionally?

What are some of the recent experiences you have had that you felt broadened you at home and at work?

How are your strengths and virtues connected with your overall philosophy of, and mission in, life?

What approach do you take to develop and maintain healthy relationships?

In your life up to this point, what ideas and beliefs have strengthened you and opened you up to see and act upon new possibilities?

Finally, which of the following sample signature strengths or supports are ones you have or need to develop further so that both daily and life phase opportunities can be seen, embraced, and acted upon?

- Creativity
- Openness and flexibility
- Hopeful, optimistic, and positive
- Responsible and dependable
- Sociable, warm, enjoyable, and friendly

- Empathic and understanding
- Analytic and a good problem solver
- Hard working
- Able to let go, so energy is available for change
- A true listener (not simply someone who remains silent waiting for their opportunity to speak) and a lifelong learner
- Considerate and sympathetic
- Reflective and takes time each day in silence and solitude
- Able to laugh at oneself
- Intrigued by ambiguity and surprises
- A balanced circle of friends

2

"If You Want to Go Fast, Go Alone. If You Want to Go Far, Go Together"*

Five Necessary Companions for the Journey

"Hold a true friend with both your hands."

—Nigerian proverb

Sometimes I am asked a question that truly gives me pause. One such question came from a highly accomplished young leader in his 30s who requested an informal mentoring session. Over tea in a small bookstore, he asked, "You have had the opportunity to work with leaders across the world in healthcare, ministry, education, politics, publishing, criminal justice, and the military. In the case of these talented individuals, what is the main challenge you have found that prevents them not only from achieving greater success professionally but—more importantly—also from taking the next leap toward psychological and spiritual maturity when it's needed?"

I could tell that this question was not merely about advancing in his field, but also about his desire to address personal transitions and delve more deeply into his own inner life. After a moment of quiet reflection, I responded, "Leaders are often paradoxically hindered by their talent. In the pursuit of many achievements, they can become blinded by a lack of humility—an inability to recognize what they don't know or to learn from sources that don't have their accomplishments or titles." The young man then paused and asked, "Well, how do you handle such people in those situations?"

In response, I smiled and said, "I simply let them be." The expression on his face showed that he was surprised by this answer, so I elaborated. "Openness is quietly difficult for the highly gifted because *their defenses can be as*

---

* Cameroonian proverb

advanced as their talents are. Hopefully, they will eventually find someone wiser and less threatening than I am, and the timing will be right for them. If that happens, they will be able to become vulnerable enough to create the inner space needed to access the wisdom necessary at that stage of life—to see and embrace new possibilities."

After a brief, quiet pause, I added, "We are not called to walk with every-one. Sometimes, the best we can offer to very talented people—who mainly use themselves as a sounding board—is simply to . . . *let them be.* However, the fact that you're asking these questions indicates that you don't just want them to be more open—you want to be that way yourself. When we seek a truly beneficial circle of friends or ask for mentorship, we're not just look-ing for answers to life's questions. Instead, we're asking for help in learning and experiencing ways to become more open—to see life, people, change, and opportunities more broadly and beneficially. Erin Matlock, an artist, author, and advocate with 13 years of leadership in the brain health and mental health fields, once said, 'There are people you meet who become impossible to forget. They were not sent to you by accident, but instead, destined to open a doorway to a different version of your life.'" In response, the young man who asked me the question nodded, and we spent the rest of the time together speaking about something both of us loved—good books we had read recently.

When I was in elementary school, I remember a teacher saying to us, "Tell me who your friends are, and I will tell you who you are." However, many of us take friendship—and its influence on us—for granted when we're young. After experiencing friends who let us down, we often become overly cautious in seeking new ones.

After a lecturing trip to India, I returned home with the saying: "When once you have been bitten by a snake, you become cautious even of a rope." Those who have been deeply hurt in relationships may find it hard to form new friendships. Additionally, most of us have experienced being let down by those close to us. If we're honest, we'll also realize that we've hurt others at times. Yet, there's an even more important reminder: "A friend knows the song in your heart and can sing it back to you when you have forgotten how it goes." Without encouraging, questioning, outrageous, inspiring, healing, and wise friends in our circle, it's easy for us to become *unnecessarily* lost.

Furthermore, in friendship, it is wise to have low expectations and high hopes. By not being blinded by a list of traits we expect of others, we can open our eyes to see the gifts they are actually offering us. Demanding more than is possible only leads to disappointment and burdens them. Yet, if we approach friendship with an openness regarding where it might lead, we increase the chance that we will truly learn more from and about relationships—and, in the process, more deeply appreciate who we are in our own eyes. It may also help us recognize how to be better friends to others, which may turn out to be no small thing for those we interact with.

People sometimes ask me, "What is one of the greatest privileges of being in the helping and healing professions?" My answer is clear: It is an honor to be among the few allowed to be present when children, teenagers, and adults cry about what they have been through—stories that hardly anyone else knows. To be invited onto such "psychological and spiritual holy ground" with those who have often hidden their pain from family and friends—sometimes behind a smile—is a simple, profound privilege. You may want to recognize this even more clearly when someone asks you to listen. In doing so, you may have the opportunity to offer a similar gift and experience the same great privilege. In turn, you will come to value even more those in your life who create such a space for you.

Sometimes, we discover this truth when life is tough. Surprisingly, when I feel temporarily overwhelmed—as a clinician with over 40 years of experience helping physicians, nurses, counselors, educators, military personnel, and relief workers under tremendous stress—I don't first think of the words of another psychologist or psychiatrist to rescue me. Instead, I recall, and have made central to my books on resilience and self-care, the simple guidance of a monk named Thomas Merton. When he saw a fellow monk looking very down, he asked him, "Brother, are you all right?" To which the monk replied that he felt quite lost and sad. Then, after a brief, quiet moment—to allow the emotion to settle—Merton smiled and said, "Courage comes and goes. . . . Hold on for the next supply."

During difficult times—and we all face them—friends can teach us that we need patience, perseverance, and sometimes even courage. *Hold on for the next supply.*

What Does a Good Friend Look Like?

Thirteenth-century Sufi mystic and poet Rumi was deeply aware of the beauty and significance of friendship—including whom he regarded as the ultimate "friend." He wrote, "From myself I am copper, through You friend,

I am gold. From myself I'm a stone, but through You I am a gem." However, he was also cautious about whom we should turn to for advice. Thus, he reminded those who sought his counsel: "When setting out on a journey, do not seek advice from those who have never left home."

Friends offer an effective presence by providing a safe space to tell our story, summarize what we have shared, and encourage sound decision-making. They also seek to avoid common mistakes such as:

- Offering premature advice
- Being uncomfortable with the psychological stress and confusion we may be experiencing
- Intimating that we should and can "get over" it when we are frozen in the face of making a choice as to how to go forward
- Nonverbally and verbally demonstrating a lack of patience with us

However, being able to tell our story and share our life with close friends, or a helping professional should we need one, even if only for one to three sessions, is so important, especially in today's insensitive and oftentimes "psychologically deaf" society, because mature friends:

- Encourage us to release both positive and negative emotions when in their presence
- Provide needed feedback and information
- Give us an opportunity to relax and regress
- Offer needed opportunity, without rushing us along, for us to tell our story
- Give us the feeling that we have truly been heard and respected

In addition, when we have been given the space to share our ideas, hopes, frustrations, fears, anger, and anxiety in a safe interpersonal environment, we are more likely to see new possibilities on our own. But perhaps, of even greater importance, when we share intense emotions, good friends do not quickly try to provide answers, fix the challenge we are facing, minimize the issue at hand, or become overwhelmed themselves to the point of pulling back. It is a reassuring, refreshing, and psychologically refreshing process— even if a solution does not arise from the encounter.

Being encouraged to tell our story is best communicated when we sit down and receive the nonverbal message: "I'm ready to listen . . . not simply hear what you are saying while waiting for an opportunity to speak." It is fostered when they ask for illustrations and start the conversation with a general question such as: "Well, I can see you are confused as to what step to take next. What exactly is involved in this call to change?" In this way, we can take a cue from them that they truly wish to listen sensitively so we feel the freedom to take the time to share in vivid terms what is going on within us and the environment in which we now find ourselves that requires careful discernment and action.

Helpful persons in our environment, after hearing our story, can help us reflect on:

- Our chief concern
- Other possibly related issues or problems
- What we did so far to deal with the situation and how effective or satisfying our efforts were
- What needs, desires, demands, joys, and frustrations we have already encountered
- The part other figures and our past learned ways of dealing with challenges such as this have played in our story

When this information is gathered and summarized by the "listener," it enables us to achieve a better understanding and a sense of what to do next. (This may simply be a recognition that we need to have patience for now, for example, in the case of newly experienced change or loss.)

Permission to Psychologically Nourish Ourselves

During a Decision-Making Process

Although there are many different decisions, changes, or problems that require reflection and action, there is an overall real need to also become more resilient through self-understanding and self-care. Given this, friends will encourage us to:

- Take care of ourselves better physically, emotionally, and spiritually when we require added energy so that we may remain healthy when facing and seeking to embrace possibility in ways we haven't before

- Take any steps we can to have more accurate self-esteem and develop a careful inventory of both our prominent and "quiet" or less-notable signature strengths
- Build greater balance in our lives by ensuring the key pieces of life and time to appreciate them are in place (reflection, work, family, outside activities, and time with friends)

When we do this on an ongoing basis, self-care can begin to replace self-condemnation and harmful types of self-denial and rash behavior.

Listening, summarizing, and providing psychologically nourishing feedback are three of the simplest, yet most important, gifts we receive from emotionally healthy friends, in their genuine desire to be sensitive to us and our needs. When we remember and feel encouraged to accept such direct and indirect feedback, it becomes possible for some degree of direction and greater clarity to emerge from the situation. It may not lead to an immediate solution, as there may not be one, but it sets the stage for a collaborative effort to identify small steps to take and the beginning of discernment regarding long-term decisions—and that, in itself, can be an essential part of the decision-making process.

In *Making Meaning of Difficult Experiences*, Sheila A. M. Rauch and Barbara Olason Rothbaum echo this sentiment, especially during times when life feels particularly stressful or traumatic:

> Our connections to other people often define how we view ourselves and our roles and expectations in life. . . . We care about people, and we care what other people think about us. When we have a difficult experience, a normal response is to consider how those around us might think about what happened to us. Do we think that they would have reacted as we did or differently? Do we think that others may feel we did something wrong or blame us for what happened? Would they think we did everything possible and want to help us feel better or even take care of us after the difficult experience? These relationships and how we perceive them can have a big impact on whether the difficult experience gets stuck in our minds or gets integrated into our life story and we move on. Years of research and clinical experience have taught us that people who reach out for help and social connection following a difficult experience are less likely to have long-lasting mental health problems. We are people who need people. . . . Unfortunately, when we are stressed, we often avoid people.

Different Voices

Psychology and the classic spiritual wisdom literature have long emphasized the importance of a strong network as a key element of emotional health, happiness, and sound decision-making. When we lack this support, the cost can be high. As the well-known Dutch spiritual writer Henri Nouwen cautions us, "We can take a lot of physical and even mental pain when we know that it truly makes us a part of the life we live together in the world. But when we feel cut off from the human family, we quickly lose heart."

An absence of at least one significant friend can even have serious health consequences. Dr. Redford Williams of Duke University tracked nearly 1,400 men and women who underwent coronary angiograms and were found to have at least one severely blocked coronary artery. After five years, those who were unmarried and did not have at least one close confidante were more than three times as likely to have died compared to those who were married, had one or more confidantes, or both.

We can listen to the voices of different types of friends who believe in us in various ways until we are able to more fully hear our own voice. In his bestselling book, *The Anatomy of a Breakthrough*, Adam Alter emphasizes this in order to help us uncover and embrace new opportunities and allow them to flourish:

> Working with new people inspires creative unsticking for at least two reasons. The first is that new people bring fresh ideas. The content of their creative thoughts is different, and novel ideas shuttled back and forth between two or more people unlock other new ideas. The second reason is that simply shaking things up has value. If part of getting stuck is about stubbornly sticking to old habits, introducing new people forces you to adopt a new style of thinking. As the researchers explained, this isn't just about new content; it's also about reorganizing old content. New blood "stimulates the adoption of new perspectives and ways of seeing thus [allowing creatives to] successfully apply old notions in different ways."

The voices of different types of friends who genuinely believe in us— listening to what we say both verbally and nonverbally—enable us to hear our own voice more clearly, leading to more careful discernment of what we are facing. This is especially valuable when we are dealing with change, transitioning from one phase of life to another, or seeking to uncover new possibilities in our day and life.

Yet, many of us believe that good friendship is something we can only fantasize about. Even when such friends are present and we say we treasure them, their presence is often not reflected upon sufficiently. Those who truly appreciate them, however, are like Abraham Lincoln, who once shared that the better part of his life consisted of friendships. This recognition is important because, when a person begins to see important relationships through grateful eyes, they can look beyond surface circumstances. We see that the famous inventor Thomas Alva Edison was clearly aware of this, noting, "I have friends in overalls whose friendship I would not swap for the favor of kings of the world." In his book *One Minute Wisdom*, Anthony DeMello describes this even more colorfully by quoting a spiritual master as saying to his disciples, "When you have the ears to hear a bird in song, you don't need to look at its credentials."

Whoever the friends or professional guides—such as psychotherapists and spiritual mentors—the safety they provide through their nonjudgmental approach hopefully fosters a willingness to respond in new ways to current demands and changes. Clinical researcher and theorist Ian Evans, in his book *How and Why People Change*, discusses this in relation to psychotherapy, emphasizing the importance of "social connectedness"—beyond casual contacts—in ways that are also reflected outside of therapy sessions. As he points out:

> As a causal mechanism for change, the key difference between social support and social connectedness . . . is in terms of the emotional and relationship intimacy that characterizes the former. Clients may have a long list of Facebook friends and spend much time texting and *Tweeting*, but still not perceive that they have someone they can turn to in times of crisis and need, both emotionally and materially. However, cultural influences, arising from the desire to belong and to identify with a larger group, share and direct behavior irrespective of the low level of intimacy involved. It is for this reason that on-line support groups can be so beneficial. When people with a common need can share often immensely intimate stories, get advice and new perspectives, and receive encouragement and the awareness they are not alone, good, if perhaps not particularly specific outcomes accrue: hopefulness, feelings of efficacy and strategies worth trying (Elgar & McGrath, 2008).

Much research on the nature of social support has confirmed that it is difficult to objectify—perceived or experienced is what is important for sustaining behavior change. Emotional support from spouses, family, and friends is surely similar to that provided by a professional therapist—having people that you can go to for assurance and sympathy. Social supporters need to be good listeners and empathic.

Once again, social support is strongest when we have people in our lives who are nonjudgmental, hold different experiences, views, and roles in our life, are open to us sharing what we feel comfortable sharing, and have enough time to cultivate mutuality. Friendship is also rich when it is:

- Based on *parity*. A friend who neither rescues nor victimizes is someone to be valued. Interdependency is a value that gives in different ways, at different times, to both friends.
- *Open* in ways that friends are free to come and go. How unfortunate it is that some people only know relationships that are imprisoning rather than freeing. We see this especially in the case of women and children involved with people who belittle or abuse them. Children who are brutally criticized often still stay connected with the abusive parent or elder . . . but they wind up not loving themselves because of it.
- *Inclusive* and not limited to only one person. Instead, there is a freedom which encourages mutuality with many different types of individuals which, in turn, leads to a broadening of outlook with respect to being open to many more possibilities in life.
- Encouraging of *growth* because friends, real friends, welcome change rather than worship the status quo.

In my own work, both personal and professional, I have found that for our interpersonal circle to be truly rich, at least five types of friends—or "voices"—need to be present (since one friend may serve multiple beneficial roles at different points in our lives). These different voices include the *prophet, cheerleader, harasser, inspirer,* and *mentor.* By having such a balanced group of voices, we increase our chances of responding effectively to change and possibility in life because these voices help us maintain perspective, balance, and openness—rather than becoming trapped in anxiety and parochialism, which can be especially dangerous in the times we are now living. With their support, feedback, and challenge to live a meaningful life, we learn to better understand and accept ourselves, while also becoming more independent thinkers. As philosopher and mathematician Bertrand Russell once warned in his book *Unpopular Essays*, "Collective fear stimulates herd instinct, and tends to produce ferocity toward those who are not regarded as of the herd." Conversely, *satsang*—a Sanskrit word meaning "gathering together for the truth"—fostered by psychologically healthy, open-minded friends, can prevent or counteract such herd mentality, which is often driven by unnecessary fear.

The Prophet

The first voice that helps us maintain balance and remain open to possibility and change in life is the one I refer to as the prophet. People in this category are not unkind or hurtful in their criticism. Contrary to what one might assume, prophetic friends do not need to look or behave differently than other close friends. The true prophet's voice can be gentle and strong at the same time. She or he lives a life guided by truth and compassion, modeling the practice of living out the truth—as Gandhi did when he proclaimed, with respect for himself: "Let our first act every morning be this resolve: I shall not fear anyone on earth… I shall not bear ill-will toward anyone. I shall conquer untruth by truth, and in resisting untruth, I shall put up with all suffering."

The message of prophets often involves discomfort because it strives to share the unvarnished truth about situations, which can lead to necessary pain. Like leaders in the nonviolent movement, they "merely" set the stage for this process, as Martin Luther King Jr. pointed out: "We who engage in nonviolent, direct action are not the creators of tension. We merely bring to the surface the hidden tension that is already alive. We bring it out in the open where it can be dealt with."

Having someone prophetic in our lives is never easy but highly beneficial. No matter how positive we may believe the ultimate outcomes will be, many of us still shy away from prophetic messages and would readily agree with Henry David Thoreau's comment: "If you see someone coming to do you a good deed, run for your life!" However, settling for comfort instead of seeking the truth may mean that, in an effort to avoid pain, we also miss important possibilities that could transform our future for the better.

Prophets point! They point to the fact that it doesn't matter whether pleasure or pain is involved; the only thing that matters is that we seek to live a meaningful life, which is reflected in what we do and how we think, feel, and perceive ourselves and the world. In other words, they remind us to seek and live "the truth," because only it can set us free.

In doing so, prophets challenge us to examine how we are living, asking ourselves: "To what voices am I listening when I form my attitudes and take action each day?" This not only refers to society's defeatist and fearful themes but also to those we have internalized unconsciously—introjected without awareness. Swiss psychiatrist Carl Jung addresses this directly, especially concerning awareness of possibility, what is holding us back, and understanding our role in moving forward: "Until you make the unconscious conscious, it will direct your life, and you will call it fate."

Conversely, even in the most difficult and dark situations, the prophet calls us to do what we can—regardless of the odds. Instead of dismissing our responsibility to see what is possible and to act accordingly, the prophet urges us to do what we can.

The following little story may illustrate this theme more clearly. As you read it, imagine the sparrow as a symbol of possibility and the horseman as the person in society who seeks comfort, flees from commitment, and only pursues what they perceive as secure:

It was a chilly, overcast day when the horseman spied the little sparrow lying on its back in the middle of the road. Reining in his mount, he looked down and inquired of the fragile creature: "Why are you lying upside down like that?"

The sparrow replied: "Oh, early this morning I heard that the sky is going to fall later today."

Upon hearing this, the horseman laughed derisively and said, "And I suppose your spindly legs can hold up the heavens?"

To which the sparrow replied: "One does what one can."

The Cheerleader

Ironically, one of the most controversial suggestions I might make regarding friendship is that we all need "cheerleaders." Some might say that encouraging this kind of friendship risks narcissism and denial.

However, to balance the prophetic voice, we also need unabashed, enthusiastic, and unconditional acceptance from certain people in our lives. Prophecy can and should invoke the appropriate concern to help us break through the psychological crust of denial. But while remorse can motivate us to do good because it makes sense, love compels us to act rightly because it feels natural.

If we only have prophetic voices in our circle, we risk burning out. Conversely, if we only have cheerleaders, we won't grow. We might be encouraged to project blame onto others and become too self-righteous to see our own misguided roles and admit our mistakes. Still, not having cheerleaders to support us and help us recognize and embrace our signature strengths creates the stage for unnecessary defeat. Both the prophet and the cheerleader are essential.

Another problem that supportive people in our community of friends help us to deal with is the presence of "deadly gnats" that plague us when we are trying to make the most of our lives. The angry, hypersensitive, passive-aggressive, and overall needy behavior of one or more people in our personal and professional lives is something we all encounter at times. Many individuals, having come from dysfunctional families, seem burdened with problems even today. However, despite this, continuously absorbing the negativity or demanding behaviors of others can become a slow, almost unnoticeable drain on our energy—one that can lead to disastrous results if left unchecked.

A number of years ago, a large search was undertaken for a chancellor of a major university system. After a long and arduous process, he was chosen— only to resign after less than a year in office. When asked about this, he said that it wasn't anything major that was overwhelming for him. It was the "gnats" that got to him. The constant bickering, complaints, obstructions, minor hostilities, hypersensitivity, and other interpersonal stresses sapped his energy and made him feel overwhelmed, underappreciated, and drained of creativity.

I didn't fully understand his situation until it happened to me a few years later. I was scheduled to go to Canada to lead a series of workshops for educators dealing with a great deal of stress. Just before leaving, I made a mistake in how I handled an issue at the university. In response, one of my colleagues unleashed various levels of anger—open sarcasm, negative comments toward others, and a disrespectful personal memo.

I knew this episode bothered me, even though I tried to handle it with calm and poise. I finally realized the full impact of it on the morning of the first workshop I was to lead. Upon waking, I sat on the edge of my bed and discovered I felt beaten and upset. It's hard to see the possibilities in your life when you are psychologically cloaked in such negativity. I then thought to myself: *My heart is so tired. How will I ever be able to reach out to those counting on me today?*

I saw that I had a very busy schedule and was unconsciously holding the unrealistic expectation that I would never encounter problems with the people hired to support my efforts. I had also conveniently forgotten my usual difficulty in dealing with people's anger and the ongoing struggle I have with over-concern about my own image. (These things always serve as reminders of my ongoing need for humility, while also embracing the signature strengths I recognize—strengths that others have affirmed are mine to enjoy and share.)

Later that morning, I was thankful that, upon seeing the faces of the teachers I was to work with, I was energized by their deep sense of commitment and their need for compassion and direction. However, I knew the issue was not yet resolved. When I returned home, I shared the episode with a close friend—someone who is definitely a "cheerleader." I explained why I felt the person who was so angry with me at the university touched a sensitive nerve. I mentioned that if another job opportunity arose, I might be tempted to take it, despite feeling called to remain in my current position. I just felt like running away from a situation where, instead of support, I was experiencing the pain of "little knives in my back." I also felt sorry for myself and kept thinking, "Where do people get the time and energy to be such a pain to those who are trying to do their best?"

But after she listened, pointed out some valid qualities I have that I was aware of, and offered a few perspectives that opened up different ways of viewing the situation and myself, I found myself well on the road to regaining a healthier and more accurate perspective.

So, while having buoyantly supportive friends may seem like a luxury, make no mistake—it's a necessity that should not be taken lightly. The "interpersonal roads" over time are often strewn with well-meaning helpers who have tried to survive without such support. Encouragement is a gift that should be treasured in today's stressful, anxious, and complex world because the seeds of involvement and the seeds of burnout are the same. To be involved is to risk, and to risk without the support of solidly supportive friends is both foolhardy and dangerous.

One of the greatest dangers is feeling like a failure when, in truth, we need not have that experience at all. American writer Kurt Vonnegut reflected on this in his own life, recalling a time when he was working on an archaeological dig at the age of 15. He shared that one of the archaeologists who spoke to him during that time changed his life. Vonnegut indicated that he was involved in art classes, theater, choir, and also played the violin and piano. However, he quickly added that he was not particularly good at any of these pursuits. To which the archaeologist replied, "I don't think being good at things is the point of doing them. I think you've got all these wonderful experiences with different skills, and that all teaches you things and makes you an interesting person, no matter how well you do them."

Vonnegut said that hearing this shifted his perspective—moving him from feeling like a failure in an achievement-oriented society to seeing himself as someone who could engage with life purely for its enjoyment. At a critical time in his life, someone turned on the power engine of a modern Renaissance person—someone with wide-ranging interests and a willingness to be involved in much more than others who had psychologically powered down because of society's worship of success.

The Harasser

When singer-activist Joan Baez was asked about her opinion of the contemplative monk and writer Thomas Merton, she said that he was different from many of the phony gurus she had encountered in her travels. She explained that although Merton took important aspects of life seriously, he didn't take himself too seriously. She indicated that he knew how to laugh at situations, and particularly at himself. "Harassers" help us to laugh at ourselves and to avoid the emotional burnout that results from holding unrealistic expectations that others will always follow our guidance or appreciate what we do for them. This type of friend helps us to regain and maintain perspective, so we don't unnecessarily waste valuable energy. They often do this through gentle teasing. Truly, this is a gift for which we can be thankful.

"The harasser" encourages us to recognize our own foibles and to develop a sense of humor. I have seen this in many groups during my travels around the world, where I have lectured on resilience and self-care. They have taught me the importance of leaning back and not taking myself too seriously.

I particularly experienced and appreciated this with the wonderful people of Newfoundland and Ireland.

I have been to Newfoundland several times. But the first time I was there doing some consulting work, I particularly remember the flight back to Baltimore. I had just sat down when a fellow dropped into the seat next to me, leaned over, and asked, "Are you from Newfoundland? Are you a Newfee?" After I responded in the negative, he quickly followed up with, "Well, then, do you know where the Newfees keep their armies?" "No," I said. To this, he replied, "Up their sleevies!" Making a face and laughing, I said, "We're not going to do this for the whole flight to Halifax, are we?"

Then, just after that, a really cheerful old fellow from one of the French-speaking areas of Newfoundland, sitting three rows in front of us, pulled down his fiddle from the overhead rack and started to sing and play—and we hadn't even taken off yet! What a joyous flight it was. I love them. Their joy and their ability to poke fun at their own simplicity made me relax easily, accept my own ordinariness and foibles more, and gain a better sense of the deep joy within me.

A similar experience happened to me in Ireland. The Irish are a beautiful nation of people who understand the richness they demonstrate as poets, artists, writers, singers, and people of deep faith and hospitality. However, in recognizing their gifts, they are also aware of some of the darkness they carry within themselves—and they freely tease about it with jokes and quips.

One Irish fellow told me he had a wonderful trip to Miami, and upon his return, he expected the weather to be bitter, cold, and rainy. Instead, he found it to be simply delightful. Overjoyed, he commented to an older woman sitting beside him on the bus from the airport, "Mum, isn't it a beautiful day?" To which she replied, "Ah, yes—and you can bet we'll be paying for it down the road!"

It's wonderful when we can laugh at ourselves, our dark side, and our foibles. Without this ability, there's a tendency to bury our negativity through denial or bravado. When we do, we reduce our own sensitivity to ourselves (rich self-awareness) and, in turn, increase our defensiveness toward others.

True self-understanding and a sense of humor go well together. They set the stage for us to relax enough to see ourselves honestly and not take ourselves too seriously—so our pride doesn't interfere with our ability to appreciate and face change, as well as explore new possibilities—even if that involves failing along the way. The joy of being at peace with oneself is key to personal growth and developing in new ways, rather than being a victim of "negative grandiosity," which prevents us from benefiting from constructive criticism and difficult questions about our motives and actions.

The Inspirational Friend

Well-known author Pat Conroy, in his book *My Reading Life*, shares two lines a girl once said about one of her teachers, which aptly describes an inspirational friend: "'Mr. Norris acted like I was the most important girl in the world,' she said. 'You were' [Conroy responded]. That was … Mr. Norris's secret. All of us were.'" This was the kind of teacher who was enthusiastic and made students excited about learning—including learning about themselves. Inspirational friends make allowances for our defenses, shortcomings, and growing edges, while calling us to be so much more—a person of courage, faith, hope, and joy.

Robert Brooks—who received his doctorate in clinical psychology from Clark University, was on the faculty of Harvard School of Medicine, had served as director of the Department of Psychology at McLean Hospital, and remains a prolific author of helpful works for the general public—wrote to me in an email:

> Years ago I had a very challenging day at McLean Hospital. When I came home I had the thought that all of the patients I saw that day seemed to be "drowning in a self-perceived ocean of inadequacy." This was followed by the thought that if there is an "ocean of inadequacy," there must be "islands of competence." This latter image was to come to include one's passions, interests, beauty, and strengths.

> In one of his website articles, "Of Micromoments and Indelible Memories: The Experiences That Change Our Lives," Brooks asks all of us to try to recall and honor those inspirational encounters in our lives, even if they were brief. As can be seen in this and his other work, he exemplifies the "inspirational friend."

Mentors of Possibility

As Adam Grant notes in his book *Hidden Potential*, being a coach—or what is here called a "mentor"—is harder than being a critic, cheerleader, or harasser. Yet, when we are open, the goals we pursue become easier for both the mentor and ourselves. In Grant's words, "The sweet spot is when people are proactive and growth-oriented. That's when they become sponges. They consistently take the initiative to expand themselves and adapt. That character skill is especially valuable when the deck is stacked against you."

Zen Master Shunryu Suzuki advised those seeking a mentor or spiritual guide to look for someone as sincere as themselves. I believe most of us have encountered individuals like that—people genuinely interested in helping us become more aware of our own sense of self in the deepest way possible. They believed we possessed the potential wisdom to find ourselves—on our own! Their goal in walking alongside us was to see if they could help in this process. They also truly embodied all the voices we have discussed here—namely, the prophet, cheerleader, harasser, and inspirational friend—to help us break through our current conditioning. The goal is tranquility and an elimination or reduction of feelings like "I mustn't," "I can't," "I shouldn't," and other limiting thoughts and attitudes, so that we can entertain the widest sense of possibility. Most importantly, the mentor is someone who demonstrates humility and shows that she or he believes in us, rather than demanding we simply trust them. They also help us realize our need to build on what we have learned in the relationship so we can eventually move out on our own. As the German philosopher Friedrich Nietzsche said, "One repays a teacher badly if one remains only a pupil."

Even such guides as the Dalai Lama—though famous and widely respected—truly immerse themselves in their own humanity. In his own words, recorded in *The Book of Joy*, he says, "When I meet someone . . . I always try to relate to the person on the basic human level… That way, there is in fact no need for an introduction. If on the other hand, I relate to others from the perspective of myself as someone different—a Buddhist, a Tibetan, and so on—I will then create walls to keep me apart from others. And if I relate to others, thinking that I am the Dalai Lama, I will create the basis for my own separation and loneliness. After all, there is only one Dalai Lama in the entire world. In contrast, if I see myself primarily in terms of myself as a fellow human, I will then have more than seven billion people who I can feel deep connection with. And this is wonderful, Isn't it? What do you need to fear or worry about when you have seven billion other people who are with you?"

Reading this, it is no surprise that people who have met him often describe the Dalai Lama as a man of such openness and simplicity—core traits of a true mentor.

Seeking the peace that comes from self-understanding—freeing us from obstacles that block our way—is vital when we walk alongside someone who has already done the necessary work to "simply find and be themselves." Such mentors or wise figures don't ask us to imitate them, but instead possess the patience and courage, as previously discussed, to help us find our own map and explore our truly unique, ordinary selves.

For many, "simple ordinariness" seems an unnecessary or overly difficult option. They're comfortable wearing the clothes of others. Yet, some—like adopted children eager to meet their birth parents—long to understand more of who they are and may be given the knowledge and space needed for genuine growth. Living out a more authentic and congruent life requires effort. Like learning a musical instrument, honoring this process involves much more than the act itself. As Russian-born American pianist Vladimir Horowitz famously said—and I believe this offers a good metaphor for the journey to full embrace of ordinariness—"The piano is the easiest instrument to play, but the hardest instrument to play well."

Given the complexities and nuances of this journey, it's sometimes necessary to undertake it in the company of wiser travelers. In the words of Reinhold Niebuhr, "Nothing we do, however virtuous, can be accomplished alone."

Occasionally, mentors use spontaneous events or humor to help people recognize that the journey toward ordinariness is about gaining one's own perceptual clarity, even when that process is facilitated by another. In his classic work *Journey in Ladakh*, Andrew Harvey shares an illustrative example of this:

> We woke before dawn, washed in icy water, went down to the prayer room for morning prayers. The Rinpoche was amused that I had stayed the night. After prayers he waved me to him and said, "So you have decided to stay with us?"
>
> "I wish I could."
>
> "You can stay as long as you like. Come when you like and go when you want."
>
> I bowed my head to thank him and my glasses fell off into his hands. He laughed and laughed and waved my glasses in the air, and then put them with a great air of conspiracy into his yellow silk shirt.

"I am going to keep them for myself," he said.

"You can keep them, of course. But I wish", I said, "you would give me back your eyes instead. You can keep mine as long as you like."

He put my glasses back on with his own hands.

"No. You must see with *your* eyes, not mine. Perhaps I can help you to see with your eyes."

"If you could help me to see with my eyes, I would be grateful to you."

"I do not want gratitude. I want you to stay a little time with us, to come when you want and learn what you need. That is all."

True mentors in ordinariness welcome people in a very unpretentious way. Steve Georgiou, in his book *The Way of the Dreamcatcher*, shared that his mentor, Robert Lax, greeted others in a manner that made them feel accepted and encouraged. He said that "he looked at them with a kind of happy awe, as if hailing a company of saints. He addressed his audience with kindness and focused on them completely, carefully, honestly, and with genuine love . . . those who left him broke into warm and carefree smiles. . . . As might be expected of a reclusive, dedicated contemplative, Lax did not talk much, nor did he desire manifold attention. Instead he preferred to maintain a low profile and listened intently, using his own silence to draw ideas out of others."

When I first sought ongoing guidance to deepen my self-awareness and to become more adept at navigating change and possibility in the best way, I looked for someone like Lax—someone who reflected a number of these traits.

The words and presence of true mentors in ordinariness are, of course, not limited solely to what has been described above. Overall, the attitude we seek in giving and receiving such mentorship—guided by the spirit of self-discovery—must be rooted in an attitude that negates the ego, allowing us to become clearer vessels for discovery rather than imposing our personal will outwardly. Sometimes, a mentor might wish to tell someone what they prefer. However, there must be openness to possibilities that go even beyond what we believe are our positive wishes.

Elie Wiesel describes such an encounter at its best in his interactions with Rebbe Menachem Schneerson, arguably one of the most influential rabbis in modern history. He said, in sharing: "I know of no one who left the Rebbe without being deeply affected if not changed by the encounter. . . . Time in his presence begins running at a different pace. . . . In his presence, you come closer in touch with your inner center of gravity. Whenever I would see the

Rebbe, he touched the depths in me. That was true of everyone who came to see the Rebbe. Somehow, when the person left, he or she felt that they had lived deeper and . . . on a higher level."

When the Rebbe was asked, "What's a Rebbe good for?" he didn't respond with insult or disrespect. Instead, he explained, according to Harold Telushkin in his biography *Rebbe*, "I can't speak for myself, but I can tell you about my own Rebbe [his father-in-law]. For me, my Rebbe was the geologist of the soul. You see, there are so many treasures in the earth. There is gold, there is silver, and there are diamonds. But if you don't know where to dig, you'll only find dirt and rocks and mud. The Rebbe can tell you where to dig, and what to dig for, but the digging you must do for yourself." May we have the good fortune to meet someone like this—someone who helps us grow, navigate external change and face necessary internal transitions, discover it is good to be lost at times, and embrace *possibility*.

Persons of Possibility: Viktor Frankl and Matthieu Ricard

In his major work, *Man's Search for Meaning*, Viktor Frankl shared insights that are essential for understanding the possibility of growth even—*especially*—in darkness. He believed it is possible to find meaning and transcend circumstances, even amid suffering.

He appreciated—much more than most of us ever will—that while we may be powerless regarding our external circumstances, the formation of our attitude, perspective, and reactions remains within our control. In this regard, he elevated the concept of the "will to meaning," and he argued that this drive, in and of itself, can be a source of strength and resilience when faced with failure, uncertainty, and adversity. Therefore, happiness and well-being are not primarily products of external factors but fostered by our outlook—particularly when we honor impermanence and vulnerability and practice gratitude in the moment.

In a later work, *Yes to Life*, Viktor Frankl encouraged people to find fulfillment by creating a meaningful work or engaging in an activity or labor of love that leaves a lasting spirit beyond our lives. Similarly, he calls us to appreciate art or examples of love that surround us in tangible forms. Finally, he urges us to confront unavoidable limits—such as illness, approaching death, and suffering—by cultivating a loving attitude amid all the horrors and pain. In pursuit of this, he reminds us that hope arises from compassion and an awareness of our eventual mortality. In his own words:

[Life's] long duration does not automatically make it meaningful, and its possible briefness makes it far from meaningless. We also do not judge the life history of a particular person by the number of pages in the book that portrays it but only by the richness of the content it contains.

Matthieu Ricard, in his book *Happiness*, echoes these themes in slightly different but equally powerful ways that I find inspiring, instructive, and a simple guide to cultivating an attitude that welcomes the possibility of a meaningful, fulfilling, and compassionate life. (If you are not compassionate, you may experience pleasure and power at times, but not the joy and peace that can only come from expressing generativity.)

Ricard shares in convincing ways how the silence, solitude, and mindfulness—mentioned earlier and discussed in greater detail later in the book—can lead to serenity and a willingness to fathom uncertainty and each day more freely and fully. He also emphasizes "renunciation" (also referred to later in this book as "letting go"), not as a way of giving up what is good and beautiful, but as a means to simplify life and create more inner space for new meaning and love.

He is not speaking about occasional "contemplative or meditative highs," but rather about a way of living and cultivating the "music" (attitude) that elevates the quality of every moment, encounter, challenge, or turn in our lives. With an exceptionally healthy mind, we can recognize that, while we may not be able to change the world directly, we can still alter the way we view it and how we choose to behave.

Like Viktor Frankl, Ricard emphasizes creating a way of being that does not rely on external circumstances as the primary source of joy or the basis for embracing possibility. Instead, he notes the following:

Changing the way we see the world does not imply naive optimism or some artificial euphoria designed to counterbalance adversity. So long as we are slaves to the dissatisfaction and frustration that arise from the confusion that rules our minds, it will be just as futile to tell ourselves "I'm happy! I'm happy!" over and over again as it would be to repaint a wall in ruins. The search for happiness is not about looking at life through rose-colored glasses or blinding oneself to the pain and imperfections of the world. Nor is happiness a state of exaltation to be perpetuated at all costs; it is the purging of mental toxins, such as hatred and obsession, that literally poison the mind. It is also about learning how to put things in perspective and reduce the gap between appearances and reality. To that end we must acquire a better knowledge of how the mind works and a more accurate insight into the nature of things, for in its deepest sense, suffering is intimately linked to a misapprehension of the nature of reality.

Just as in the philosophy of critical thinking and the overarching goal of cognitive clarity in psychology, Ricard seeks to help people value truth rather than society's tendency to foster "mental anesthesia." To this end, he encourages reflection rooted in honesty and humility—calmly looking inward to better understand ourselves and our situations. From this foundation, possibility becomes . . . well, more possible!

In encouraging us to emulate mindful individuals, he is not asking us to be monks, but to sit quietly and reflect regularly, taking a moment at the end of each session to savor the warmth and joy that arise from a calmer mind. This becomes possible as we free ourselves from egocentric tendencies, approaching ourselves more honestly, hopefully, and with a sense of curiosity. Such an approach leads to a form of selflessness that, rather than stripping us of the opportunity to become who we truly are, opens the door to inner freedom—allowing us to explore our thoughts and relationships with greater ease.

Furthermore, as Ricard points out—and as we will discuss later—positive psychology teaches us that when we are more in tune with our signature strengths and positive emotions, the world opens up, offering us a broader perspective on ideas, life, and possibilities. The question of what we truly desire from life then expands; it invites us to go beyond meeting trivial needs and opens us to joy rather than fleeting pleasure, compassion rather than self-interest, and generativity rather than entitlement.

In this light, renunciation and letting go, according to Ricard and aligned with the philosophy of this book, "does not come down to saying no to all that is pleasant, to giving up strawberry ice cream or a nice hot shower after a long walk in the hills. It comes down to asking ourselves, with respect to certain aspects of our lives: 'Is this going to make me happier?' Genuine happiness—as opposed to contrived euphoria—endures through life's ups and downs. To renounce is to have the daring and intelligence to scrutinize what we usually consider to be pleasures in order to determine if they really enhance our well-being."

A natural question to ask, and one that invites reflection, is: How did Ricard come to this understanding of happiness and how to approach it?

He couldn't have been this way since birth. His answer? "The good fortune of meeting with remarkable people who were both wise and compassionate was decisive in my case, because the power of example speaks more forcefully than any communication." In seeking the possibility of a meaningful and rich life, may we seek and find "friendly voices" and mentoring models like this as well. They are key to uncovering and dealing with the resistances to change all of us must encounter at different turns in our life.

For Review and Reflection . . .

Characteristics of an Ideal *"Possibility Mentor"*

- Helps you uncover and navigate unnecessary fears that are causing you to give up opportunities.
- Is attuned to psychological attachments and unnecessary preoccupations that are "psychologically too expensive."
- Provides insights into those problems that are really alerts to the fact that you must change at a certain point.
- Asks questions you are not considering that invigorate thinking to see both possibility and challenge in new, possibly innovative, ways.
- Enables a clearer understanding of *both* your defenses and signature strengths—including minor, as yet not fully explored ones—that can be used in facing doubt and change.
- Employs a balance of gentleness and clarity in the questions asked so that you can return to the noise and commotion of your life with a greater sense of humility, dignity, and confidence in today's sometimes anxious and confusing world.
- Listens to your story with attention in ways that you become more aware of how to listen to yourself.
- Offers the "psychological room" to be more fully yourself.
- Introduces the need to investigate "social factors" and your history, not simply personal limits, which may be in play and holding you back. (As American social psychologist, Christina Maslach, who is one of leading experts on "burnout" notes: "If we were to investigate the personality of a cucumber to discover why it changed into a pickle, without examining the vinegar barrel in which it was submerged, you wouldn't get very far.")
- Paces you so you don't unduly procrastinate on the one hand nor feel overwhelmed by the mentor's expectations on the other.
- Provides guidance without giving pat answers by offering support without removing your own independence and faith in yourself to discover a personally suitable approach given your own personality, history, experiences, and current circumstances.
- Offers guidance on how to experiment with new ways of thinking, perceiving, and understanding.

- Indicates approaches to recognizing when fear of rejection, personal hypersensitivity, and over-concern about ridicule and failure are preventing appropriate risk-taking.
- Encourages action after proper discernment.
- Reinforces your willingness to mentor others because of what is psychologically referred to as "the tutor effect" and results in the development of greater self-confidence because of your work as a guide to others.
- Reviews with you when and how to seek necessary information of change.
- Helps you develop a greater appreciation of the value of self-knowledge as a never-ending process.
- Models ways to be more appreciative of the current friends and possessions one has so that you can move ahead from a position of strength rather than a sense of deficit and deprivation.
- Is aware of the need to let go of the intensity of the mentoring situation when the timing is right because, in the words of Romanian sculptor Constantin Brancusi when he was being guided by greatly admired Auguste Rodin, "Nothing grows under big trees."
- And, as is contained in the following Hindu proverb, an ideal mentor recognizes: "There are hundreds of paths up the mountain, all leading to the same place, so it doesn't matter which path you take. The only person wasting time is the one who runs around the mountain, telling everyone that his or her path is wrong."

3

Invisible Fences

Understanding the Psychology of Personal Resistance to Growth and Change

"He who knows all the answers has not been asked all the questions."

—Confucius

"When you are fooled by something else, the damage will not be so big. But when you are fooled by yourself, it is fatal. No more medicine."

—Shunryu Suzuki

Swiss psychiatrist Carl Jung once purportedly quipped, "If the path before you is clear, you're probably on someone else's." Even when we believe we are open to new possibilities, understanding that there are still personal resistances to growth and change can be very helpful. However, uncovering and overcoming these resistances is often easier said than done. As Thomas Merton, the contemplative and author of the classic autobiographical work *The Seven Storey Mountain*, laments: "All day I have been uncomfortably aware of the wrong that is in me. The useless burden of pride I condemn myself to carry, and all that comes with carrying it. I know I deceive myself...but I cannot catch myself in the act. I do not see exactly where the deception lies."

Therefore, understanding as much as we can about our hesitancy to confront resistance—and acting more effectively to address the areas we need to change—is essential if we wish to truly embrace possibility each day, both in small ways and at key turning points in our lives.

The concept of "resistance to change" has evolved significantly in psychology over the years. A brief review of this evolution can be helpful for anyone seeking to overcome their own barriers to personal and professional development. In the early days of psychology, resistance was often viewed simply as a motivational problem. When a person struggled to change or welcome new possibilities, the mentor or clinician might have thought, "I did my job in pointing out your difficulties. In return, you didn't do yours!" The responsibility for the resistance was placed on the individual claiming to want change, and the goal was to eliminate that resistance and re-motivate the person.

Today, we recognize that when someone resists change and growth, they are not deliberately trying to hinder those who seek to help them. Instead, their resistance often unconsciously conveys critical information about past issues, personality style, history, and current circumstances. This material, when viewed in this light by a skilled mentor, can become a valuable source of wisdom—helping foster psychological growth, personal development, and deeper insight. While motivation remains a key element in progress, we now understand that individuals seeking change must also acquire self-knowledge and act on it to truly embrace the possibilities before them. In a nutshell: Motivation or positive thinking alone are not enough!

One of the primary reasons that motivation alone often fails to produce change is fear—fear that the demands involved may be too costly. We may need to acknowledge our own role in missing opportunities and confronting the need for change. Even when growth is beneficial, it can be surprisingly upsetting to those accustomed to the "devil they know"—their usual defensive style. They may resist change because of discomfort or fear of being challenged by new styles or actions, or because they feel "left behind" by the progress others are making. Additionally, recognizing our role in avoiding possibilities might evoke painful reflections on the past and how much time we've wasted by failing to act.

The "advantages" of staying the same are often very costly. Conversely, the insights and freedom gained through genuine change can greatly benefit us and those around us. Therefore, when it comes to breaking the tyranny of habit, it is vital to take practical steps that make the pursuit of self-knowledge and growth both realistic and inspiring. Alongside improving our self-awareness, we must develop the ability to acknowledge and accept change, recognize defensiveness in ourselves, and outmaneuver tendencies to project blame onto others or circumstances. Anthony de Mello points this out in a dialogue from his book *One Minute Wisdom*: "To a disciple who was forever complaining about others, the Master said, 'If it is peace you want, seek to change yourself, not other people.'" He then added, "It is easier to protect your feet with slippers than to carpet the whole of the earth.'"

Change

Truly, nothing remains the same. Yet, it is often hard for us to see and accept this reality. A friend who hadn't seen me in a year—since his move from the neighborhood—illustrated this point. When he returned, we walked around the area together again, giving him a chance to reconnect with old acquaintances. After we returned, he remarked about one of his former neighbors, "My gosh, he's aged." I was surprised to hear him say this because I hadn't noticed it. After thinking about it for a while, I realized that the reason I hadn't observed it was because I saw that neighbor almost every day. Change can be hard to notice when it happens gradually and steadily right before our eyes.

The change we must confront within ourselves is often even harder to notice and face—yet it is essential if we wish to grow and respond to new possibilities. When we consciously take steps toward needed change, especially since the circumstances that once justified our current positions are now different, sometimes unimaginable things can happen. As the Zen saying goes: "Face reality clearly in an unvarnished way, and unwilled change will take place almost of its own accord." To follow such a principle, we must not only have the passion to continually seek the truth but also, as was emphasized at the beginning of this book, we must remain alert to the areas where we believe we are right but are actually mistaken now. Seeing honestly and straightforwardly what our current opinions are about situations, others, and ourselves is a crucial step toward embracing new realities and uncovering the truth.

In *Transitions*, the seminal work by the late William Bridges (later updated by Susan Bridges), there is an acknowledgment of how challenging it can be to make sense of life's changes—especially once we move beyond the teenage years. In their words, "The transitions of life's afternoon are more mysterious than those of its morning... everything that once worked for him now works against him." Thus, external change is a product of an internal transition—moving to a new "place" psychologically.

What puzzles many who are eager to make changes in their lives and open new doors to greater possibilities is that obstacles often remain—even when they know the steps they need to take are beneficial. It's as if routine, habit, and past successes with certain approaches have emotionally intoxicated them. To truly see and embrace new possibilities, one must be psychologically and spiritually sober.

Transitions humorously illustrates this point with the following brief vignette:

> The old radio comedian Bob Burns ("The Arkansas Traveler") used to tell the story of eating army food for the first time after eighteen years of his mother's deep-fat frying. A week of bland GI fare was enough to cure something he had never realized he suffered from: heartburn. But rather than feeling relief at his improvement, Burns rushed into the dispensary, clutching his stomach and yelling, "Doc, doc! Help me! I'm dying. My fire went out!"

Jeffrey Kottler, in his book *Change*, points out that real beneficial alterations tend to lead to reduced stress and improved functioning in the daily activities in which we are engaged. He also highlights various levels of change, such as an attitudinal shift that dramatically improves self-acceptance and acceptance of events, an increased ability to experiment with alternatives, a greater capacity to tolerate ambiguity, knowing how to reach out to supportive individuals who can facilitate necessary change, and developing the skills to take steps that foster a healthier perspective. Importantly, he stresses the crucial role of having a higher purpose or a profound sense of true meaning in driving lasting transformation.

Kottler also notes that many psychological theorists have proposed reasons why positive change can be inhibited. For the purposes of this book, with respect to the theme of possibility, I would particularly frame such factors as:

- Limiting behavior modeled for a person early in life by parents and other significant persons
- Unhelpful, unexamined ways of thinking, perceiving, and understanding
- Vague goals
- Lack of commitment to living a rich life of meaning and compassion
- Unstructured goals and steps to meet one's objectives
- Failure to have a clear understanding of personal signature strengths and growing edges (defenses, resistances to change)
- Possessing an incomplete self-narrative or one overly influenced/determined by others
- Absence of a rich circle of friends to inspire, challenge, and guide one with respect to personal and professional development

- Limited or an absence of time for reflection as well as ignorance on how to most profitably approach mindful meditation
- Unwillingness to let go of styles of behavior or attitudes which are no longer relevant or productive
- Inability to learn and deepen from negative or traumatic events
- Feelings of impotence as to how one might lead a truly beautiful life

In line with Kottler's work, Ian Evans, in his book *How and Why People Change*, also examines resistances—concepts that are important not only for professional mental health practitioners but also for anyone seeking to benefit from the possibilities of change. In his book, Evans discusses the wide range of excuses we tell ourselves for not changing, including:

- "It's too hard."
- "We're too busy."
- "Change is too fearful or upsetting."
- "The timing wasn't right for me—I'll do better next time."
- "Different behavior removes my freedom to be myself."
- "A new repertoire of behavior would take too much practice."
- "I don't have the skills necessary to change."
- "The rewards of staying the same are too important to me."

Due to our unique perspectives, we see everyone and everything in a way that can either blind us to the wonder of the world or continually inspire us with it. For me, each morning is an ideal time to seek new wisdom that can help me open myself more fully to the day ahead. This involves examining my beliefs about my psychological and spiritual challenges in the world around me, and, as Swiss psychiatrist Carl Jung recommends, withdraw my projections and stop blaming others for my problems. Doing so allows me to better see what I need to learn about myself and what I must let go of in order to become freer from prejudice and the narrow thinking I currently hold. As Indian philosopher Jiddu Krishnamurti observed: "The story is there, but we don't read the story. We are telling the book what it should say." When gentle, clear self-questioning takes place, it opens us up in ways that help us "read the story" with fresh eyes—revealing new possibilities rather than sticking to a story we simply wish were true.

Often, we deny our role in mistakes, justify actions, absolve ourselves for crossing boundaries in relationships that we shouldn't have, rationalize failures, and focus on the negative roles others have played—all while removing ourselves from the equation. We do this partly out of a tendency to overreact when trying to take responsibility for our part in unpalatable events. Instead of understanding what part we played so we can learn from it, we move from remorse over our actions to shame about who we are. This pattern leads us to condemn ourselves, become hypercritical of our behavior, set unrealistic standards, and take excessive responsibility for the impact we have had—and can have—on others.

A better approach is to recognize the need to take a step back from the event, attempt to frame the situation objectively—as if it involved someone else—and cultivate curiosity about our own role. In this way, we increase the potential for meaningful change. At the same time, we are more likely to avoid blaming others, condemning ourselves, or becoming discouraged when results do not occur immediately. Accordingly, in the spirit of mindfulness and to further reduce resistance to change, I often offer several caveats to help overcome the blocks to growth in myself and others. They are:

- Anything discovered does not have to be changed immediately.
- No area should be condemned . . . just neutrally observed as if it were happening to someone else.
- No area should be defended—no one is criticizing or attacking, just observing where the energy is being spent.
- Observations—even disturbing ones—should be embraced as a wonderful treasure trove of information.
- After each period of observation, the areas of concern should be written down so some record is kept of discoveries.

With these considerations in mind, we can approach the following principle with a greater sense of openness: Where there is energy—whether positive or negative—there is usually an element of grasping or fear underneath. When the smoke of a strong reaction is present, the fire of desire is often also burning nearby, and it's important to understand what it is. Otherwise, our passions may be rooted in unexamined attachments, and rather than being a source of good energy, they can become barriers to truth.

These attachments tend to keep us connected to views and convictions that obscure or distort the reality, rather than helping us discover it. Classic signs that we are holding on include: arguing, withholding information or motivations from others during discussions about the event, complaining that change in certain areas is impossible, stonewalling others with icy silence or monopolizing the situation, feeling misunderstood or completely ignored, and exhibiting other strong emotions or off-putting actions.

Conversely, there are also classic signs that a person does value change, growth, and insight—both professionally and personally. As author Paulo Coelho once said, "When I had all the answers, the questions changed." Some of the signs of this openness, which are discussed in *It's Good to Be Lost Once in a While*, include:

- An ability to let go
- Being receptive to new lessons
- Humility
- A desire to understand one's own emotional hot-button issues
- Feeling disgusted with the endless wheel of suffering that comes from grasping and bad habits
- Curiosity, openness, non-judgmentalism
- Valuing experience
- Recognizing the danger of attachments which prevent experiencing new gifts
- Being awake to the present; attentive and mindful
- Appreciative of quiet meditation
- Generous and alive
- Learning, reflecting, and applying wisdom to daily life
- Not taking oneself too seriously

Years ago, a psychiatric nurse who worked at what was then known as Lancaster Osteopathic Hospital asked me as I was preparing to make rounds, "What do you think is one of the most important things you do for people here, in your books, and in your clinical practice, to help them better understand themselves?" I replied, "Most people either don't know the right questions to ask themselves or, if they do, still don't ask themselves what they truly need. Those are the very questions I try to ask them—at the right time and in a way they are most willing to hear." "Sounds simple," she quipped. "Oh, it is," I responded, "but not easy." Today, as we look around at who people vote for, the leaders they follow, and the issues they defend, we see that the problem has not lessened in society. Self-interest, fear, compartmentalization—in which we hide a portion of our attitude and behavior from ourselves—reigns. And so, all of us need to see if we are asking ourselves questions that are big enough and will lead us to the truth, rather than being persons who yell the loudest when we know the least. In the end, we need to remember that we may be traveling on a "psychological and sociological boat" with others who happily agree with us . . . but we may be traveling in the wrong direction. However, if we ask ourselves questions in a spirit of discovery, hope, and a desire for concrete action, we might ask simple but powerful questions such as: What do I feel needs to change? What is the first step I can take in response? What might be uncomfortable if I do this? Who can I ask to walk with me as I move forward? What options do I have for progressing? What would be rewarding for me if I made this change?

Many people's concerns about personal security and pleasing others are so ingrained that they remain unaware they are essentially trapped. This often leads to forgoing change and failing to envision who they might become in the future. Instead of recognizing, welcoming, and pursuing those deep callings, they dismiss these longings as fantasies for others. Others remain bound by past failures and guilt—which is unfortunate, because, as we will see later in this book, even those who take measured, creative, and reasonable risks will face failures at times. What truly matters is how we react to those failures. As Zen Master Sheng Yen wrote in *Footprints in the Snow*: "I have been asked whether there is anything in my life that I regret. I have experiences where I did embarrassing things. I still do plenty of embarrassing things. But there is nothing I regret. When I make a mistake, I repent, accept responsibility, and keep going."

People often share with me a sense of regret about something from their past. The defining feature of this feeling is guilt—an emotion and faulty way of thinking that repeatedly pulls them back into the past, leaving them helpless, sad, and sometimes hopeless about the future. Others may feel just as remorseful about certain events. They are honest and clear about their past mistakes, but there is a crucial difference: remorse doesn't trap them in the past. Instead, with a remorseful attitude, they are guided by the reminder to try to be different going forward. They seek to learn so they can make the most of the present moment—because this is the only moment we truly live in during our brief lives. Such an approach to the past is beautiful and brimming with both reality and hope. That's how I aspire to be, so I can help others live the same way. But first, I must recognize and embrace the critical difference between unhelpful regret and life-affirming remorse. Take a quiet moment each day to reflect on this difference yourself.

A rich, healthy life that embraces new possibilities requires a willingness to let go of old views, routines, and ways of approaching each new day and phase of life. To do this, we must stay alert to the blocks that hinder growth and change—though, of course, this is easier said than done.

Conditioning from family, friends, colleagues, and society—sometimes from well-meaning individuals, for "the right reasons," or even in the early stages as a way of behaving—can be very resistant to change. In the words of Housden, in his book *10 Poems to Change Your Life*, "Whatever your circumstances, people will start to give you advice as soon as you disturb the status quo. That advice is likely to be bad. It will be bad because they're seeking not to understand and further your calling but to perceive the world as they know it."

That we are often partially or entirely unaware of our blocks to growth and development—because of such influences—inevitably makes life more difficult. One common result is the use of a primitive psychological defense: projection. In this defense, blame (and the perceived power to change) is shifted onto factors or people in the environment—it's their fault that I am unable to see or respond to new possibilities.

Alternatively, attempts to accommodate what was not initially imagined as a possibility often lead to rationalizations—excuses for why we fail. Once again, it's not about the person trying to change. Along with this defensive pattern, withdrawal or expressions of anger replace understanding and a deeper appreciation of what positive insights can be gleaned—even from "dark situations" or losses.

However, understanding the sources and manifestations of resistance, as well as recognizing the futility of self-blame, can foster a new mindset. This shift opens doors to change and allows us to benefit from what, and how, we have been blocked from appreciating and acting upon in the past.

Among the 20 countries I have worked in, I have traveled and spoken in nations under immense stress, such as Lebanon, South Africa, Haiti, and Cambodia. Despite these challenges, the people in those countries have always impressed me with their gratitude, resilience, and sense of wonder. I learned a great deal from them. And so, I was surprised recently when I found that I was upset here in America by someone who seemed to have so much yet was always ungrateful and looking for what he missed or how people took advantage of him. I could see this reflected in his children, who responded to his sense of neediness and sense of entitlement by living out their lives in strange ways. One was always trying to impress him and was aggressive. Another was immature and behaved like a child even though she was an adult. The question for me was: Why was I letting his behavior impact mine?

I knew this was a unique experience, so I asked a friend about it. She simply replied, "Oh, that's just the way he is. So why would you let his misbehavior bother you? He has decided he's in permanent need, behaves that way, misses so much in the process, and turns people off. I feel sorry for him and those in his family he has impacted negatively without their really knowing it."

This conversation made me realize I sometimes give away my power to others—and I need to understand why. By learning about this sensitivity, I can not only live more freely but also conserve the energy that I might otherwise waste, and use it to make better decisions and offer help to others who turn to me. Recognizing what and who affects us most in negative ways—without dismissing it because of who they are or how they behave—is a vital inner journey. I am currently on this journey, and for some reason, it makes me feel young and adventurous again. I also sense that the energy I have been giving away is returning, driven by a desire to see life more clearly than I ever have before.

One of the natural arcs in any movement toward greater openness—and positioning ourselves to maintain the healthiest perspective at any given moment—is to uncover our resistances to growth and change. Achieving this is challenging because thawing our outlook—particularly during emotionally charged moments, so we do not remain frozen by habits and responses conditioned by society, family, and (sometimes) outdated, inaccurate, or unhelpful beliefs—requires a gradual, step-by-step process of dismantling, which is rarely straightforward.

When this process is completed, it can be incredibly powerful. William James, the father of American psychology, recognized that even the smallest insights, a slightly clearer perspective, or a minor change in behavior can ultimately lead to astonishing results. In his own words:

> Sow an action, and you reap a habit;
> Sow a habit, and you reap a character;
> Sow a character, and you reap a destiny.

A healthy perspective and openness lead to actions that often reflect a freshness in one's outlook.

The "people" influencing us may be voices from those around us or internal voices ingrained within us—impressions from the past that once impressed us with their caution and practicality. In seeking a healthy perspective, we must uncover and confront these voices with the question, "Is this, should this, be my voice now?"

I remember once working with an adult child of Holocaust survivors. The understandable neediness and fears of those who raised him drained his early life of carefree spaces and failed to provide the joy and simple security that positive parenting can freely offer. The consequences for him included an inability to see life's nuances, a short emotional fuse, and a deep, persistent hunger to be emotionally fed constantly. He viewed disagreement as rejection. Close friends were not cherished but consumed. As a result, others responded in one of several unsatisfying ways: They would run away, become angry at his demands, tread carefully, or avoid him altogether.

A healthy perspective is much like poetry. Once again, in the words of Roger Housden in his book on free verse, "Poetry at its best calls forth our deep being, bids us live by its promptings; it dares us to break free from the safe strategies of the cautious mind; it calls to us, like the wild geese, from an open sky . . . a great poem can open a door in us we may never have known was there." Yet, he also quite rightly adds:

> A new life requires a death of some kind; otherwise it is nothing new, but rather a shuffling of the same deck. What we die to is an outworn way of being in the world. We experience ourselves differently. We are no longer who we thought we were. But I do not suggest for one moment that it is easy. Nor that there are any guarantees. If you start down a new road, you cannot know where it will take you.

To "break free from safe strategies," we must see perspective in a dramatically different way. It is not the pearl of great price that, once gained, will give us all that *we* desire now. Instead, a healthy perspective opens us up to see reality more clearly so we can appreciate new, unforeseen possibilities that we could not have conceived of if we only received what we wished for. A healthy perspective based on openness doesn't change reality into what we want; rather, it reveals the full range of what is available within the given circumstances of life, so that we may recognize and shape what it might become. That is "the pearl of great price"—often sitting right in front of us—yet remaining unrecognized, untouched, and unengaged.

One of the most precious gifts of life is inner freedom. To truly change, move, *really* grow, we need "space" within ourselves. Habits, worries, emotions, defensiveness, stubbornness, and fear all take up room. Perhaps that's why Zen masters suggest that, to find joy and peace, we don't need to add anything to our lives; instead, we need to let go of something—so we can see clearly and live more freely. Spiritual figures often refer to this as gaining "unobstructed vision" or "purity of heart." Psychologists are less poetic but just as clear: They recommend getting rid of "expensive defenses" that drain our energy. Their advice is to uncover and eliminate old, useless habits and unfounded, erroneous, negative beliefs. The result? A newfound sense of freedom.

However, although the goal—creating space, emptiness, or inner freedom—sounds good, it is obviously not easy. Why? Because the first step goes completely against the grain of our "common sense" and presently limited self-awareness. To be free, we must first realize that, in many ways, we are not!

There are all types of hidden addictions, ingrained habits, and unexamined beliefs that are guiding us automatically through life and negatively impacting our having a healthy perspective on life, *our* life. One of the best ways to find out what they are is to continually monitor our emotions and ask the right kinds of questions—questions that ultimately reveal information capable of freeing us.

Yet, self-awareness and sensitivity to what we "fill our psyches with" often seem elusive. I believe Thoreau was right when he said, "It is as hard to see oneself as it is to look backward without turning 'round.'" Much of my work involves helping a "professionally sensitive" population—those who consider themselves in tune with themselves and their environment because of their roles as helpers and healers. Yet, the truly sensitive are those who seek to learn new lessons and "unlearn" old habits every day.

To cultivate such awareness, we must maintain a questioning attitude fueled by an appreciation of our emotions. In other words, we need to be willing and able to listen to what our emotions can teach us. When we feel angry, sad, thrilled, anxious, fearful, or depressed, we are tempted to think that an external event caused the emotion. That's only partly true. The interpretation we attach to the event plays a major role in eliciting that emotion. We often haven't asked the right questions—we haven't questioned far enough.

Typically, we ask questions about the other person(s) or event(s) that trigger our emotions—especially those who are unduly or unfairly critical of us. This is a natural initial response. It's common to ask: What is wrong with him? Why does he behave so critically? Doesn't he realize he's pushing potential friends away with his dissatisfaction with the gifts or suggestions offered? While these questions may yield answers, they are often not the most helpful when it comes to seeking a healthy perspective on our interactions.

And so, after asking these outward-directed questions and allowing our emotions of anger or annoyance to diminish, it becomes time to pose more meaningful questions—such as: Why did I allow myself to become so upset over someone else's behavior? Or, given my reactions, what can I learn about my own insecurities and agendas that would increase my self-awareness, reduce my defensiveness, and make me more free? Shifting the focus and depth of our questioning like this helps cleanse our perceptual palate and reclaim the power to alter our future responses.

If we don't ask these questions, or if we stop the questioning process too soon, we end up uncovering only information that may be useful for the other person but not for ourselves. The sad truth is that it probably won't be helpful to them either. Since their behavior is often unconsciously motivated or tied to unexamined beliefs about themselves and their worldview, they are unlikely to accept our interpretation—even if we present it to them on a silver platter. Besides, when we're annoyed by someone's actions, we are probably the least capable of helping them. In such cases, our motivation to assist may be compromised, and our response more likely aimed at paying them back or proving how they hurt us rather than genuinely helping.

However, in irritating or unpleasant situations, we can help ourselves by tilling the psychological and spiritual soil—planting new self-knowledge that opens pathways to necessary growth and change. Wouldn't that be a better option than simply sulking over others' silly behaviors and our own wounded feelings? Wouldn't it be more effective to reclaim the power we're wasting in interpersonal exchanges—to change both our internal reactions and our outward behavior? The way we question ourselves—especially when annoyed, hurt, or overwhelmed with negative emotions—is a key to self-understanding, breaking destructive patterns, and creating space for new learning. These elements are all essential for gaining a healthier perspective.

Sweet Disgust: When Being Fed Up Is Good

In therapy, one of the main reasons people are willing to attempt a program of change is that they are thoroughly fed up with their lives. Such a situation offers a favorable time to risk new attitudes, perceptions, and behaviors in lieu of remaining stuck in the status quo. The same holds true for those interested in spiritual wisdom. People turn to Hindu swamis, Buddhist rinpoches, Christian mystics, Taoist sages, or Jewish rebbes with the wish to live differently and to discover a deeper sense of meaning at the center of their lives. They want their perspective of the world transformed, made new.

Whether you call it ingrained habits, unexamined erroneous beliefs, or early life experiences that have led to crippling attitudes in the present, people at this juncture want to both see and experience life differently. They want to change. As the process unfolds, the therapist or guru often realizes that what is truly being asked is: *Can I change without really changing? Can I alter only those parts of my life that are causing me pain but essentially remain as I am?* Or, more to the point: *Can I have relief but no real cure that will require me to work to significantly alter my style, perspective, or beliefs?*

This basic resistance to change to a greater sense of openness is natural and to be expected in others and ourselves. Whenever we look at a challenge or problem, we must first and foremost include ourselves in the examination. However, people are trained to be protective of their energy with respect to self-examination and self-change. The preference is to look outward, when life becomes so difficult that someone finally wants to break free from the treadmill of worries, stop being strapped to the wheel of suffering, and genuinely feels disgusted with how they are living, that moment presents a wonderful opportunity. It's an ideal time to increase self-awareness and vulnerability—two key ingredients for profound openness to change.

When our attitude and outlook change, our perspective on the whole world also changes. For example, if a poor man feels grateful, his watery soup can taste much better than a wealthy man's fine meal. Furthermore, a person who experiences joy within will more often look with a sense of wonder at those around him—as well as at her/himself.

That is why spending time looking in disgust at the negative patterns in our lives as part of our daily reflection need not be an exercise in masochism. Instead, with the right outlook, it can be a step forward in enlightenment! If this is so, then why don't we do it? Why don't we look at the compulsion, anger, greed, narcissism, and stress in our life directly and honestly?

Well, I think we fear seeing the truth, and worry about what such insight might demand of us—namely, in our own mind we may believe we would need to:

- See our *own* role in making our life a painful web of grasping demands, insecurities, anger, envy, and resentment, and do something about it.
- Become more aware of the time we have lost behaving in a way that has been nonproductive and frozen because we have projected blame outward as an excuse for not doing something inward.
- Face the other's reaction to our new movement toward freedom, love, and peace and away from competition, defensiveness, and inauthenticity. (The reality is that while other people say they want us to grow and change, they often feel quite uncomfortable when we do.)

Still, despite our hesitation, being truly fed up with our current ways of perceiving and coping can be the crucial catalyzing factor prompting us toward necessary change. Repeatedly witnessing the negative consequences of our thoughts, feelings, and behaviors can drive us to exclaim, "Enough! I don't want to live this way anymore!" This realization provides a powerful motivation to begin the process of change. However, maintaining that motivation and staying committed over time is another story.

In therapy, when people start to get better they are often tempted to take a "leap into health" and stop their program of change. In response, the therapist seeks to help them continue challenging themselves so that their overall attitude remains open to new ways of seeing—ways that can open the door to a healthier perspective. To facilitate this kind of movement, how we and they view life plays a crucial role in determining whether growth continues or stalls.

Personal Intrigue! Not Arrogance or Ignorance

The two greatest enemies of openness and change are arrogance and ignorance. These two extremes waste more energy than any other defensive maneuver. In fact, if we could avoid both of them, growth would happen almost spontaneously and naturally. To reiterate a powerful Zen Buddhist proverb that illustrates this: "Face reality and effortless change will take place."

Arrogance manifests when we export (project) the responsibility for our failures and mistakes. The words that reflect that this process is going on are:

- Blaming
- Excusing
- Absolving
- Rationalizing
- Mitigating
- Contextualizing

The more subtle the words and sophisticated our excuses, the more we hide the following central truth from ourselves: *We* have a primary role in removing the blocks to openness and change.

At the other end of the spectrum is *ignorance*. This occurs when we accept all responsibility for our failures in a way that leaves us feeling negative about ourselves. Such self-debasement does not lead to insight or personal growth; instead, it only results in feelings of guilt, shame, or seeing ourselves as failures.

Moreover, because behavior that we wince at turns into behavior that we wink at, such self-blame eventually burns itself out. So, we feel overwhelmed rather than empowered, discouraged rather than enlightened, and we avoid further understanding rather than delving deeper for information that could set us free.

Some of the ways we describe this process are:

- Self-condemnation
- Over-responsibility
- Being hypercritical of self
- Overly perfectionistic tendencies

As a positive alternative, experienced therapists, mentors, and coaches encourage those seeking guidance to be *intrigued* by their behavior. They want them to become detectives exploring the mystery of the self. Spiritual guides offer similar encouragement. For example, Buddhists recommend that people watch themselves objectively—neither condemning nor excusing—so they can see their own grasping tendencies and the evil results such attitudes cause.

Psychological mentors of all sorts often tease people to get them to realize how overly serious they are about their mistakes. In response to people condemning themselves, their comment may be: "I don't think anyone in the city or state has ever made such a creative mistake before!" Breaking up the tension to understand the dynamics, rather than being involved in rumination, is an essential part of intrigue. Furthermore, at the other end of the spectrum, projection of blame onto others is discouraged by those who coach us as well: "If the source of the problem resides fully in the world outside of us, then we will have to change everyone else for it to improve. Quite a job for us!"

When we relinquish the blame, we also give away the power to change. But if we neutrally look at our own role with a sense of intrigue, not self-condemnation, we can increase the power that lies within us. This takes practice. Accordingly, I suggest people go through several steps to encourage intrigue:

> *First*, anytime you have a strong feeling about something, immediately act as if it is someone else experiencing the feeling.
> *Second*, observe any temptation to blame others or condemn yourself.
> *Third*, be a detective who is awed by the subtle temptations to be arrogant/ignorant and get intrigued about the process of uncovering the mystery of the real cause of the problem.

Bring the Responsibilities Home: Not with Vindictiveness but with Love, as You Would a Prodigal Child

Clarity is the medium of both new freedom and the ability to change. Many people never gain this state because they view the challenges and questions in their life without including the most important factor: themselves. Knowing and loving ourselves allows us to be more objective in how we see things. Ignorance, fear, and self-dislike cloud our vision, and sometimes we become so overwhelmed with emotion, rationalization, and denial that we are completely blind. But no matter—once we recognize this, we can begin to open our psychological and spiritual eyes and truly see again. With that clarity, we can stand firmly on our own two feet and walk toward our next goal, fully appreciating and learning from the journey itself. Nothing—no pain or failure—is ever wasted.

So, what will enhance the possibility of being more honest with ourselves as part of gaining a healthier perspective? The answer is that whatever increases the likelihood of others accepting questions and feedback from us will also increase our own willingness to embrace such understanding within ourselves. Included among these are:

- Style of approach
- Awareness of the positive
- Toughness
- Willingness to deal with unpleasant specifics
- Need for action based on insight

The way we approach ourselves is crucial if we are to learn the most from each event. Without treating ourselves with the right attitude, learning is hindered by defensiveness or self-condemnation. Fundamental to our attitude toward ourselves must be gentleness, love, and unwavering honesty. But as our mood changes, so should our approach when examining situations that can offer valuable insight into ourselves.

For example, when we are stressed, we should adopt a gentle curiosity: "Let's see what is happening so we can break things down a bit." A soothing desire to understand ourselves is an appropriate antidote to anxiety. When we are moody, bored, defeated, or passive, we need to be passionate and encouraging—perhaps even giving ourselves a little push to reach out to others so we remember to be grateful for what we have.

Another effective way to move toward clarity is to illuminate the darkness of negative situations. As we've seen, both cognitive behavioral therapy and positive psychology suggest that this can be achieved by increasing our awareness of the positive. Often, when we seek greater self-awareness—whether for psychological or spiritual reasons—we tend to amplify our sensitivity to ourselves. The goal is to bring into consciousness those pre-conscious patterns that remain hidden from our everyday awareness.

We do this by examining moments when we become upset and saying to ourselves, "Aha, here is another area where I am holding on!" We may also look more closely at times when we are angry, cowardly, blaming others, pompous, proud, or in denial of our own role in creating difficulties for ourselves and others. We tend to excuse or minimize the negative actions we continue to do in life.

Recognizing our faults in the light of day is beneficial. It enables us to address them. However, a problem arises when we let these "clouds" gather so that we no longer see our positive achievements and growth. To counteract this, just as we would in mentoring others, we must remember where we have successfully changed for the better in the past and avoid dismissing those successes, especially if we are struggling now. Once we've turned up the volume on our defensiveness, we can also recall moments when we experienced the freedom to act and break free from habits, fears, and petty addictions.

Toughness is also essential for clarity. While numerous techniques can make change and self-awareness easier, they won't make seeing things clearly and acting on our insights easy. We must seek to toughen ourselves up so that we can face *and act upon* the difficult insights about ourselves in the same way that we embrace the progress.

One spiritual master said to his disciple, "Tell me what you see in me, and, in turn, I will tell you what I see in you." His disciple replied, "You are a good person, but a little harsh." In response, the master said, "You are good, but your spirit is not tough enough yet." The obvious goal: Build a good and tough spirit in looking at our own foibles, escapes, and excuses.

A willingness to deal with unpleasant specifics in our lives significantly enhances the possibility of becoming increasingly honest with ourselves. Too often, our journey remains on the level of "the general"—it doesn't reach the depths of our daily experience. Yet, that is precisely where change must occur. If we aspire to be an author but never sit down to write, how will our dream come true? If we claim we want to be more compassionate but treat those who live and work with us poorly, what is the real value of our commitment? Bringing our responsibilities into our awareness allows us to see clearly our role in any difficulties and to take action to change them. When we do this, the rest of life will naturally follow. However, all of these steps must be taken without self-vindictiveness. The part of us that needs attention should be seen as a prodigal child—welcomed home, understood, and helped to change, not beaten up—especially by ourselves.

Looking More Closely: Sharpening a Healthy Perspective Through Daily "Self-Debriefings"

Annie Dillard, in her book *The Writing Life*, notes that "in working class France, when an apprentice got hurt or when he got tired, the experienced worker said: 'It is the trade entering his body.'" Similarly, when the daily pressures of our lives seem to tip the scales, we too become tired and frustrated; yet it can also be seen as a sign that a rich, meaningful, and compassionate life is entering our body.

A life of caring is never easy and sometimes pushes us into irritation. After a day especially filled with aggravations and ridiculous requests, a pastor sat down to dinner with his hair all askew, said a prayer of thanks, and turned to his dinner guest with a sigh, "I get the feeling that early this morning, someone put a sign on the door that read: 'If you're nuts, knock here!'"

Sometimes, things become much worse than this. Listening to stories of terrible things that happen to family members or coworkers, we catch glimpses of their futility, fear, vulnerability, and hopelessness—rather than merely feeling frustrated or concerned. We realize that no matter how professionally prepared we are, we are not immune to the psychological and spiritual dangers that arise from living a full, involved life with others. I learned this the hard way myself.

In 1994, I conducted a psychological debriefing of relief workers evacuated from Rwanda during its bloody civil war. I interviewed each person and gave them the opportunity to tell their stories. As they related the horrors they had experienced, they seemed to be grateful for an opportunity to vent. They recounted the details again and again, relating their feelings as well as descriptions of the events that triggered them. Their sense of futility, feelings of guilt, alienation, and emotional outbursts all came to the fore.

In addition to listening, I gave them handouts outlining what they might expect in the future—such as problems sleeping, difficulties trusting and relating to others, flashbacks, and similar challenges. As I progressed through the debriefing process and offered information to help them understand and frame their experiences, I thought to myself, "This is going pretty well." Then, something happened that profoundly shifted my entire experience.

During one of the final interviews, a relief worker recounted stories of how certain members of the Hutu tribe raped and dismembered their Tutsi foes. Suddenly, I realized I was holding onto my chair for dear life—I was doing what some young people call "white-knuckling it."

After the session, I did what I usually do after an intense encounter—a psychospiritual countertransferential review—if time permits, I do this at the end of every day. This process involves getting in touch with my feelings by asking myself: What made me sad? Overwhelmed me? Sexually aroused me? Made me extremely happy or even confused? Being brutally honest, I try to identify the core of my emotional response.

The first thing that struck me about this particular session was how tightly I was holding onto the chair as the relief worker's story unfolded. I asked myself, "What was I feeling when I did this? Why did I do this?"

It didn't take long to realize that the terrible stories had penetrated my defenses, momentarily shattering my usual sense of distance and detachment. I was holding onto the chair because I was, quite simply, terrified—that if I didn't, I might be pulled into the vortex of darkness myself.

That recognition alone helped to lessen both the pain and my fearful uneasiness. I then proceeded with a combination of countertransferential review and theological reflection—tools often used by therapists and ministers to prevent slipping into unnecessary darkness and to learn—and thus benefit—from the events of the day.

For therapists and counselors, a countertransferential review helps them become aware of the feelings triggered during treatment sessions. They seek to discover whether their intense encounters with clients have activated distorted thoughts or beliefs. By examining their own reactions, they not only gain insights about themselves but also develop a deeper understanding of the people and situations they encounter, often seeing them in new ways.

For ministers, a theological reflection is a spiritual review of the day. In this process, they stop at day's end to take stock of their lives. Like the countertransferential review, it helps them recognize when they are slipping into unnecessary darkness and allows them to learn from difficult or intense events.

The process of a *structured reflection*, which could be modified according to individual needs, includes the following steps:

- Picking events during the day that stand out
- Entering into the event and describing what happened (the objective) and how we felt (the subjective)

- Avoiding the temptation to be discouraged, blame others (projection) or ourselves (self-condemnation); instead, see what we can learn from the event about ourselves and our vulnerabilities, needs, addictions, fears, anxieties, worries, and desires
- Reflecting on the day in light of what we believe (our philosophy, psychology, ethics, and spirituality)
- Deciding on how what we learn from our reflections should change us personally, interpersonally, and professionally
- Altering the way we behave in light of these new insights

In the Buddhist tradition, Zen roshis teach that feelings, past hurts, shame, questions, and needs will come to the surface during meditation. These can teach us—if we are willing to pay attention and refrain from judging, blaming, indulging in, or rejecting our feelings. Instead, we must be open to learning from these experiences, just as we would hope others would learn from us.

In his informative work, *A Path with Heart*, Jack Kornfield points out, "Spiritual transformation is a profound process that doesn't happen by accident. We need a repeated discipline, a genuine training, in order to let go of our old habits of mind and to find and sustain a new way of seeing. To mature on the spiritual path we need to commit ourselves in a systematic way."

We can all benefit from these processes—be it counter transferential review, philosophical/theological reflection, or Buddhist meditation. People who wish to live truly aware lives need to take time out during the day, or at day's end, to quietly sit with their feelings and cognitions in an objective, nonjudgmental way. The more we can do this on a regular basis, the more we can avoid unnecessary darkness and live through the unpleasant events of life in a way that provides direction and learning.

Debriefing ourselves can also be enhanced by sharing this process with someone we trust to accompany us on the psychological and spiritual journey. When we get feedback from those we trust, we will cut down on the distortion and discouragement that can arise when we seek to be truly honest and loving with ourselves. The importance of having the patience and determination to go deeper in our lives sometimes can't be seen until someone else—much wiser than we are—helps nudge us along in the self-discovery process. A sensitive guide who was aware of the important role balance plays in exploring our inner life once told me this story, which nicely illustrates my point:

> As I reflected on a call I felt to metaphorically "put out into the deep water and lower my nets for a catch," a childhood memory came to mind. My aunt would advise me on how to draw a cup from a fresh pail of milk. The cream and froth would be gathering to the top, and if you put your mug in straight, it either filled with froth (no substance, shallow) or with all the cream (too rich for your system).
>
> Instead she showed me how to bend over and blow gently on the top, about three gentle blows. The froth and cream would glide over to the sides and I could then put my mug in deep down and draw up milk and angle my cup in such a way to gather just a little cream as well.

Beautiful! But we have to be willing to patiently, gently blow the froth and to reach into the depth and draw up such a full, balanced catch. A "full, balanced catch" involves discovering:

- What we were *feeling* (affect) at different points in the day
- What we were *thinking* that caused us to feel that way
- What we were *believing* that made us think or come to the conclusions we arrived at.

Not taking time to review and learn from our day is foolish. Moreover, if we don't consistently spend time asking ourselves why we feel, think, and believe what we do, we risk missing the chance to live a freer, more satisfying life. In contrast, when we adopt practices that enhance our openness to change and increase our clarity, we cultivate both a healthier perspective and a way of greeting each day that helps us discover more about ourselves and those around us.

If we avoid looking at ourselves, we miss the opportunity to uncover the hidden programming that may be driving us in directions we need not go. On the other hand, by taking the time to examine ourselves during the day and at day's end, we give ourselves the chance to cut the psychological strings held by the "hidden puppeteer" (our unconscious or erroneous beliefs) and begin to live in a clearer, more intentional way. This is essential if we are to live a peaceful, full, and compassionate life—and to maintain a healthy perspective.

Bringing Role Models Closer So They Can Help Us

There is a tendency to keep potential role models at a distance. The media colludes in this. First, it elevates individuals who are very different from us. Then, investigative reporters dig up every bit of dirt they can to show that the idols they presented to us have feet of clay. This creates a see-saw effect on our psyche and can be discouraging. We receive a disheartening message: namely, that real figures of wisdom and truly good people are rare—if they exist at all!

This message is pure nonsense! Moreover, it is destructive to the natural and necessary movement in society to both seek and become mentors. All of us should strive to be role models for others—not by being fake or putting on a good face for a particular role, but by becoming all that we can be. Each day (trying for longer periods can be too discouraging), we need to accept the challenge to be our best—at home, in the office, even in the grocery store.

Again, I don't mean we should practice "chronic niceness" or put on a plastic smile. Nor do I mean we should try to imitate someone famous or familiar whose lifestyle or personality is completely different from our own. What's essential is that we aim to be healthy role models while also seeking a personal standard-bearer for ourselves. Our role model should be the kind of person we believe we could become if we dropped some of our defenses and allowed our true personality to flourish.

In psychotherapy, patients are able to change partly because the therapist functions, on some level, as a role model. The patient thinks: "I trust that this person—while not perfect—is living in truth, with greater flexibility and an openness to possibility, more than I am right now. I can follow her lead. I can borrow her strength and, step by step, take the risk to change, to explore new possibilities, and to see myself and the world in a healthier way."

In spiritual guidance, the role of a sage is also essential. In Buddhism and Hinduism, it is expressed as devotion to a guru (literally meaning "one who removes darkness") and a deep desire to align one's will with that of the spiritual master. In Christianity, it may be Christ—who, according to the Gospels, did not cling to his divinity so that others could see their own humanity and possibility reflected in him.

In daily life, we all encounter lessons and opportunities like these. In business, there may be someone we admire. In our families, an older sibling or cousin may share our personality style but be more personally integrated.

Or, in a well-developed saga or biography, we may recognize qualities in others that we aspire to emulate.

For years, I felt a need to be gentler, as a way of softening my passion. In Shirley du Boulay's biography of Bede Griffiths, *Beyond the Darkness*, I saw that his desire for gentleness was somewhat like mine. I saw that his nature, like mine, needed tempering—and still does. But du Boulay's words about Griffiths gave me hope when I first read them, and they continue to do so:

> It is clear that as a young man Alan was not easy to live with; that the saintly man he was to become was the result of his determination, the fruit of a life of . . . meditation, rather than the path of a man born with a naturally easy temperament. The search for holiness, the journey on which he was already embarking, is a hard road. If he sometime overrode the needs of his companions, it was the blindness brought on by the intensity of his own struggle and he certainly paid for it in the remorse that later swept over him. Much later [one of his companions] summed up the way Alan had been and the man he became in a single phrase: "He is much more now a pervasive light than a consuming flame."

One of the key elements of change, then, is to seek out role models we can emulate, rather than keep at a distance. To increase the likelihood of this happening, we need to find role models who are right for us at this particular point in our lives.

Role models vary from person to person. One person may seek someone who is inspirational; for another, the most valued trait may be clear thinking or a calm demeanor. However, when we consider role models in relation to the concepts of *inner freedom, growth, change,* and *a healthy perspective,* certain talents or qualities are consistently present in all truly healthy role models—regardless of their personality style or background. It is important to know what these qualities are. Not only does it help us choose the right person to emulate, but it is also essential when we seek to develop our own inner freedom. In this way, we can actively welcome growth and change, rather than resist it.

Some of the key qualities of a person with inner freedom and a healthy perspective—someone we should strive to model ourselves after—include:

- An ability to let go
- Being receptive to new lessons

- A countercultural attitude that is not self-righteous
- A sense of intrigue with one's own emotional flashing lights
- A feeling of disgust with *samsara* (the endless wheel of suffering that comes from grasping and attachments) and bad habits
- Curious, not judgmental
- Values experience
- Recognizes danger of preferences which prevent experiencing new gifts in life
- Awake to present; is mindful
- Appreciates quiet meditation
- Generous and alive
- Learns, reflects, and applies wisdom in daily life
- Rests lightly in life
- Knows the difference between "freedom to be" versus "freedom to choose"

To gain a sense of people who possess a healthy perspective—one that leads to greater inner freedom—we need to pay attention to the kinds of questions commonly asked of mentors known for their mindfulness and clarity, as well as the responses they typically give. These responses often represent composites of the oral answers reportedly shared by such individuals. It is by grappling with the right questions in our own lives that we can move forward, avoid missing opportunities, and better navigate both internal transitions and external change.

Several Final Things to Remember on the Psychology of Resistance to Change

As we have seen, even when we are motivated to be open to change and excited about its possibilities—whether at different phases of life or during the turns of a single day—there are still many factors that can hold us back. Habits are quiet, comfortable ways of drifting through the brief time we have in "a life." Once ingrained, we may not even realize that we are following an invisible script rather than responding beneficially to the particular challenges and opportunities before us.

Also, our need for acceptance by those in our past and those currently in our circle of friends and family is a pressure not often reflected upon. Once we move through the teenage years into young adulthood, another factor comes into play: our personality, which represents the consistent, unique way we view the world. Our personality style also influences how we interact with others, perceive the world, communicate, and live through both "good" and "bad" times. Who we are, what challenges we face, the overall education we have received, and the people in our support group—all combine to make a significant difference.

This is why the discussion of resistance to change was examined here, as well as the type of friends that lead to optimal recognition of the factors impacting our lives. It is also why the topics of unlearning, letting go, and the importance of taking time in silence and solitude will be explored in the next two chapters.

Each of us has a different sensitivity to what is happening around and within us, a unique pain threshold that signals the need for change, and a distinct way and pace of learning. But as Kottler notes in his book *Change*, "Once you become more educated about your own processes and patterns, you can significantly enhance the magnitude, power, and pace of change you'd like to make"—which is the purpose not only of this chapter but also of the chapters to come as we keep our eyes on *possibility*.

For Review and Reflections . . .

In Pursuit of Clarity: Careful Self-Questioning

"The world fears a new experience more than it fears anything. Because a new experience displaces so many old experiences."

—D. H. Lawrence

Simple exploration of events, feelings, and cognitions (ways of thinking, perceiving, and understanding) can provide a valuable resource for reflection, adjusting dysfunctional thinking, shifting to a healthier perspective, and ultimately producing important changes in both attitude and behavior. Below are some sample questions inspired by principles from critical thinking, cognitive behavioral and schema therapy, as well as classic spiritual discernment literature.

When I fail do I:

- Ask myself what I feel most badly about for not succeeding?
- Catch myself when I am tempted to see everything as a failure instead of this one event?
- Give myself the alone-time necessary to be upset, understand, and move on?
- See how my own ego is preventing me from being open to all the agendas and learning possible?
- Appreciate what I can learn about myself that would not have been possible had I succeeded?
- Learn what contributed to this failure both in myself and in the situation surrounding it?
- Appreciate how to avoid or minimize failures like this in the future without feeling I must totally withdraw from the scene as a way of dealing with this lack of success in this instance?
- See the role of unrealistic expectations and how my own thinking may have contributed to my having them?
- See how failure and the pacing of efforts in my life are possibly related because I was moving too fast, slow, or precipitously?
- Acknowledge personal and professional limitations in my life that can be improved?

- Miss early warning signs that if addressed could have averted this result?
- See this as an impetus to initiate new interpersonal approaches to the challenge in question?
- Truly recognize that failure is part and parcel of involvement and that the more I am involved, statistically, the more I will fail?

Do I emulate cognitive behavioral and schema therapists as well as critical thinkers and spiritual discerners by seeking the wisdom, intellectual power, and a healthier perspective that can result from more carefully:

- Examining comfortable, but unsatisfying patterns with an eye to practicing a step-by-step approach to undo and replace them?
- Recognizing my own gifts, growing edges, agendas, negative emotions, attitudes, motivations, beliefs, and ways of thinking, perceiving, and understanding when a feeling or reaction arises?
- Seeing "the grays" of life rather than simply shunning ambiguities and seeking only so-called right or wrong answers to the questions of life?
- Entertaining both the possible and probable as I reflect on a challenge, problem, or question?
- Appreciating (and then enjoying more fully) the positive elements already present in my interpersonal circle?
- Uncovering when I over-predict worrisome events and challenge them so even little potentially beautiful encounters in life aren't missed?
- Appreciating those times when I tend to exaggerate, catastrophize, minimize, "awfulize," or can't see the humor or nuance in events or interpersonal encounters?
- Dealing with disagreement, rejection, or change?
- Searching for what I can understand and let go of when I encounter personal emotional hot-button issues?
- Picking up "self-talk" that is defeating in nature such as: minimizing or disqualifying the positive, if I feel it, it must be true, if I don't succeed at something then I am a total failure, etc.?
- Balancing the way I am looking at an event by exploring alternative possibilities/interpretations?
- Recognizing an inclination to see negative and self-defeating behaviors as being a "natural" part of one's life rather than a schema/belief to be

uncovered, challenged, and replaced with a healthier perspective/life pattern?

Do I seek further clarity in examining something during my daily debriefing by discovering:

- What emotions are elicited by this particular topic, event, or area and what is the thinking behind them?
- What mature and immature agendas do/did I have in this interaction?
- On what am I basing my conclusions/interpretations regarding this and what might be some other possible ones that I might see now that I have stepped back a bit from the interaction/event?
- What makes this challenge a possibly more difficult or emotional one for me?
- What might be some other ways to look at this that I haven't yet considered?
- Are there additional details or input I could obtain which might help me broaden or deepen my understanding?
- Why might I resist changing my opinion on this? (i.e., What consequences or vulnerabilities are in play here?)
- What was unexpected and surprising in what I am now examining?
- What is the first thing that comes to mind when I think of this topic/event/person and what can this reaction teach me about *myself*?
- Am I giving enough time for reflection and consideration of the issues at hand?
- Am I picking up the "voices" of self/other's blame, discouragement, and unhelpful labeling of people and events and responding to them so they don't prevent critical thinking?
- What factors do parental/family/corporate/religious/other values and notable past events in my life play in preventing me from thinking more openly about this issue?
- What would it take for me to replace possible hypersensitivity with a sense of intrigue about these events or occurrences?
- How I can use this particular issue as an opportunity for building resilience and strengthening a healthier perspective by (1) leaning back emotionally from the event, (2) reappraising it, and (3) renewing myself through gaining new wisdom through humility and new learning?

- This as an opportunity to increase my sense of intrigue about where I am spending my energy and learning what the emotional centers of gravity are in my life?
- New abilities in: asking myself questions; developing logic and abstract reasoning; clarifying my values and collecting as much information as possible in ways that my self-knowledge and enjoyment of all of life (both what is perceived as bad as well as good) is accomplished?
- Innovative approaches to: track dysfunctional styles; enhance life-giving activities and approaches; and become fascinated with learning more and more ways to loosen the grasp of ongoing unproductive habits?
- Possibly opposing views to mine which may balance or enrich my understanding?
- The unfamiliar as well as the familiar in how I understand my actions?
- Where immediate self-interest blinds me to new information that may lead to a broader, healthier perspective for me in the long run?

As a final reflection before moving on to the second series of questions on gaining and maintaining a healthy perspective, asking the following questions during a period available for quiet, slow consideration would be helpful.

Am I aware of:

- Both my signature strengths and growing edges *in detail*?
- The values which represent the "music" (attitude) I have playing in my mind as well as the "lyrics" (thoughts and actions) that follow?
- My priorities in life at this phase of it and whether they have/should change?
- The ability to delay or postpone immediate gratification in pursuit of a greater good?
- How I determine the difference between taking a measured risk and being rash?
- The levels of stress/distress I am experiencing and how I am dealing with them?
- How disappointment derails my sense of purpose so I know how to get back on track?
- Ways to set both incremental and far-reaching goals that are *both* optimistic and attainable?

- The importance of being *both* clear and gentle in undertaking self-reflection when dealing with failure, mistakes, and uncertainty?

Sample Questions to Consider to Gain a Healthier Sense of Perspective

What is the psychological essence of inner freedom?

Don't prejudge. Picasso used to lament that it was a shame we couldn't pluck out our brains and just use our eyes. Too often, past experiences fasten a biased perception onto what we encounter. This prevents us from seeing things simply as they are. Instead, we see things as we wish them to be, as we fear they might be, or as we feel they should be. Wishes, fears, and "shoulds" cloud our eyes and prevent clarity.

Are there signs I should be aware of that I'm not being open to the help I've sought from others to help me grow or change?

Classic signs that we are resisting help from others that would enable us to be more open to change include:

- Frequently arguing or taking issue with suggestions being offered
- Holding back on sharing information because of shame or lack of trust
- Making excuses for not doing the agreed-upon tasks between session/meetings with your growth/change consultant/mentor
- Complaining that real progress is too difficult for you to accomplish
- Blaming others for your lack of advancement
- Focusing on the differences between you and your mentor as a way of excusing your lack of compliance with suggestions offered for consideration
- Monopolizing time together to the extent that the other person can't get in a word
- Being late or missing helpful encounters with others
- Not taking responsibility for bringing information to a meeting, but expecting that the consultant will provide the agenda
- Repeated, extended silent periods.

Are there ever times when I disagree with someone guiding me, and it is not resistance to change but a healthy difference?

Yes, this often happens when people have different philosophies about what one's goals should be in life. The situation where this occurs most frequently is at work, during feedback from someone who, in the organizational chart, is responsible for helping you grow professionally. For example, in an end-of-year evaluation, a supervisor said, "You are so talented, I'm surprised you're not more ambitious." After reflecting on this feedback, the employee replied, "Oh, I think I'm very, very ambitious. However, I believe we may be ambitious for different things." When the supervisor asked him to explain and heard what he meant, both realized there were true differences in what was being valued, rather than simple resistance to taking risks or expending energy to move ahead.

If I work with someone (a coach, supervisor, mentor, therapist, or spiritual guide), what are some of the ways I can reduce my resistance to the change and growth I seek?

If you are willing to consult someone to help you change and grow, you have already overcome the first barrier that most people never get past: the simple admission that you need assistance. You can't do it alone. Once you've taken that step, there are additional ways to make the most of the consultant you've chosen by following some simple—but often not easy—guidelines, including:

- Be honest.
- Avoid second-guessing or preparing answers while your consultant is speaking. Instead, listen carefully.
- Achieve as much clarity as possible as to what your goals are in seeking this relationship; ensure you both are in agreement regarding the objectives.
- Recognize that though the principles of change, growth, and achieving greater freedom in life are usually surprisingly simple, they take work.

Is there a style of thinking I should seek to incorporate which encourages growth, change, and the search for a healthier perspective?

Yes. If you see yourself as an adventurer—or as part of a group of psychological and spiritual pioneers—like inventors Edison and Buckminster Fuller were—your enthusiasm for the process of change will grow. Even failures will become sources of learning and intrigue. The key attitude that fosters this mindset is this: I will enjoy the process and journey toward greater freedom, change, and enlightenment, rather than solely focusing on the end result.

What about the other side of the coin? What tip-offs do I have that my thinking is resisting change by being defeatist, inappropriate, or negative, and how can I short-circuit self-defeating thinking?

Real change becomes difficult when we are ambushed by negative beliefs and unhelpful attitudes. True growth and maintaining a healthy perspective require that we surface and confront the messages that have held us back—perhaps even for years.

The best way to recognize this is to catch yourself in the act of making broad, negative statements and to respond to them constructively:

- When you think, "I'm a failure," reply, "I didn't succeed this time. What can I learn from what happened?"
- If you catch yourself thinking, "I guess I am just not meant to change or grow," ask, "What happened today that I found discouraging?" "Why am I feeling so discouraged?" and "Did I set my goals in a way that was meant to deflate rather than challenge me?"
- Instead of saying, "Changing is impossible! It's just too hard," remind yourself, "Progress does take effort, but each step is manageable."
- And rather than thinking, "My life is hopeless; I need to win a 'psychological lottery,'" remember that "When things don't go our way, it may feel hopeless. But if we break things down and take it step by step, there is always reason for hope."

4

Preparing Space for Possibility

Letting Go, Kenosis, Unlearning, Traveling Lightly . . . and the Delicate Role of Grieving

"The best way to keep a prisoner from escaping is to make sure he never knows he's in prison."

—Fyodor Dostoevsky

"The mind, once stretched by a new idea, never returns to its original dimensions."

—Ralph Waldo Emerson

Years ago, a tale was told about how a group of people in Africa would catch monkeys. They would take gourds and cut off the large ends to empty and fill them with peanuts. After attaching the gourds to a tree, they would then cut a small hole in the narrow end and leave the scene for a while. Once they were gone, the monkeys higher in the trees would feel safe enough to come down. As they approached, they would see the gourds and inspect them. They smelled the peanuts and wanted them. And so, they would reach into the gourds, grab the peanuts, but then find themselves unable to get their hands out through the small hole. Some monkeys would realize the problem, release the peanuts, and leave. Others, equally frustrated but unwilling to relinquish the peanuts, would remain tethered to the gourds by their clenched fists filled with peanuts, screaming in frustration. Those who had earlier secured the gourds to the trees would then return, capture the monkeys, and send them to zoos, where they would be imprisoned and miserable for the rest of their lives. Those who shared this tale would then tell those listening to them, "Before we project your scorn too quickly onto these poor animals, the questions for you and for I are: What are we still holding onto and refuse to let go of that results in our forfeiting our own freedom and making us miserable? Possibly without being fully aware of it, why are we continuing to entertain limiting, poisonous thoughts and beliefs that are holding us back, making us psychologically sick, and suffocating our potential?"

These are really tough questions for all of us to answer, but they are ones we must face because possibility is often missed, refused, or taken depending on how willing we are to release what is holding us back. Ancient Chinese philosopher Lao Tzu puts the potential cost of our fears and concerns about uncertainty by saying, "If I let go of who I am . . . I become who I might be." To this, the Buddha would add, "In the end, only three things matter: how much you loved, how gently you lived . . . and how gracefully you let go of things not meant for you." From a psychological point of view, we need to recognize there are true helps for us at each phase of our journey, but we must carry only what we need *now*. The rest, even if it were helpful in the past, is too much for us to hold within our minds and hearts and must be let go of.

Possibility is encountered by those who see themselves as pilgrims—individuals who listen to the new and different voices around them so they can live more robust and meaningful way. Yet, the temptation is to be merely a *tourist*—watching life from the sidelines, with only occasional moments of pleasure and comfort.

Researcher and renowned scientist Louis Pasteur explained the importance of honoring a true journey by setting the stage for a pilgrimage: "In the field of observation, chance favors the prepared mind." Many possibilities are missed by those who are too busy to notice them at a deeper level. The wise words of Phil Cousineau in his delightful book *The Art of Pilgrimage* underscore this point: "To set out on a pilgrimage is to throw down a challenge to everyday life. . . . Attentive travel helps us to see this because the continually changing outward scene helps us to see through the world's pretentions."

When the question arises as to why someone might forsake the spirit of pilgrimage as a way to form a healthier, more open perspective and attitude toward life, Cousineau explains that pilgrims who came before us recognized the need to "be prepared to discover that from the spiritual point of view that the journey is always a two-edged sword because of the dispersion which can result from contact with so much that is new." He adds, "We cannot simply shut ourselves off from this newness or we might just as well stay home—if we are going to travel we naturally wish to learn something. But if the newness threatens to overwhelm us, it can occasion periodic hardenings of the ego, as if in reaction to the fear of losing ourselves through dispersal we find it necessary to shore up our identities."

To have an attitude of "pilgrimage" like this psychologically in our daily lives, we must be willing to learn to:

- Travel lightly and appreciate kenosis
- Understand the import of *un*learning
- Honor the process of "letting go"
- Expect transitions within us, even when they are difficult, to be potentially valuable experiences
- Fathom the essential role of "grieving" the loss of people, security, and possessions since this process is part of the journey in living a meaningful life

Travel Lightly . . . Appreciate Kenosis

Making psychological room within ourselves is essential so we have the inner freedom to welcome possibility. *Kenosis* refers to an emptying of ourselves of all that is unnecessary now, so we can be prepared for more. To accommodate change, move, and *really* grow emotionally and cognitively, we need "space" within ourselves. Habits, worries, emotions, defensiveness, stubbornness, and fear all take up room. Spiritual sages and philosophical wisdom figures have known and pointed this out through the ages. Maybe that is why Zen roshis, for example, suggest that to find joy and peace, we don't need to add something to our lives. Instead, we need to drop something so we can see more clearly the possibilities before us. Psychologists have been less poetic. They simply suggest that we get rid of those "expensive defenses" that take up too much of our energy. Their suggestion? Uncover and *let go* of old, useless habits and unfounded erroneous negative beliefs and the result will be new freedom during the day and at each turn in life.

Once, while teaching a course on the integration of psychology and classic spirituality, I noticed a fascinating dynamic between two students. One was a Buddhist, modeling a sense of serenity, while the other was an Evangelical Christian, quite passionate and often expressive. I observed that when she was so outgoing with her feelings and opinions, it disturbed the Buddhist sitting right in front of me. In response, he made facial expressions that only I could see. I kept my observations of his reactions to myself.

Then, one day, the student became so effusive and excited about something that she actually threw an object at the board just missing me. She, of course, was mortified and later told me she recognized the need to reflect on her behavior—which I reinforced, knowing that with some mentoring, her deep passion could find greater focus and produce better results for herself and those she interacted with.

However, after this outburst, the young Buddhist counseling student in front of me could not contain his disdain for her behavior. I felt it was time to "use" his reaction to help him explore his inner self further. I asked him to stay after class.

When everyone else had left, I said to him, "You noticed the behavior of the student who threw something at the board." He responded quite vehemently that he had, and the psychological barriers opened as he expressed his negative feelings toward her. Once he finished, I said to him in a low voice, "She is your spiritual guide." His face showed an incredulous look before he composed himself and replied, "I'll have to think about that." I responded, "I didn't ask you to think about it. She is your spiritual director." With that, I walked out, leaving him to reflect on what I had just said so firmly.

My point to this very psychologically and spiritually mature student was that anyone capable of eliciting such strong negative emotion is actually a "teacher" of sorts—about what he finds most upsetting, fearful, anxiety-provoking, or anger-inducing rather than sorrowful. Listening to those whose behavior we despise offers an opportunity to examine our own virtues and outlook. If we do so gently and clearly, little remains to be projected onto others.

When we are filled with unexamined opinions, attitudes, and assumptions, there is little room to intellectually and emotionally mature. I believe Lao Tzu articulated this well when he said, "The usefulness of the cup is its emptiness." Over the past 40 years of being a psychotherapist, spiritual companion, and clinical supervisor of helping professionals, I've often wished I could ask certain questions. Surprisingly, they mostly revolve around one theme: traveling lightly or letting go.

Perhaps I didn't ask them earlier because, in pacing sessions, they seemed inappropriate at the moment. Maybe, as I walked beside individuals on their psychological journeys, I felt the questions would ask too much of them. Or, even in my own life pilgrimage, I hesitated because I was afraid of where those questions might lead me. Whatever the reason, the result was the same: less inner freedom and a failure to fully understand the paradox of letting go—even as it opens us to life's possibilities, both small and significant, at each turn. Traveling lightly means not only releasing unnecessary possessions but also shedding old habits that prevent us from being a person without guile who can meet others and the challenges of living a full life while wearing our psychological clothes loosely and being willing to change them when they no longer fit.

Welcoming Change

So much energy is spent holding onto things that it is no wonder people feel too exhausted to become involved in a program of change. Change takes energy, openness, and honesty. And, once again, to be honest, *really* honest, with ourselves requires us to recognize that, in many subtle ways, we are not very clear and candid in our self-analysis. As a result, instead of knowing when we are grasping or trying to control life, we remain in the dark, which prevents us from gaining a healthy perspective.

There are many good things: health, wealth, success, friends, and feeling physically attractive. Desiring and enjoying them is wonderful. However, being dependent on any of these for happiness and feeling anxious about losing them is not helpful. In our hearts, we must be free to appreciate and enjoy all that we have without falling into the trap of spending so much time and energy trying to secure them, so they will never be lost.

Many people feel as if holding on tightly is "only being practical." In reality, though, it is foolish. If we were to stop for a few minutes to reflect on our own and others' experiences, we would see this to be true. There are people who are in ill health, poor, unsuccessful by worldly standards, appear to have few friends, and may not be especially attractive by usual norms—yet they are happy. There are also others—maybe including ourselves at times—who seem to have so much and are not as happy as we could be. Why? Because people who are truly happy are grateful for the process of being alive and have learned to be free to change and enjoy everything that is before them. Others, however, have centered in on certain things that they feel are the only things/people that can make them happy. So unfortunately, when change or loss of people and possessions eventually takes place, as it surely will, they become unhappy—even in anticipation of this occurring.

In various aspects of our lives, we need to ask a simple question: When do I get upset, or feel the happiest? How we answer this question will lead to wonderful information about our values and preferences. It will also guide us to those places where we have become frozen, excluding other possibilities for ourselves and others. Once again, feeling joy is wonderful and being upset on occasion is natural. The problem is not with the emotion or experience but in being unaware as to why we really felt this way. By questioning ourselves further, there is much helpful information for us to mine, which will lead us to gain or maintain a healthy perspective. To reinforce this, we should also seek to emulate those persons we admire for their openness and psychological health—particularly how they view themselves and life, no matter what is going on around them.

When people speak of "releasing" or "letting go," it is often in reference to a specific desire, possession, or relationship. But while jettisoning a particular attachment can be the source of new inner "lightness," releasing is much more than that, although we shall address that as well. What this attitude or spirit offers can be an almost indescribable gift if it is fully understood and becomes the cornerstone of an overall attitude of freedom that is constantly renewed and experienced.

There is a relief when you release your grasp—even of something that may initially have been beneficial or practical. When the timing is right, the movement toward new freedom is wonderful. To be honest and realistic, though, such freedom is often short-lived. The room swept clean no longer remains that way. The empty space that originally opened up new opportunities for creativity, compassion, wisdom, and the experience of freedom in our lives soon starts to fill up again. It need not be with something bad or addictive, but it still fills nonetheless; our life no longer has the sense of the fresh possibility that it did for a while.

Unfortunately, the harm this causes is not normally felt for some time. And when it is finally discovered, a sense of self-betrayal or remorse is often experienced. This feeling may even lead us to think, "I am back where I started—or even further back than that!"

However, when there is a sense of openness to nurturing an attitude of releasing or letting go, even when grasping becomes temporarily prevalent again, all is not lost. There is at least a recognition that our new free space has slowly and quietly become contaminated again. This should not be surprising, because habit (or the influences from the past and the society in which one lives) can be very persuasive.

There is the "secondary gain" experienced when we feel like a martyr and can project the blame onto others, allowing us to take the easy way out rather than involve ourselves in the hard work of change. There is a degree of comfort in remaining helpless and gaining sympathy from others. Working to attain inner freedom is not easy to maintain.

Still, the good news is that when we are mindful of the natural tendency to retreat to the familiar, a reservoir of integrity always remains within us—one that values both honesty and clarity. Paradoxically, this awareness of having been pulled back again can also seed an even more intense desire to practice letting go anew—maybe this time with greater wisdom concerning the challenges we all face.

And so, when new idols and fears appear—though they may be temporarily bowed to—the pilgrimage to experiencing life more directly and fully never truly ceases. The rewards of avoiding grasping and ego tight-fistedness are experienced more quickly. The loosening of one's psychological grip and being able to smile at the amount of peace and joy during the day is felt. Yes, deeply felt. Then everything becomes easier because the art of releasing is experienced and honored more often—not because it should be, but because it simply makes sense.

For this to happen, though, knowledge, discipline, and commitment to enhancing our outlook and practice regarding opening ourselves up to life are essential companions. And so, with this reality before us—and to dispel any notions of psychological romanticism about the process being easy, automatic, or magical—several "field notes" on letting go will be explored. They are designed to put the experiences of others (both their successes and failures) at our disposal. They are also intended to encourage each of us to write our own reflections, tracking the ongoing unfolding of our lives. This is a simple yet powerful tool for learning from personal experiences and reactions.

By utilizing the information assembled here, the goal is to help us appreciate and record personal breakthroughs as well as possibly unnecessary mistakes. In developing our own set of field notes on inner freedom, we immediately undertake a search for what works best—given our unique background, circumstances, personality style, and beliefs.

By unearthing this information, we can begin to enjoy the pilgrimage to greater inner freedom more intentionally, making space for the experience of life and our relationship with it. We can also see that attending to the flow of life—rather than merely drifting with it—is an intriguing and rewarding daily endeavor in itself. Even when it is difficult and we stumble, we learn from these encounters as well. There can be an ultimate satisfaction—even in failure.

Creating Your Own "Field Notes"

Field or clinical notes are about a person's experiences of what is happening around and within them. They are notations made by social and behavioral scientists about what they have observed in others—as well as themselves—while undertaking research and/or treatment of others. For instance, anthropologists have long been known for their written personal observations of cultures. Reading the works of Margaret Mead and Colin Turnbull (author of *The Forest People*) enlightens us not only about the people being studied but also about the researchers themselves. Formal clinical notes or informal journal entries are similar to this.

They are prepared by psychotherapists and some mentors to record the course of the lives of people who come to them for assistance. They also usually offer assessments of the interventions that were recommended and the resistances to such changes encountered in the process. These findings are relevant—they speak to the helpers about their own human state and psychological situation as well.

Since all of us must face transitions, losses, and the requirement to see things in new ways as we move forward in life, this information is essential not only to those who seek some form of help but also to ourselves.

In my own case, I recall the efforts I made to observe and fathom people's feelings, attitudes, and cognitions—ways of thinking, perceiving, and understanding. I also sought to note their actions, psychology, philosophies, and hesitations to act in ways that might lead to greater inner freedom, a more powerful desire to be compassionate toward others, and their openness to the ongoing revelation of offering compassion in new ways.

I also know that in preparing my own field or clinical notes (by seeking to put my psychological "fingers" on the pulse of my feelings and thoughts during sessions), I could discover a great deal not only about those seeking help but also about myself—because of the reactions they elicited. Certain people have particular effects on us, so we can begin to see patterns that teach us a great deal about ourselves as well as those with whom we interact.

In seeking to accomplish this, I sought wisdom from the writings of other guides I knew or had read about, to see how their reflections and "field notes" were guiding their own self-understanding. It is especially beneficial if, in our reading and reflection, we use as psychological lenses both a sense of the value of releasing as well as what seems to be holding us back from encountering a deeper, richer sense of self. And so, from both classic wisdom and the findings of contemporary psychology, actual approaches to greater inner freedom are there for the taking. All we need to do is look at them more intentionally with this purpose in mind. By doing so, we can better incorporate helpful attitudes and activities that can have both immediate and long-term impacts on the amount of freedom we experience in our lives.

Preparing our own "field notes" at the end of the day is simple and only takes a few moments. However, those moments can be invaluable—especially at this delicate stage in life—because they record essential information to track one's emotions and thoughts going forward.

The first step is simply to sit back and reflect on the peaks, valleys, and plateaus of the day. Once a clear picture emerges (what happened), it becomes possible to reflect on our emotions and what we were thinking, perceiving, and understanding about the events of the day. Such an activity can help us see more clearly the vague perceptions and beliefs that often foster our emotional reactions and conclusions. In this way we can recognize our philosophy and psychology of life more readily and address or correct it in ways that will free us to live our life more intentionally.

Then, when the end of life eventually comes—whether suddenly or slowly—it will be with a spirit of releasing and openness to new experiences at the heart of our lives. We will know that the present moment is being encountered as fully as possible—almost to the point of astonishing awareness. We will have the sense that releasing our grasp and opening up to appreciate ourselves—acting out of a deeper honoring of who we are:

- Is both a practice and an attitude
- Involves small daily actions and large decisions
- Can be fed, not distracted, by memories of past joys as well as by possibilities for the future
- Rarely ends with a final breakthrough but rather is, more accurately, a journey during middle through late adulthood of recognizing and embracing inner freedom
- Manifests itself differently depending upon one's personality
- Is worth the time, effort, and respect we can afford understanding and incorporating it into our overall outlook and daily experience

- Is a way of living to help us avoid wasting so much of our short precious life by postponing fulfillment until something else happens in the future

Greater inner freedom and more fruitful encounters with others can begin now—if we are willing to act upon what we decide is relevant for us in reflecting on these lessons and then putting them into practice in a way that makes sense for us.

The specific reward? A flexibility, openness to grace, and lightness of being that an attitude of letting go and being present can bring to us.

The cost? As a starting point, time spent in reflection on the ongoing themes in this book, the courage to change based on what is learned, and the discipline necessary not to turn back but to keep our hands on the wheel of our lives—even when it shakes.

Not a bad deal when you think about it.

So, Where Do We Begin?

In order to release, we first need to realize that we are holding on—whether in terms of material possessions, our identity, or our way of interacting with others. Surprisingly, this may not be as easy as it seems. Finding our emotional center of gravity can be elusive. For instance, what initially was truly beneficial or rewarding behavior may, over time, have quietly slipped into being something quite different: *grasping*. In some cases, society may also collude with this change, making it even harder to recognize and address.

Once, a famous Buddhist monk recalled a moment of awakening in his own life. He was staring intently at a beautiful piece of pottery. Just then, his abbot walked by and said as he passed, "Stop committing adultery." The comment, from someone wiser and more experienced about what was actually taking place in his heart, provided new enlightenment. He could now see what was truly happening. It obviously had nothing to do with a sexual encounter inside or outside the monastery. Instead, it was about the fact that he had moved from admiration of a beautiful piece of pottery—which is a wonderful attitude—to a desire to possess the vase, something unhelpful to someone committed to inner freedom. Admiration allows us to fully enjoy and then move on. With lust, we become captured by the object, person, or cause. We are caught by it in ways that prevent us from appreciating everything else that is also before us as a gift.

If we went to a beautiful garden and were only captivated by one flower, it would be a waste. Likewise, if we heard only one instrument during an overture, so much would be missed. The sad thing is that we often do just that with many small and large things in life—sometimes without even realizing it. We become captured not only by our basic style of dealing with life but also by what seems new, different, or supposedly perfect—until it dawns on us that we have been duped by induced needs or society's salesmanship. Eventually, the new becomes familiar, the different becomes part of the same, and what was once deemed perfect is finally unveiled for what or who it truly is.

So, the question we may ask is: Why do we continue to fall for the lure of what doesn't turn out to be truly rewarding when, in our hearts, we actually know better? A bombardment of both formal and informal advertising has replaced a psychology and philosophy of hope. Instead, an "anxiety of entitlement" and a fear that our needs won't be met unless we are aggressive on our own behalf are promulgated. Once again, though, why do we continually fall for it? After all, we are pretty bright and have had some pretty revelatory experiences in our lives, haven't we?

John Berger, in his book *Ways of Seeing*, offers some guidance on this:

Publicity speaks in the future tense and yet the achievement of this future is endlessly deferred. How then does publicity remain credible—or credible enough to exert the influence it does? It remains credible because truthfulness of publicity is judged, not by the real fulfillment of its promises, but by the relevance of its fantasies to those of the spectator-buyer. Its essential application is not to reality but to daydreams. No two dreams are the same. Some are instantaneous, others prolonged. The dream is always personal to the dreamer. Publicity does not manufacture the dream. All that it does is to propose to each one of us that we are not yet enviable—yet could be.

Ruth Marcus Goodhill's book *The Wisdom of Heschel* pointed out that Rabbi Abraham Joshua Heschel's writings reflected a profound understandings of what life can offer when it is lived nobly. She noted his work reflected in part on the question of "needs" as follows:

Needs are looked upon today as if they are holy. . . . Suppression of a desire is considered a sacrilege that must inevitably avenge itself in the form of some mental disorder. . . . He who sets out to employ the realities of life as a means for satisfying his own desires will soon forfeit his freedom and be degraded to a mere tool. Acquiring things, he becomes enslaved to them; in subduing others, he loses his own soul. We feel jailed in the confinement of personal needs . . . we must be able to say no to ourselves in the name of a higher *yes*. . . . Every human being is a cluster of needs, some of which are indigenous to his nature, while others are induced by advertisement, fashion, envy, or come about as miscarriages of authentic needs. . . . We usually fail to discern between authentic and artificial needs and, misjudging a whim for an aspiration, we are thrown into ugly tensions. Most obsessions are the perpetuation of such misjudgments. In fact, more people die in the epidemics of needs than in the epidemics of disease.

In these words, he is following up his famous dictum: "What I look for is not how to gain a firm hold on myself and on life, but primarily how to live a life that would deserve and evoke an eternal Amen."

Heschel obviously appreciates the fact that we must begin to see (1) how we have confined our identity to our perceived needs and (2) where the centers of gravity in our days are. In the process of responding to this call to see these truths, we must ask ourselves:

- Have I imprisoned my identity within my needs?
- Are these needs really the most important things in my life?
- Are these the areas worthy of my life and ones to which I want to give most of my attention?

In addition, by reflecting on the aspects of the process listed below, the fuse can be lit to see both how exciting and meaningful the process of letting go can be. The true search for inner freedom is *not* for the romantic or those who fanaticize. It is for those who truly want what is left of their lives to be a real journey in living:

- Attending to the spirit and process of letting go each day so we know more clearly what and who need to be let go of
- A willingness to take risks, be courageous, and unlearn what may have been valid but is now stale
- Recognizing the enchantment and vitality of experimenting with our life and the way you approach people, premises, and desires

- Incorporating a childlike playful nature and right brain sense of the world and ourselves rather than being captured by an image of adulthood that is deadening
- A desire to expand our repertoire as a way of exploring a broader narrative of ourself rather than confining our voice to what others or society has thus far dictated it to be so we can better see what the possibilities are that wish to become new realities
- Having the discipline to pursue a spirit of "releasing" in all aspects of life
- Being a learner all our life by taking practical steps to be open, observe clearly and nonjudgmentally, and absorb the cardinal virtue of psychological sages through the centuries: *humility*
- Seek friends who encourage and also practice a commitment to inner freedom
- Choose and emulate a person who models a life based on "letting go" so we have a human compass to follow
- Retrieve memories of when we felt truly free or that we were flowing with our life rather than merely meeting certain dictates
- Becoming more sensitive to what areas in our life are in transition
- Imagine ourselves 10 years older and ask what changes we are glad to have made over the past 10 years

Changing the Memory You Have of Yourself

For our purposes here, "releasing" involves more than simply letting go of things or attachments to others. Middle through late adulthood is a particularly important period when we must be willing to change the limited memory we have of ourselves. In his book *A Path with Heart*, psychologist and spiritual teacher Jack Kornfield shares the following story:

An older man, a lifetime smoker, was hospitalized with emphysema after a series of small strokes. Sitting beside his bed, his daughter urged him, as she had often done, to give up smoking. He refused and asked her to buy him more cigarettes. He told her, "I'm a smoker in this life, and that's how it is." But several days later he had another small stroke, apparently in one of the memory areas of the brain. Then he stopped smoking for good—but not because he decided to. He simply woke up one morning and forgot that he was a smoker.

To this, Kornfield adds with a sense of simple directness, "We do not have to wait for a stroke to learn to let go." However, when we see that our true identity is being compromised by something—perhaps a "spiritual stroke"—it awakens us to the fact that we need not be chained to an identity. A spirit of releasing or letting go is what we truly need.

The same can be said of our identity when it is tied to the reputation we have with others. When I read a dialogue between a master and a disciple in the book *One Minute Wisdom* by Anthony deMello, I recognize how foolish all of us are to be tied to this. In the story, the master's disciples knew that he was quite impervious to what people thought of him so they asked him how he had gained such inner freedom. In response, he laughed aloud and said, "Till I was twenty I did not care what people thought of me. After twenty I worried endlessly about what my neighbors thought. Then one day after fifty I suddenly saw that they hardly ever thought of me at all!"

There had to be a decision to let go of one's concern—whether reasonable or not—about what people thought regarding the change. In a broader sense, we can see that the question of who holds the rights to our own story is an important issue to resolve when it comes to letting go and inner freedom. Terry Hershey, in his enchanting book *The Power of Pause*, tells the following story about a girl labeled as ADHD that makes this point clearly:

In the 1930s when Gillian was a child, her teachers considered her learning disabled, one of those students who didn't pay attention or focus, and who could not sit still. ADHD was not yet a diagnosis, so Gillian was labeled "difficult." And her parents were deeply troubled. A school counselor arranged a meeting with Gillian and her parents to discuss the options. Through the entire meeting, Gillian sat on her hands, stoic, doing her best to act natural and well behaved. At the end, the counselor asked to see Gillian's parents privately, outside the office. Before he left the room, he turned on his radio. Music filled the office. Outside the office door, the counselor asked Gillian's parents to look back inside at their daughter. No longer seated, Gillian now moved about the room with the music—free, untroubled, and blissful.

"You see," the counselor told the parents, "your daughter isn't sick. She's a dancer."

This story could have gone another way. Gillian could have been labeled and medicated. Problem solved.

Instead, she was given the freedom to live from the inside out. The result? A lifetime of dance on stage and in films, and an extensive career as choreographer for such shows as *Cats* and *The Phantom of the Opera*. Difficult little Gillian became the great Gillian Lynne.

Being Open to Changing Our Narrative

Actress Liv Ullman once shared the following deeply felt sentiment regarding her own narrative:

> I am learning that if I just go on accepting the framework for life that others have given me, if I fail to make my own choices, the reasons for my life will be missing. I will be unable to recognize that which I have the power to change. I refuse to spend my life regretting the things I failed to do.

What Ullman is struggling with is the narrative of her life. A very creative approach to achieving a healthier, richer sense of self is through narrative therapy. Learning a few things from this psychological school of thought can certainly support an inner journey toward openness and a desire to make all things new in our lives.

Narrative therapy, as a process, is associated with the groundbreaking work of Michael White and David Epston. They were interested in how people's life stories—attributed to them, but not by them—could be problematic. In one of their key maxims, they state, "the person is not the problem; the problem is the problem." The problem is often a result of a labeling that overshadows alternative stories of possibility that people hold within themselves but may not be in touch with at the time.

This is not simply the case in clinical settings but also in how we perceive life and our lives in all settings. In the words of educator and author Parker Palmer:

> When we lose track of true self, how can we pick up the trail? One way is to seek clues in stories from our younger years, years when we lived closer

to our birthright gifts. A few years ago, I found some clues to myself in a time machine of sorts. A friend sent me a tattered copy of my high school newspaper. . . . [I said in it] that I would become a naval aviator and then take up a career in advertising.

I was indeed "wearing other people's faces," and I can tell you exactly whose they were. My father worked with a man who had once been a navy pilot. He was Irish, charismatic, romantic, full of the wild blue yonder and a fair share of the blarney and I wanted to be like him. The father of one of my boyhood friends was in advertising, and though I did not yearn to take on his persona, which was too buttoned-down for my taste, I did yearn for the fast car and other large toys that seemed to be the accessories of his selfhood!

These self-prophecies now over forty years old, seem wildly misguided for a person who eventually became a Quaker, a would-be pacifist, a writer, and an activist. Taken literally, they illustrate how early in life we can lose track of who we are. But inspected through the lens of paradox, my desire to become an aviator and an advertiser contain clues to the core of true self that would take many years to emerge: Clues, by definition, are coded and must be deciphered. . . . From the beginning, our lives lay down clues to selfhood and vocation, though the clues may be hard to decode. But trying to interpret them is profoundly worthwhile—especially when we are in our twenties or thirties or forties, feeling profoundly lost, having wandered, or been dragged, far away from our birthright gifts.

Narrative therapeutic views help us to see more and more of life anew, in ways that broaden our perspective and open us to possibility. This process involves isolating our assumptions about ourselves, examining them, and considering alternative views—especially ones that we develop ourselves, rather than merely mimicking authority figures (parents, educators, the pre-dominant culture, therapists, etc.), no matter how noble their intentions may be.

As Stephen Madigan, the author of a small work *Narrative Therapy*, notes:

From the beginning, a central poststructural tenet of narrative therapy was the idea that we as persons are "multistoried." . . . Simply stated, narrative therapists took up the position that within the context of therapy, there could be numerous interpretations about persons and problems. . . .

And the very interpretations of persons and problems that therapists bring forward are mediated through prevailing ideas held by our culture regarding the specifics of who and what these persons and problems are and what they represent (abnormal/normal, good/bad, worthy/unworthy).

Madigan recognized that people often hold a reputation with themselves that aligns closely with prevailing ideologies and, in extreme cases, prejudices or opinions that have nothing to do with their own values. The goal of narrative therapy is to explore many stories and interpretations within people's lives, so they can resist being cast in a way that may have held them back. This is precisely what we should wish for ourselves—and what we can put into practice—by embracing a healthy perspective on life and maintaining an openness to new views and necessary change.

Understanding the Sources of and Points of Psychological Light within the Emotional Darkness

When we focus our attention on the past and present with an aim (in my case, gentleness), we begin to see how we have failed in the past and are truly failing in the present. For example, if you wish to be more assertive at this stage of life—especially when you are known to yourself and others as someone who is first receptive to others' wishes—looking back at times when this was not so might evoke pain. This is because you will notice the many moments you may have stepped back, and now you realize you should not have done so. Similarly, in my own case, as I seek to gain more clarity on being gentler now, I can see perhaps more starkly than ever before the times in the past when I was not gentle. Moreover, in the present, as I try to practice gentleness, it also causes a level of upset and disequilibrium because I realize how unnatural it is for me to be the way I now wish to be, and how challenging it is to accomplish this goal.

A natural danger at this point is that guilt over past failures and discouragement over currently unsuccessful efforts to change in my way of being may lead to profound despair. This can evoke a sense of helplessness that might result in serious dysfunctional thinking—and, as French philosopher Alain might say, make progress even more impossible: "You don't have to be a sorcerer to cast a spell over yourself by saying, 'This is how I am. I can do nothing about it.'"

Of course, it is to be expected that feeling incompetent, discouraged, and a failure at changing our central style of interaction with others and even ourselves can lead to a sense of confusion about who we are at this point. Naturalist Peter Matthiessen, in his journal *Nine-Headed Dragon River*, notes during this very stage that, "It is difficult to adjust because I do not know who is adjusting; I am no longer the old person and not yet the new." Frustration and confusion at this stage are natural and to be expected. One of my own patients, who happened to be a psychologist herself, said in an exasperated voice after I gave her some feedback—which I intended as a bridge to the next level for her—"You expect entirely too much mental health!"

Yet, I think writer and contemplative, Thomas Merton, balances the challenge and a more modulated sense of this stage when he first writes and later balances his initial comments by noting, "What matters is the struggle to make the right adjustment in my own life, and this upsets me because there is *no pattern* for me to follow, and I don't have either the courage or insight . . . in freedom. Hence my fear and my guilt, my indecisions, my hesitations, my back tracking, my attempts to cover myself when wrong, etc. . . . The ordinary answers tend to be confusing and to hide the truth, for which we must struggle in loneliness—but *why in desperation*? This is not necessary." And it isn't.

We need to be open and able to let go. The problem for all of us is that we don't realize we are full of things that don't allow us to let go and leave room for the appreciation and embrace of new information and, thus, possibility in our present lives. Harriet Tubman, one of Maryland's most legendary women who was admired by presidents and poets and had her image on two postage stamps for her work in leading hundreds of slaves out of bondage via the underground railway, was often praised for her work. In response, instead of smiling she would say wistfully, "I could have freed thousands more only they did not know they were slaves."

In the journey of releasing, the goal is to pick up where we are "slaves" to an identity that is no longer sufficient and where we are captives to inner dictates either because we are not aware of the invisible puppeteers in our lives or we feel we have no choice. "This is how I am. I can do nothing about it."

Kenosis, the emptying of self, so we can receive more says the opposite. It believes that we cannot expect to find out what our future can be if we are full of ourselves as we are and allow ourselves to remain captured by the narrative we have absorbed from others and our own culture. One of the alluring things about a narrative is that it can give us a sense of security, comfort and assurance because those around us support it, are used to it, and would be threatened by something different. Yet, like taking a ride on a boat in which everyone is having a good time, it still can be drifting in the wrong direction.

"Releasing" recognizes this, as well as the psychological understanding we refer to as "predominance theory," in which we internalize the values and fears of others so completely that it fills our minds and hearts to the extent that we are not able to see the world afresh through our own eyes, allowing us to see our lives clearly. Otherwise, how do we expect to help others see theirs in a fresh way as well?

Since these roads to clarity and uncovering what represents the center of gravity in our lives—that we need to unearth and replace consciously with what we want to be predominant—are not easy, some preparation would seem wise. Included among these should certainly be seeking help from sessions with actual mentors or reading the words of "virtual" mentors—not just in passing, but with carefully thought-out values in mind as we go forward. In addition, a more useful understanding of "failure" is also important since most people see it merely as something to be avoided at all costs, and this framing of a lack of success will only unnecessarily deplete the energy of those who wish to experience the personal joy of being committed to what is good.

Grieving, Regret and Endings

Grieving is not simply a process to attend to when a person dies. It includes a range of external losses: friendships, employment, previous routines, and financial status. It also includes those interior transitions in response to external events. As such, the process of grieving should not be taken lightly or regarded as limited solely to the physical death of someone. Similarly, the natural response of regret to our perceived past losses, disappointments, failings, and shame is also not a feeling to be dismissed lightly. Both are worthy of our attention as we move from one phase in life to another. We need the "psychological space" and flexibility to close certain doors and open new ones when change is necessary to meet possibility in the best way possible in the present.

Moreover, the loss of identity and familiar ways of coping and thriving can help us find the bedrock of what gives our lives meaning. We move beyond habit, routine, and what we take for granted in a new search for meaning and possibility. We recognize, once again, that in some way, we will always be a beginner. It also leads us to find additional approaches and a better appreciation of what truly gives us life. Grieving helps us recognize and share with good friends what we experience deeply within ourselves after a loss or significant change.

Grief, on a greater scale than simple doubt, shakes our assumptions and our ways of thinking, perceiving, and understanding. We begin to see, as the Buddhist saying teaches, that everything gathered is dispersed—all that is gained is eventually lost... life is fleeting. While we, on one level, know this to some extent, when a loss occurs, we often protest and deny that change within is now necessary. This is a natural event not to be overly concerned about—unless, of course, it does not eventually change us to accommodate the new situation.

One of the major reasons for resistance to accepting loss is that it is a refusal to embrace the breadth of life we are called to each time the one constant—change—happens. As Francis Weller, in his book *Entering the Healing Ground*, notes by sharing Diane Ackerman's words: "I don't want to get to the end of my life and find that I lived just to the length of it. I want to have lived the width of it as well."

What Weller then shared in his work on grieving was an experience from his grief work with others. In it, he uses the word "soul"—for which I would substitute "inner life"—but whatever term is used, I found this illustration and the questions posed important to reflect upon as we seek to be more open to possibility:.

Several years ago, I was working with a group of men in Southern California in a workshop on love and death. On the second day of our time together, I posed the question, "What is the vow your soul is waiting for you to make? This generated an intense discussion and a good deal of grief as men recognized that this longing in their soul was something that was often denied or ignored. They spoke about their desire to be more vulnerable, to take greater risks in love, to hold a commitment to their creativity and more. This question called forth what was not being lived, the outcast, the silenced part of their soul. After that, I posed a second question: "What will you have to sacrifice in order to honor that vow? Once again, it became clear that they were holding on to patterns and strategies designed to keep them safe and living within a prescribed radius where no one could hurt them. . . . When we gathered together again on Sunday morning, I asked a third question: "Imagine that it is some time in the future and you are near the hour of your death. You know this. You look back on your life and see that you have honored your vow and have been able to stay true to the sacrifice you made. Now, for what would your soul like to be remembered?"

What Weller was seeking to do was help those present face themselves completely—gifts, desires, hopes, and fears—and to cast themselves as facing their end days as a way to free them from what may offer them true joy, peace, and meaning in the present. He wanted them to be released from unnecessary disappointment, emptiness, and loneliness going forward. Rather than avoiding the losses, hurts, and fears in their lives—being denied, minimized, or ignored—he wanted them to face their lives in a way that their tears would cleanse the lens of their perceptions of the world . . . their world. He wanted them to see the possibility that their grief might soften their souls rather than harden their outlook on life. (This will be discussed more thoroughly in Chapter 8.)

As in all processes of change, Weller also recognizes the importance of interpersonal safety for this to happen. That's why the previous chapter on friendship was so important. Experiencing our pain privately at times allows us to reflect more deeply. However, the need to share it with others is just as important, so the confines of suffering can be psychologically melted, fears can be shared out loud with someone who can walk with us as we traverse uncharted routes, and new dreams can be realized.

There is a platitude: "Time heals all." The psychological reality, although it may not sound as poetic, is this: New intervening variables heal all. The quality of what happens after a loss determines whether life continues in new, meaningful ways or no. Key to this occurring is a willingness to realize that:

- We need a safe psychological place to heal.
- Grief is cyclical and doesn't end once and for all. Instead, it remains as a wonderful reminder of the good experiences of love that once were physically present and now are in a new form.
- As we remember the past and can integrate it, life's newness can be greeted more readily.

- Friendship is an important factor in healing and redirection.
- Structures and routines (a time to take a walk, a time to cry . . . and, yes, a time to shop) should be honored.
- If needed, professional support (psychotherapy, spiritual sage, etc.) can be a lifesaver.
- How regret is dealt with can be a crucial factor in how one lives after a loss.

In looking back during a period of change or after making choices, a degree of regret is normally present. Such negative reminders of choices one wished one could forget or hadn't made can sap energy from being available for decision-making going forward and from feeling gratitude and contentment in the present.

Robert Leahy, author of *If Only . . . Finding Freedom from Regret* and founding director of the American Institute for Cognitive Therapy, is quite aware of this. Yet, he notes that if we can also see regret as an opening to learn and self-correct moving forward, it can serve as a bright psychological signal pointing to changes that need to be made cognitively and behaviorally. He also points out that when regret is used not only as a way to learn from the past but also as an anticipatory approach, it can help us avoid rash decisions and avoidable mistakes.

Whether it is regret for actions taken in the short term or a failure to act at certain points in one's history, we can learn from such emotions the thoughts and beliefs underlying them. Leahy points out that utilizing regret—rather than simply allowing it to cause emotional discomfort—can help us accept reasonable risks in decision-making and live with the integrity and clarity to bear the consequences of past errors. This is aided by not ruminating about what was done or idealizing the alternatives to the decisions we made, while simultaneously discounting the positive results of what was done, which we should be grateful for. With such a sense of appreciation, not only personal happiness will have the possibility to increase but, on a broader level, the personal signature strengths or virtues, such as compassion, have a greater chance to result in an enhanced life of meaning.

Transitions—Dealing with Endings . . . and Beginning Anew

In the preface to the 40th anniversary edition of the groundbreaking book *Transitions,* Bridges notes that a difference exists between change— which is situational—and transition—which is psychological. She states that a transition "is not those events but rather the inner reorientation and self-redefinition that you have to go through in order to incorporate any of those changes in your life. Without a transition, a change is just a rearrangement of the furniture. Unless transition happens, the change won't work, because it doesn't take. Whatever word we use, our society talks a lot about change, but it seldom deals with transition. Unfortunately for us, it is the transition that blindsides us and is often the source of our troubles." Susan Bridges, in the latest edition, then adds the following important note: "However you learned to deal with them, endings are the first phase of transition. The second phase is a time of lostness and emptiness before life resumes an intelligent pattern and direction. The third phase is that of beginning anew."

Although we would like such periods in our lifetime to be identifiable, as we move through the stages of our maturity, there is also a recognition by the author and reviser of the book *Transitions* that "adulthood unfolds its promise in an alternating rhythm of expansion and contraction, change and stability." In addressing the desire to go back in time to realize earlier wishes and hopes, late 18th-century writer and philosopher Johann Wolfgang von Goethe indicates that each phase of our life "has its own fortunes, its own hopes, its own desires."

And so, it is important for us to recall, when the timing for a transition is necessary, to be aware of our style of ending so as not to be caught off guard by our emotions and approach. Again, Bridges advises us in this way:

> One of the benefits to reviewing your experience of endings is to see how often they have cleared the ground for unexpected beginnings. But reviewing these elements in your past may also uncover the times when the ending did not provide a starting point, as well as the times when you started a new journey without unpacking your baggage from the old one. Right now, at the new transition point in your life, remember some of these aborted transition points from your past. Poke around among them as you might explore an old house you once lived in. Some of these unfinished transitions might be ones that you could still complete, and if you did that, you would bring more energy and less anxiety to your present situation as a result. Completion may involve no more than a belated farewell, a letter, or a call to someone. It may involve an inner relinquishment of someone who outwardly you left behind years ago, or some old image of yourself, or some outlived dream or outworn belief that you have kept in your baggage long past its time. You'll travel more easily if you lighten your load.

Handling endings like this includes being able to, once again, let go of former professional identities, relationships, beliefs, and self-images. For this to occur, taking regular time each day for periods of silence and possibly solitude is necessary. In addition, having longer periods for reflection is also needed. However, simply providing the time and space is not enough. Knowing how to gently and clearly meet our thoughts, perceptions, and ways of understanding is equally important.

For Review and Reflection . . .

Skills Emphasized by Narrative Therapy Proponents

Narrative therapy encourages the very skills that all of us need to open up our perspective as to who we are, can be, and how we might live each day. This also includes our vocation and long-term goals. Some skills worth practicing with these goals in mind are:

- Listening to our hopes, dreams, and ideas so they are not eclipsed or crushed by the attitudes of culture, family, work, or our own previously limited self-definition
- Reflecting on those "little" events and experiences which gave and give us joy so that they can be given further opportunities for expression
- Having a chance to reframe our difficulties in light of possibly unexplored gifts and talents
- Giving ourselves the power to author our own stories, since we—not others—hold the "copyright" to our identity
- Being sensitive to our self-talk (what we mentally tell ourselves about events, people and ourselves) in order to pick up interpretations and criticism that are not centered in us but in the outside world's set of values and ethics
- Opening ourselves to an array of stories that color our lives (volunteer work may not be considered "important" because the culture doesn't seem to value unpaid activities but after exploration *we* may see the good we are doing and the joy it may be bringing us) but have been underrated
- Participating in rituals/activities that reinforce and stabilize new, more life-giving identities

5

"Don't Just Sit There in Silence and Solitude. Do Nothing!"

A Mini-Guide to Patience, Reflection, and Mindfulness

> "Sometimes simply by sitting, wisdom is collected."
>
> —Zen Saying

> "Who looks outside, dreams; Who looks inside, awakes."
>
> —Carl Jung

Novelist James Joyce once said of one of his characters, "Mr. Duffy lived a short distance from his body." Without time for silence and solitude each day, and without a reflective spirit, we never seem to fully catch up with all we are doing. This is dangerous. Moreover, without quiet attentiveness, we miss the renewing presence and "voice" of natural gifts such as the wind, the rain, the sun, and the waves. When we pause to be still—whether for a few moments in our day, during a holiday at the shore, or in the mountains—these realizations often come to the forefront.

During the reflective process, the more personally meaningful items we are willing to entertain, the greater our motivation to reflect. We become willing to unlearn what is no longer true for us and to adopt new ways of approaching life. This involves seeing more clearly how we think, perceive, and understand events and ourselves. As Virginia Woolf poetically describes, we will take our minds out of their "iron cages" during these times, opening ourselves to new possibilities and greater appreciation of what is happening within us—how we meet change and challenges at each new phase of life. In those quiet moments, we are not merely absent of sound around us, but rather creating a space inside to be more gentle and attentive, allowing new insights and lessons to surface.

When a healthier perspective is gained through reflection, alone-time, and mindfulness, it can be filled with promise that was previously absent.

At the very least, it can help reduce unnecessary worry and rumination, conserving our limited energy so we can notice and embrace new possibilities. To reach this state of clarity and openness, a time for inner stillness is essential—even in the midst of noise, distraction, and daily stimulations that drain our spirit.

During a lecture trip to Japan this was explained to me quite vividly in such a captivating way by a gentle, insightful man. I had just finished delivering a series of lectures in Tokyo and was invited to visit one of Japan's most sacred Shinto shrines: Ise Jingu. I was especially intrigued when I learned I would receive a personal tour from a former woodsman, now the director of the temple grounds. His comments were to be translated for me by someone fluent in both English and Japanese, who had taught his children.

When my interpreter and I arrived, the director greeted us at the gate, and we bowed to each other in traditional Japanese fashion. The tour involved a careful, sensitive explanation of the symbolism and rituals that mark the seasons and the life of the tranquil temple grounds and their visitors. As we continued, he led us up to a slightly arched, simply but carefully carved wooden bridge. He then stopped and urged me to look down at the water. When I did, he asked, "What do you see?" I responded, "Water that is clear, fresh, and at peace." He smiled and replied, "*Hai*" (Yes). Then, with a serious look in his dark brown eyes, he asked, "Now, what do you hear?" After a pause, I thought I could hear a small frog and told him so.

"Ah so," he said softly, then added with quiet seriousness, "You will not hear this species of frog anywhere else on the temple grounds but here." When I asked why, he simply answered, "Because this species of frog only lives near water that is clear, fresh, and calm."

I understood enough about the animistic beliefs of Shintoism to realize he was not just talking about frogs and water, but about my way of living—and the opportunities (or lack thereof) that this way of life could offer. Would I take time for silence and solitude to truly experience calm, clarity, and peace? Or would I simply rush through life, believing that doing so was "practical," "natural," and "necessary"? After all, doesn't everyone live that way?

Much later, naturalist Peter Matthiessen reflected on this in his book *Nine-Headed Dragon River*. His words made me revisit that experience more deeply, especially as he shared thoughts from the spiritual master, Yasutani-Roshi:

"The mind of a buddha," Yasutani once said, "is like water that is calm, deep, and crystal clear, and upon which 'the moon of truth' reflects fully and perfectly. The mind of the ordinary man, on the other hand, is like murky water, constantly being churned by the gales of delusive thought and no longer able to reflect the moon of truth. The moon nonetheless shines steadily upon the waves, but as the waters are roiled, we are unable to see its reflection. Thus we lead lives that are frustrating and meaningless. . . . So long as the winds of thought continue to disturb the water of our [real] nature, we cannot distinguish truth from untruth. It is important, therefore, that these winds be stilled. Once they abate, the waves subside, the muddiness clears, and we perceive directly. . . . The moment of such realization is *kensho*, enlightenment.

Leaning back from the pressures and busyness of life can open the gates to pathways of greater inner freedom not yet traveled. Yet, today most of us leave a number of these potent portals unopened. We may not even know they are there, or think they are only discoverable through some kind of magic, luck, fame, or winning a major psychological or spiritual lottery—in other words, believing that once we find the "perfect" relationship, job, or financial stability, we will be free. But as alluring as these images are, constantly entertaining them only leads us into emotional and intellectual cul-de-sacs. Conversely, stepping back intentionally—perhaps during periods of "alone-time" when in solitude or silently reflecting inward—can provide the inner space we need—not only for our own benefit but also for those around us: our family, friends, and colleagues who turn to us for support. Having a healthy perspective is something we can help "export" through a presence that is open, welcoming, and encourages freedom that is borne out of having some quiet time alone. In this sense, it truly enables us to be "the calm within the storm."

Silence, solitude, and mindful moments have the power to stop us in our tracks and prompt us to ask the question: Why are we continuing to live so driven and mindless? This may be a disconcerting question for us adults who believe we're already familiar with being responsible people. And often, we justify our busyness with statements like, "We must live this way. We have no choice. It's practical and normal." Paradoxically, acknowledging this is so because in our hearts, in defending our avoidance of silence and solitude, we already know at some level that what we are telling ourselves is not true. Consequently, once this initial portal of reality—which can give us space to gain a healthier, freer perspective—is nudged open a bit (even though the need for alone-time may still be presently ignored or temporarily forgotten by us), it will never close completely again. That is the true gift of reflecting on our desire to step back from our packed lives and preoccupations, even if we haven't yet fully embraced such "spaces" consistently.

The first step often involves examining the objective geography of our day: what happened, who was involved, where and when it took place? Then, we examine the *subjective* geography of the ups and downs of the day: How did I feel about it, and what thoughts, perceptions, and beliefs fired up our emotions and views. In doing this, we give ourselves a chance to pause before reacting or continuing beliefs that may no longer serve us. Throughout history, sages and wise teachers have emphasized the importance of silence and solitude as essential to living a conscious, meaningful, and compassionate life.

The reflective process uncovers insights that are easy to overlook. As novelist Walker Percy famously asked, "What if I missed my life like a person misses a train?" Taking the time and space enables us to see events, pick up feelings, and examine the thoughts and beliefs we have that may only appear in the "psychological corner of one's eyes." Whether it is a few quiet moments at the beginning of the day or a formal self-debriefing at day's close, the primary question all of us must ask ourselves is: Do we sufficiently value time in silence and solitude where we seek to be open to the stream of thoughts lying just below the surface of our consciousness. Henri Nouwen, the spiritual writer, posed a profound question in his book *The Genesee Diary*: "Is there a quiet stream underneath the fluctuating affirmations and rejections of my little world? Is there a still point where my life is anchored and from which I can reach out with hope and courage and confidence?" He recognized how fragmented our lives can become amid the many agendas and demands on our attention, leaving us feeling less integrated, alone, and bored instead of centered and mindful.

Nowhere do I feel this is more evident than when we dedicate significant periods of time to quiet ourselves, reflect, breathe deeply, and simply enjoy our ordinary selves. Although I initially followed Henri Nouwen's suggestions for a brief time each morning, when I took longer periods for alone-time, they would prove crucial in my life and psychological travels with other helpers and healers who turned to me for guidance in their own lives and clinical practices.

As I created gaps—vacuums—in my schedule and consciousness, thoughts, feelings, beliefs, and suppressed experiences that had lingered just beyond my immediate awareness began to surface. By allowing them to flow freely—without judgment, interference, or the need to fix, deny, or entertain them—they became inner mentors of ordinariness. When I observed them nonjudgmentally, they revealed how I had constructed an identity, needs, and responses that were actually alien to my ordinary self. To some extent, these experiences are similar to those Sara Maitland describes in her book *A Book of Silence,* when she shares: "I felt oddly foxy—I'd slipped my leash and got away. I felt open to whatever might happen and hungry for the silence." She also noted, "It took a little while to realize how much I loved it. It was not a sudden plunge into solitude and silence; it was a gradual shifting of gears, a gentle movement toward a new way of living that gave me increasing deep satisfaction." In my own experience, then and now, I resonate deeply with Ezra Pound's words: "I did not enter silence. Silence entered me."

The impact of those times of quiet can be truly transformative. In his biography of Zen master Shunryu Suzuki, David Chadwick shares a brief but powerful vignette illustrating how moments of retreat and connection with new support groups can profoundly free us—to be our authentic, ordinary selves again, or perhaps for the first time:

A Stanford professor told Suzuki that many college students were smoking marijuana all the time and taking LSD. Maybe it was good in some ways for them to experiment, but it was interfering with their studies. What did Suzuki [who led a local Zen center] do about this problem? "Oh, nothing," said Suzuki. "I just teach them how to sit zazen [quiet meditation], and they forget about those things pretty soon." For Suzuki, "Life without [sitting meditation] is like winding our clock without setting it. It runs perfectly well but doesn't tell time."

Yet, the attentive quiet of meditation—an intense form of alone-time—is more than a fantasy or an act of self-centeredness. It is an education in wise living. As Matthieu Ricard notes in his book *Happiness,* "Indeed, meditation is not about sitting quietly in the shade of a tree and relaxing in a moment of respite from the daily grind; it is about familiarizing yourself with a new vision of things, a new way to manage your thoughts, of perceiving people and experiencing the world." To this he also adds:

We willingly spend a dozen years in school, then go on to college or professional training for several more; we work out at the gym to stay healthy; we spend a lot of time enhancing our comfort, our wealth, and our social status. We put a great deal into all this, and yet we do so little to improve the inner condition that determines the very quality of our lives. What strange hesitancy, fear, or apathy stops us from looking within ourselves, from trying to grasp the true essence of joy and sadness, desire and hatred? Fear of the unknown prevails, and the courage to explore that inner world fails at the frontier of our mind.

To appreciate this more deeply, we sometimes need specific places where we can truly feel the space to enjoy alone-time. It may also require guidance from those who know how to embrace both ordinariness and alone-time. Buddhist psychologist and meditation teacher Jack Kornfield notes that you wouldn't want to go hiking in the Himalayas without a guide, so why would you attempt the even more demanding journey of the inner life without the guidance that is available?

Places and People of Alone-Time

In Peter France's book *Patmos: A Place of Healing*, he describes how this island held a profound sense of possibility for him, noting that Patmos is a place of power. "It changes people. They come here for a brief summer visit and find themselves returning, year after year, for the rest of their lives. If you ask them why, they all give the same answer: they are responding to a force which they can recognize but not explain. And which they find nowhere else."

There are, of course, other powerful stories of places and people of solitude whose experiences highlight how their comments impact their own sense of discovering their authentic selves, rather than remaining caught in societal or destructive cycles which need to be released. One such story is by Erwin James, who wrote in *The Guardian* (Thursday, September 30, 2004), reflecting on his time in prison: "I have never minded having those 20 years taken from me. . . . If I had not had them taken away, they would most likely have been wasted anyway. . . . My cell then was a reinforced concrete box, and I spent the biggest part of my days locked behind its steel door. I spent a lot of time reading and meditating on what I had read, until the fear and anxiety I had felt from being held in those conditions gradually subsided. . . . I could not say exactly when it happened—and I am not sure that I realized it until sometime afterwards—but there was definitely a period in that cell when for the first time in my life I experienced peace. I had not expected to miss any aspects of my imprisonment when I had been released. But more than once during these past few weeks of being out and about full-time in the modern world, I have missed that."

Another example of extreme solitude was described by Christine Ritter in her book *Woman in the Polar Night*. She recounts her extended stay in Svalbard, Norway, demonstrating how one can experience the self so deeply in silence and solitude:

> How varied are the experiences one lives through in the Artic. One can murder and devour, calculate and measure, one can go out of one's mind from loneliness and terror, and one can certainly also go mad with enthusiasm for the all-too-overwhelming beauty. But it is also true that one will never experience in the Artic anything that one has not oneself brought there.

She also added later in her book, "In centuries to come, men will go to the Artic as in biblical times they withdrew to the desert, to find the truth again." In his introduction to her book, Lawrence Millman wrote, "I can't imagine any [other] polar explorer making a statement like this."

In a similar setting, polar explorer Admiral William Byrd wrote a sentiment akin to Ritter's and James's: "[I had] one man's desire to know that kind of experience [of solitude] to the full, to be by himself for a while and to taste peace and quiet and solitude long enough to find out how good they really are." He also said, "Now, I wanted something more than just privacy in the geographical sense. I wanted to sink roots into some replenishing philosophy."

After his ordeal alone, he wrote several years after his experience, "I did take away something that I had not fully possessed before: appreciation of the sheer beauty and miracle of being alive, and a humble set of values. . . . Civilization has not altered my ideas. I live more simply now, and with more peace."

The capacity to be alone is certainly recognized today as an indicator of emotional maturity. British psychiatrist Edwin Storr suggests no less in his book *Solitude: A Return to the Self.* Relying on the insights of psychoanalytic thinker Donald Winnicott—one of the first modern psychologists to explore the positive aspects of solitude—Storr highlights the connection between the ability to be alone and vital processes such as self-discovery and self-realization.

He also states that practices like meditation or silent prayer can "facilitate integration by allowing time for previously unrelated thoughts and feelings to interact." Being able to connect with one's deepest thoughts and emotions, and giving them space to reorganize into new formations, is crucial not only for the creative process but also as a way to relieve tension and promote mental health. It appears that developing the capacity to be alone is essential for optimal brain function and for fulfilling our highest potential. Human beings can easily become disconnected from their deepest needs and feelings. Learning, thinking, innovating, and maintaining contact with one's inner world are all facilitated by solitude.

It is therefore not surprising that a deep understanding of one's true ordinariness depends so heavily on taking time in silence, embracing solitude, and opening oneself up in ways that are impossible amid constant stimulation or unreflective group activity.

Is it any wonder, then, that American novelist, memoirist, biographer, literary critic, and essayist Doris Grumbach, in her book *Fifty Days of Solitude*, reported that after experiencing a significant period of solitude, what I refer to as "our ordinary self"—a way of living out one's life—becomes more accessible? She writes, "There was a reward for this deprivation. The absence of other voices compelled me to listen more intently to the inner one. I became aware that the interior voice, so often previously stifled or silenced by what I thought others wanted to hear, or what I considered socially acceptable, grew gratifyingly louder, more insistent."

However, she is also aware of our natural resistance to such periods of detachment from society. She adds, "...How right Rousseau was about the modern person. Our points of reference are always our neighbors, the people in the village or our city, our acquaintances at school, at games, at work, our close and distant families, all of whom tell us, with their hundreds of tongues, who we are. . . . Rarely if ever did we think to look within for knowledge of ourselves. Were we afraid? Perhaps, we thought we would find nothing there."

Solitude and silence share with the virtue of ordinariness the need for courage in facing such fears—and others like them. In this sense, they are virtues for the truly self-aware, sane individual who possesses inner freedom.

Regarding possibility, Jack Kornfield, in his book *The Wise Heart*, sees meditation as a space to confront life's essential questions—our own questions. Reflecting on this mindfulness practice and Buddhist psychology, he raises the questions: "Was it a need to take a deep breath and find a wiser way to cope with conflict, stress, and fears so common in modern life? Was it the longing for a psychology that included the spiritual dimension and the highest human potential in its vision of healing? Was it a hope to find simple ways to quiet the mind and open the heart?"

Thomas Merton, a monk and author of numerous books, including his autobiographical *The Seven Storey Mountain*, spent much of his religious life living in community. Yet, at a certain point, he was granted permission to live in a hermitage. His joy in this new solitude echoes the experiences of others across the ages. In his words, "What a thing it is to sit absolutely alone in the forest at night, cherished by this wonderful, unintelligible, perfectly innocent speech... the talk that rain makes all by itself all over the ridges.... As long as it talks I am going to listen. But I am going to sleep, because here in this wilderness I have learned to sleep again."

Such periods of solitude need not require physical separation; they can occur in moments of quiet within everyday life—perhaps in the early morning before the house awakens, during an evening bath after everyone is asleep, or during a quiet moment a mother finds while nursing her baby at night.

Periods like this can be truly renewing, refreshing, and enlightening because the "dust of the day" has settled, allowing us to hear the inner thoughts that have been drowned out by the noise and activity of daily life. It is during these times that extended periods of silence can hold greater significance in relation to our broader sense of our ordinary selves—our personal narrative. Once again, Sara Maitland recognized this during some time apart early in her experiments with silence and solitude.

> One of the things I gained during this week, in this specific silence, was a much stronger narrative of my own life. It was not until after I went home that I became aware of how much—how many anecdotes—I had added to my conscious memory bank. The effort to eliminate ego and silence the mind, heart and imagination destroys a clear sense of time and therefore of narrative, but the attempt to use silence deliberately to stimulate internal states of imagination has exactly the opposite effect.... You go out into the wild and you "discover who you are", "establish your individual voice", or "your authentic identity". One of the definitions of identity or selfhood being explored at present in both philosophy and psychiatry is the idea

that the ability to construct a coherent narrative of one's own life circumscribes identity—to be an individual is to own a narrative of self. Choosing to be alone, solitary, particularly in a place that is "sublime", is one way of establishing contact with such a narrative, unmediated by other people's interpretation.

Andrew Weiss, in his book *Beginning Mindfulness*, echoes this with respect to placing ourselves in the now with our eyes wide open. He comments that "Meditation is not just something you do on a cushion or chair. Anything you do is an occasion to engage yourself mindfully in the present moment. . . . Ultimately the path of mindfulness will lead you to a place within yourself where you may encounter the world without ideas or preconceptions, where you can disengage from your habitual narrative and free yourself from mental constructs [which] . . . gives us a way through suffering to joy."

Beyond this, in simple terms, Jack Kornfield recognizes that mindful periods "allow us the space of kindness. There is beauty in the ordinary. We invite the heart to sit on the front porch and experience from a place of rest the inevitable comings and goings of emotions and events, the struggles and successes of the world."

The Capacity to Be Alone: Recognizing We Are Not Used to Silence . . . Much Less Solitude!

Early in my professional career, an unexpected opportunity arose—an unforeseen invitation that has, to this day, profoundly changed my life. After the publication of one of my books, the director of a graduate program at St. Michael's College in Vermont asked whether I would be willing to teach a three-week summer course. Given the beautiful setting near Lake Champlain, I thought it would be a wonderful opportunity to enjoy the scenery and accomplish some work, especially since the teaching load was light and they provided a townhouse for my stay.

My expectations were more than fulfilled regarding the natural beauty of the area. Rudyard Kipling once noted that the two best locations for sunsets over a lake are Lake Victoria in Africa and Lake Champlain from the Vermont side. The lush mountains, scenic ferry rides, and beautiful walking trails up Mt. Mansfield made relaxing walks a special delight.

Additionally, I had time to write and prepare lectures for a new faculty position I was about to begin in the fall, and I was able to interact with wonderful faculty and students. However, the real hidden jewel—something less tangible but more life-changing—was the discovery of extended periods of silence and solitude.

Initially, I responded to these moments with a sense of urgency or discomfort—how was I supposed to "productively" fill this space? Yet, recalling a conversation I had with Henri Nouwen a few years earlier, sitting in his kitchen in his small apartment off Harvard Square, I finally realized something new: I actually needed more space to simply be.

During that meeting with Henri, I was enthusiastic about the importance of being available to others—especially since my work as a therapist, clinical supervisor, mentor, and presenter was primarily focused on helping professionals in medicine, nursing, psychology, social work, counseling, education, and ministry. He responded with encouragement and appreciation for my efforts. However, he also made a point that struck me deeply: "Availability is not simply a gift for many of us. It is a problem."

After saying this, since Henri Nouwen was also a priest, I wasn't surprised when he suggested that there must be a theme from sacred scripture that addresses this issue. When I asked him what it might be, he admitted that nothing specific come to mind at that moment, so we simply let the question drop. Finally, just before I was about to leave for the airport to fly home, his face lit up, and he said with emphasis, "Pruning! That's it. That is the theme from the Bible that I was trying to recall. When you prune something, it doesn't blossom less; it flowers more deeply."

He then shared with me a way to begin a deeper appreciation for this concept. From it, one can naturally develop an understanding of pruning—where it is necessary and, as I would later learn on my own, the pain involved in the required trimming of psychological branches—our activities, thoughts, and beliefs—that had driven me to the point of burnout on several occasions.

Silence and solitude—the "places" or "spaces" where we can pause and take a breath—are surprisingly no longer in favor. Today, they may even be viewed with suspicion. Thoreau recognized this long ago when he wrote, "If a man walks in the woods for love of them half of each day, he is in danger of being regarded as a loafer. But if he spends his days as a shearing off those woods and making the earth bald before her time, he is deemed an industrious and enterprising citizen."

Thankfully, such Thoreau-styled protests against the neglect of solitude are increasingly common. More and more people are recognizing that even intimate relationships—though good and essential—also heavily depend on our having quality time alone. As psychologist and spiritual writer Henri Nouwen points out in his book *The Way of the Heart*:

We have been made to believe that feelings, emotions, and even the inner stirrings of our soul have to be shared with others. Expressions such as "Thanks for sharing this with me," or "It was good to share this with you." show that the door of our steam bath is open most of the time. In fact, people who prefer to keep to themselves and do not expose their interior life tend to create uneasiness and are often considered inhibited, asocial, or simply odd. But let us at least raise the question of whether our lavish ways of sharing are not more compulsive than virtuous; that instead of creating community they tend to flatten out our life together. Often we come home from a sharing session with a feeling that something precious has been taken away from us.

He then goes on to note, "It is in solitude that this compassionate solidarity grows. In solitude we realize that nothing human is alien to us, that the roots of all conflict, war, injustice, cruelty, hatred, jealousy, and envy are deeply anchored in our own heart. In solitude our heart of stone can be turned into a heart of flesh, a rebellious heart into a contrite heart, and a closed heart into a heart that can open itself to all suffering people in a gesture of solidarity."

Once, I was leading a couple of days of recollection on the theme of resilience for Methodist ministers at the Jersey Shore. On the first day, I suggested—a bit timidly since they were all prayerful, professional people—that each morning, they take at least two minutes of silence and solitude, wrapped in gratitude, to center themselves before beginning their busy day of service to others. My mention of "two minutes" was intentional—to encourage regularity—because I believed anyone could manage just two minutes. It was also an attempt to circumvent the usual resistance I encounter when suggesting periods of alone-time, such as "I just don't have time in my busy schedule."

The next morning, one of the ministers in line for breakfast asked if she could sit with me. I said, "Of course," and after gathering what they wished to eat, we sat down together. I smiled and asked if she would like to say grace before the meal, which she did. We ate slowly, and eventually, over coffee, she shared the question she had been pondering. She asked, "Do you really take those two minutes each morning as you suggested yesterday?"

When I replied that I truly did, she paused, then said, "I tried it this morning. Two minutes felt like an incredibly long time!" We both burst into laughter.

Surprisingly, short periods of silence and solitude may not be easy for us—even when we seem to be in "the mindfulness or prayerfulness business." People who take alone-time seriously understand this all too well. In his diary *A Vow of Conversation*, contemplative Thomas Merton posed a thoughtful question that reflects the respect we should have when approaching quiet time alone: "Solitude is a stern master who brooks no nonsense. And the question arises—am I so full of nonsense that she will cast me out? I pray she will not."

The Psychological Capacity to Be Alone

Psychiatrist Edwin Storr, in his seminal work *On Solitude*, initiated a discussion among psychotherapists about the value of alone-time. He cited the work of therapeutic pioneer Donald Winnicott to underscore the significance of the capacity to be alone. One of the most intriguing points he made in this context is the following:

> Winnicott suggests that the capacity to be alone in adult life originates with the infant's experience of being *alone in the presence of the mother*. He is postulating a state in which the infant's immediate needs, for food, warmth, physical contact and so on, have been satisfied, so that there is no need for the infant to be looking to the mother for anything, nor any need for her to be concerned with anything. . . . I find his conceptions illuminating. He is suggesting that the capacity to be alone originally, depends upon what Bowlby would call secure attachment: that is, upon the child being able peacefully to be itself in the presence of the mother without anxiety about her possible departure, and without anxiety as to what may or may not be expected by her. . . . But Winnicott goes further. He suggests that the capacity to be alone, first in the presence of the mother, and then in her absence, is also related to the individual's capacity to get in touch with, and make manifest, his own true inner feelings. It is only when the child has experienced a contented, relaxed sense of being alone with, and then

without, the mother, that he can be sure of being able to discover what he really needs or wants, irrespective of what others may expect or try to foist upon him.

The capacity to be alone thus becomes linked with self-discovery and self-realization; with becoming aware of one's deepest needs, feelings, and impulses.

Storr then goes on to draw a connection between Winnicott's concept of the capacity to be alone and the value of meditation. He notes that this form of alone-time enables a person to integrate previously unconnected thoughts and feelings by providing the necessary time and space to achieve this important goal. From his perspective, he then emphasizes that:

Being able to get in touch with one's deepest thoughts and feelings, and providing time for them to regroup themselves into new formations and combinations, are important aspects of the creative process, as well as a way of relieving tension and promoting mental health.

It appears, therefore, that some development of the capacity to be alone is necessary if the brain is to function at its best, and if the individual is to fulfill his highest potential. Human beings easily become alienated from their own deepest needs and feelings. Learning, thinking, innovation, and maintaining contact with one's own inner world are all facilitated by solitude.

Yet, time for reflection is often not regarded as a priority—even by those of us who should know better or who claim to value meditation and reflection, despite the pressures in our lives. Insightful author Anne Lamott often uses autobiographical material in her nonfiction books to illustrate sound psychological and spiritual realities. When it comes to silence, solitude, and mindfulness, she is especially articulate. On the one hand, she encourages us all to carve out time for reflection. In her words, "Almost anything will work again if you unplug it for a few minutes… including you." On the other hand, she openly shares her own—and our—hesitancy and resistance to taking that time for self-reflection: "My mind is like a bad neighborhood. I don't like to go there alone."

Additionally, in many cases, mindfulness or simple periods of quiet reflection are undervalued, even among the most talented and committed helping and healing professionals.

Once, I was delivering a presentation on resilience, self-care, and maintaining a healthy perspective at Walter Reed Army Hospital, when one of the physicians approached me during a break. "Do you have a moment?" he asked. "Yes, I do. How can I help?" I responded. He immediately shot back with emotion, "I'm blowing my whole life through my rear end. Can you help me?"

After a few seconds of taking this in, I responded, "Can you be more specific?"

He then explained that he had just returned from a war zone, expected to be redeployed there soon, and was primarily involved in serious surgeries—for example, amputating legs of soldiers who had stepped on landmines or triggered improvised explosive devices. With a hint of a smile, he added, "I'd just like to do a damn gall bladder for a change." Then, he said he planned to go home afterward, upstairs to the bedroom, and putt a few golf balls to unwind.

He described how, after a little while, his wife would come upstairs, see him hitting golf balls into a plastic cup, and say, "You're at work all day, and now you're up here hitting golf balls instead of being downstairs with me and the boys? This marriage is going down the tubes!" and then slam the door shut.

After listening to him and waiting a few seconds, I asked, "So, what do you do immediately after work?" At first, he seemed surprised by the question, then appeared to get upset, and responded in an angry tone, "Well, what else would I do? I go home!" I then replied, "Well, you can't just do that."

He asked, "What do you mean?"

I explained to him in a concise way the importance of taking a short period of silence, solitude, self-debriefing, and role change as a prelude to mindfulness with his family at home. I said, "When you're in a restaurant and need to use the bathroom, what does the sign over the sink say? It says, 'If you work here, after you go to the bathroom, you must wash your hands before returning to work.' However, those of us who work with patients in the hospital must not only wash our hands after using the bathroom but also before touching patients. Otherwise, we risk physically contaminating ourselves with what we encountered on the floor, and then unintentionally passing it on to others. From a mental health perspective, the same holds true. You're leaving the hospital 'psychologically and spiritually contaminated,' and if you don't take time to cleanse yourself, you might carry that negativity home and negatively impact your family—by feeling discouraged, helpless, jaded, or preoccupied—because of what you've encountered during the day."

He looked at me and asked, "Well, what can I do about it? Is it really that big of a deal?"

I responded, "It's quite straightforward. After your shift, take a few moments to walk around within the hospital. If that's not possible because patients and colleagues might see you and call out, 'Doc, doc . . . got a moment?' then simply sit in your car for some quiet time. You can even drive to a peaceful spot nearby. During that time, briefly review the objective geography of the day—what happened. Then, reflect on the subjective experience—how did you react to what happened? How did you feel about the events? What thoughts, perceptions, and understanding led to those feelings? And what underlying beliefs shaped your interpretation of the day's events?

By doing this, you give yourself a chance to pause, create some distance from the events, and understand what triggered your feelings. It also provides an opportunity to identify and correct any dysfunctional thinking that may be causing unnecessary darkness or discouragement."

After I said this, he looked at me with a different expression—one that seemed to suggest he had understood. In our subsequent discussion, we contemplated why he hadn't thought of such an approach himself, or, if he had, why he hadn't prioritized it, given that it seems both sensible and quite instructive. Certainly, it is a cornerstone for enhancing the possibility of post-traumatic growth, as we discussed earlier. Yet, no matter how intelligent or seemingly committed to reflection one may be, in an action-oriented world—with so much that needs to be done—meditation and simple quiet alone-time can quietly fall by the wayside without us realizing it.

Once, when I was speaking in Cambodia to helping and healing professionals working to rebuild the country after years of terror and torture, a Buddhist nun approached me to ask for some advice. She said, "A young Buddhist is a chaplain at the hospital unit responsible for the rehabilitation of farmers who have had their legs blown off by landmines and he is getting very discouraged and overwhelmed. What can I do about this to help him?"

In response, I said, "Well, Sister, if you tell me what comes up during his brief meditation in his car before he returns to the temple, I could give you a more focused, helpful answer." She looked at me with a surprised expression that resembled a deer caught in the headlights, and in a sad voice, she said,

"Oh, doctor, I'm so embarrassed." That caught me off guard, and I replied, "Sister, why do you feel that way?"

Finally, she admitted, "I am a Buddhist nun, and I've never suggested or asked him about his meditation." Even when we publicly affirm the value of meditation or reflection, action takes precedence because the culture values it so much. Yet, if meditation truly becomes a priority, it will assume a central place in our lives and ultimately foster more careful, beneficial actions. The essential first step is cultivating a deeper understanding of what genuine awareness and mindfulness really are.

What Actually Is True Awareness and Mindfulness?

A sense of mindfulness—being fully present with our eyes wide open—is the foundation of any meditative or informal reflective practice aimed at increasing awareness. While it is essentially quite simple, it often requires us to relearn it repeatedly as adults, regardless of how committed we believe we are to being aware and appreciative of what is before us. In fact, mindfulness is actually a state that young children often experience naturally, almost effortlessly. Jerry Braza discusses this in his book *Moment by Moment*, reflecting on the awe of the "now" as seen through the eyes of his daughter:

> I recall a time driving my young children somewhere when we approached a railroad crossing as the lights began to flash and the safety gate went down. My first thought was "Oh no! We're going to be held up by a train and be late." Just then, my daughter called out from the backseat, "Daddy, Daddy, we're so lucky! We get to watch the train go by!" Her awareness of the present moment was a wonderful reminder to stop and enjoy what the journey had to offer along the way.

In this story, taken from a book on the art and practice of mindfulness, we can see the importance of paying attention to where we are and what we are doing. Often, "the now" is filled with many gifts—if we have the eyes to see— and this awareness can be cultivated by learning the basics of mindfulness.

As Chris Germer, a leading voice on the psychology of mindfulness, explains and suggests in an essay within the edited volume *Mindfulness and Psychotherapy*, "Any exercise that alerts us to the present moment, with acceptance, cultivates mindfulness. . . . Examples are directing attention to one's breathing, listening to ambient sounds in the environment, paying attention to our posture at a given moment, labeling feelings, and so forth. The list is endless. . . . Two common exercises for cultivating mindfulness in daily life . . .involve slowly walking and slow eating."

In his subsequent book, *The Mindful Path to Self-Compassion,* Germer also clearly explains what mindfulness is *not.* (See the section "For Review and Reflection . . ." at the end of the chapter for a helpful summary of this important information.)

Paying Attention Differently in Solitude

Being alone can mean many different things for different people. For some, it may be an opportunity to engage in mindless activity. For others—whether they are tidying a closet or planting a row of tulips—spending time sitting quietly or engaged in activity can be a mindful experience. The key difference lies in approach: not only in how we understand what we're doing, but also in the results that follow and how we greet them.

Mindfulness allows life to emerge before us without judgment during periods of silence and, perhaps, solitude. (It sounds a bit like the ideal process of counseling, therapy, or mentoring, doesn't it?) It involves leaving nothing out while not indulging anything—neither negatively nor positively. In a spirit of mindfulness, we observe, experience, and learn. The process simply entails watching, breathing, and living in the present moment—ideally with a sense of wonder. But it's certainly not as "simple" as it sounds.

Many writers and mentors of mindfulness offer guidance on how to keep the process as elementary as an unpolished stone. Among their advice is a reminder that, with mindfulness:

- Everything is fresh each time. Expectations—even if they be based on history of how something originally happened in the past—defeat this.
- Awareness of even *mindlessness* doesn't lead to regret that we are not in the present but "merely" encourages us to return to the now when we get trapped in the past or preoccupied with the future.
- The real rather than the ideal is included rather than focusing on positive or negative fantasies or concepts.
- An appreciation is held deeply that everything, *every* thing changes.

- We are encouraged to see—honestly and completely—how every action and comment have an impact on others in our interpersonal network—and to some degree on ourselves.
- We appreciate not general philosophies as much as specific impacts of the words and actions taken.

And so, with a heightened sense of awareness—often referred to as "mindfulness"—we recognize that the openness we truly embrace can make all the difference in how we perceive and value a life rooted in truth, presence, and awakening. This awareness, in turn, shapes how these qualities manifest in the many facets of our lives.

Mindfulness ensures that we are truly awake. It also sets the stage for important learning during the difficult times in our life "*if* only we have the eyes to see." In contrast, "mind*less*-ness" not only keeps us blind to all that we should be grateful for, but it also prevents us from being all that we can truly be, which comes with having a healthy perspective—no matter what is going on in our life at any given time. And so, as part of our journey to become more awake (so we can perceive more accurately what is going on in and around us), we must be able to pick up and attend to the unique characteristics of mindfulness. Some of these include:

- A clear awareness of what we are experiencing, thinking, or feeling without judging ourselves or others
- A sense of intrigue about ourselves and others without projection (blaming others), self-condemnation, discouragement, or expectations
- More interest in discovering the gifts of life rather than merely focusing on our accomplishments
- An appreciation of being in the now and a willingness to return to the present when we are drawn into the past or begin to be preoccupied by the future
- A spirit of "unlearning" and a willingness to see life differently that is inspired by the call to "make all things new"
- A non-ego-centered approach to life that recognizes that it isn't all about *me*
- A willingness to recognize, embrace, and flow with change
- A spirit of receiving life as it is without reaction or rejection
- A focus on those activities that create well-being instead of suffering for others . . . and *ourselves*

- Appreciation of the beauty of patience and enjoying the process of life rather than solely looking forward to completions or successes
- An interest in letting go of the "training" we have received in grasping, being envious, angry, and unkind; and instead having an openness to sharing without an expectation of getting anything in return, being intrigued by our responses so that we can learn from them rather than responding by being defensive or self-indicting, and slowing down rather than straining toward goals (even perceived good ones)
- Avoidance of comparing ourselves favorably or unfavorably with others
- A greater desire to be sensitive to how our words and actions affect others
- An interest in seeking—even in little ways—to contribute to well-being rather than suffering for others and ourselves
- Openness to "mindfully touching" all of our denials, loneliness, shame, and negative feelings about ourselves with compassion rather than running away from them
- Allowing information, negative and positive, familiar and unfamiliar, to flow to us without being obstructed or modified by our ego or fears
- An increased desire for transparency and being persons without guile in the way we live so we can help purify—rather than contaminate with our defensiveness—the psychological and spiritual atmosphere in which we and others live

Practicing—rather than merely knowing about—these characteristics of mindfulness can help us become more open to receiving all that life has to offer. Moreover, and perhaps even more importantly, actively cultivating mindfulness will assist us in facing life's difficulties, gray periods, and sad experiences, deepening us in ways we may never have imagined. In doing so, we also become a gift to those around us.

Releasing Previously Unaccounted for Energy

Whether we recognize it or not, much of our day is spent in front of a mental mirror, whose distortions can be dramatic due to the positive and negative characteristics attributed to us by the people we interact with. This is often shaped by their personal needs and personality styles. These external distortions can, in some cases, also trigger our own longstanding characterological and situational blind spots. Fortunately, meditation and clearer awareness can bring these patterns to the surface of our consciousness—especially when we have a gentle, clear-minded mentor to process them with. When this happens, all that's required is to keep our "perceptual eyes" open. Yet, psychologically, often without realizing it, we tend to "squint"—narrowing our perception instead of fully observing.

In *A Path with Heart*, psychologist and Zen Master Jack Kornfield, aware of this tendency, recalls the guidance of his teacher, Achaan Chah. He said that in meditation, metaphorically, "Just go *into* the room and put one chair in the center. Take the one seat in the center of the room, open the doors and windows, and see who comes to visit. You will witness all kinds of scenes and actors, all kinds of temptations and stories, everything imaginable. Your only job is to stay in your seat. You will see it all arise and pass, and out of this, wisdom and understanding will come."

By doing this, Kornfield suggests, we create space within ourselves where memories and emotions can rise and teach us about the unaccounted-for energy hidden in unresolved sadness and shame, resentment and regret, desire and loneliness, and even happiness and joy. We are given the opportunity to experience how mindfulness can guide us to a healthier perspective— one that allows us to see ourselves more clearly and respond more wisely.

Creating Familiar Places of Solitude

One of the most practical steps we can take to incorporate mindfulness meditation into our daily lives is to establish familiar places where we can practice it. However, such places in the world seem increasingly limited today, meaning that we must take extra steps to discover them. As Sara Maitland suggests:

> Silence, even as an expression of awe, is becoming uncomfortable. We are asked to be silent less and less; churches and public libraries are no longer regarded as places where silence is appropriate . . . silence is not experienced as refreshing or as assisting concentration, but as threatening and disturbing. . . . Nonetheless, despite the rising tide of noise, there are some real pools of silence embedded in the noisiest places and I began to search them out.

Sara Maitland reflects further in *A Book of Silence* on how silence and solitude are particularly important for a writer. She also shares that when she moved to a house away from everything, her friend responded negatively. I believe this incident highlights once again society's often negative perception of alone-time today, and how those who love both inner and outer space may view it quite differently from those who see solitude as unnecessary or even threatening:

> Virginia Woolf famously taught us that every woman writer needs a room of her own. She didn't know the half of it, in my opinion. I need a moor of my own. Or, as an exasperated but obviously sensitive friend commented when she came to see my latest lunacy, "Only you, Sara—twenty mile views of absolutely nothing!"
>
> It isn't "nothing," actually—it is cloud formations, and the different ways reed, rough grass, heather and bracken move in the wind, and the changing colours, not just through the year but through the day as the sun and the clouds alternate and shift...and it is the huge nothing that pulls me into itself. I looked at it, and with fewer things to look at I see better. . . . I can see occasional, and apparently unrelated, strips of silver, which are in fact the small river meandering down the valley. . . . I think about how beautiful it is, and how happy I am.

Thoreau, one of the most prominent advocates for the importance of silence and solitude, believed he could not maintain his health and spirits unless he spent significant time sauntering "through the woods and over the hills and fields absolutely free from worldly engagements." We may not have as much time as Thoreau did for such pursuits. Additionally, many of us may not wish to find ourselves in a rural setting. In fact, some may view solitude as a back-to-nature movement—something Thoreau and, later, Maitland seemed to suggest. However, this need not be the case.

Hugh Prather humorously notes that "what is conducive to concentration for one person is not for another. Solitude is often associated with the fact of getting away from people, and into nature, but my wife Gayle, for example, is more at rest in a large city than in the wilderness. 'Nature makes you itch,' she says. She's convinced that camping out invites angry bears and ax murderers. And certainly it makes no sense to say that in order to feel what connects us all, we must always get away from each other."

However, with an appreciation of mindful silence, any time—regardless of duration or location—can have a profound, positive influence on us. In her book *Contentment: Wisdom from Around the World*, Gillian Stokes notes, "You do not have to live in a cave on a mountaintop to realize spiritual contentment, but if you have become habituated to noise and bustle, you might find it easier to reach a sense of contentment in a less hectic environment, at least in the beginning." The goal is not to run away but to find those spaces that are conducive to us—even in, especially during, times of difficulty.

As Viktor Frankl, Holocaust survivor and author of *Man's Search for Meaning*, aptly noted, "To live you must choose; to love you must encounter; to grow you must suffer." Yet, this doesn't happen spontaneously. Such growth during times of sadness needs to be fed by a sense of informal mindfulness—and whenever possible, its formal counterpart, meditation.

A graduate course I led focused heavily on cultivating these forms of awareness. One of the counselors attending, reflecting on her reasons for being drawn to reflection, meditation, and staying present in the moment, clearly heard this message and took it to heart. She said:

> I so well remember a few years ago when I was invited to a Buddhist place of meditation in Washington, DC. There was a week-long retreat taking place, and my friend and I were allowed to join them for a few hours of sitting and walking meditation that day. I then had the unexpected opportunity to have a few moments to speak privately with the Vietnamese monk who was leading the retreat. I asked him quite bluntly: "Why do you meditate? He answered in his almost perfect English, "I meditate to be happy. When I am in the present moment, I am happy. If I think on the past, then I am often sorry. If I think about the future, I often worry. So then I am often sorry, worry, sorry, worry, sorry, worry. But when I meditate I am in the present, and I am happy."
>
> The simplicity and accuracy of this simple explanation struck a deep chord in me, and I have related this story many times to friends. I am all too familiar with the "sorry-worry" obsession that plays in my head all too often. Author Eckhart Tolle expresses it so well when he writes: "Stress is caused by being 'here' but wanting to be 'there' or being in the present but wanting to be in the future. It is a split that tears you apart inside." This is one reason that meditation is a lifeline for me. It is a time for me to quietly remember to be present and, hopefully, it will spill over into the rest of my day.

No doubt, we would want the same level of commitment to be said of our commitment to having mindfulness meditation at the core of our lives. However, for this to become a reality, we must not only have the motivation but also employ the basic approaches to meditating in silence and solitude that have been passed down through the ages. This is particularly worthwhile to consider, as we have simple yet profound wisdom on mindfulness that those who came before us have left for us to reflect upon and apply. Our only response to such guidance should be: Understand it, absorb it, and, most importantly, put it into practice. Yet, to do so, we need to have the time and space necessary to undertake this essential discipline.

Time and Space to Be Mindful

Regarding time and space, George Prochnik, in his recent popular work *In Pursuit of Silence: Listening for Meaning in a World of Noise*, notes that "We probably do not need a pervasive silence—desirable as this might seem to some. What we do need is more space in which we can interrupt our general experience of noise. What we must aspire to is a greater proportion of quiet in the course of everyday life."

He then highlights an important reality about taking significant periods of silence—one worth reflecting on—so that it does not become a source of resistance to setting aside any time at all:

> I cherish the memory of the time I spent on a silent retreat at an ashram, gazing at a group of people scattered across a grassing hillside like roosting birds—all of them concentrated on doing nothing but being still and listening to the natural world. But the people who go to ashrams, vipassana centers, and all the rich variants of silent-meditation retreats are, for the most part, reasonably well off. Like me, they had the money, the time, or simply the social context that enabled them to wake up one day and say to themselves, "You know what? I'm going on a silent retreat." I'm worried about all the people who, for one reason or another, lack the resources to discover what silence can bring.

Still, there are many places accessible to all of us if we have the eyes to see them—places we can use as refuges for silence and reflection. These include places of worship in our cities that are open during the day, perhaps between services. Libraries, small urban gardens, large parks, walkways along rivers and streams, and quiet coffee houses during off-hours are just a few that come readily to mind. We need to become aware of these options and recognize that they can serve as "double" as places of refuge, rather than dismissing them with thoughts like, "There's no place for me; I can't do it."

Additionally, we must put in the effort to create a conducive space in our homes and offices. That way, when the opportunity for silence spontaneously arises or when we have established a ritual—such as morning meditation or quiet reflection—we will know exactly where to go and how to make that time meaningful.

Simple Approaches to Formal Mindfulness Meditation

Once we have identified the places conducive to silence and reflection, the question of how to approach the practice naturally arises. In addition to enhancing our general sense of nonjudgmental mindfulness and awareness, we also need to pay attention to our formal meditation practice, if we choose to include one. To assist readers who are unfamiliar with meditation, the following simple suggestions are offered to help develop a beginning practice:

- *Have a conducive posture.* As we sit, with our back straight, we look just ahead of us at something that can hold our attention (a candle, etc.) as we breathe naturally and gently.
- *Be patient.* Rushing or expecting something only injects unnecessary pressure into our time of meditation. Be the apple slowly ripening.
- *Don't unduly entertain, judge, or run away from your thoughts.* Just observe and let them move through you like water in a slowly running stream. To help accomplish this, you can label thoughts ("judging," "guilt") that come your way or use a centering word/mantra like "gentle" or even count your breaths (1-2-3-4) and keep counting this way until you are present again.
- *Accept where you are in meditation and don't compare.* After all, what choice do you have than to be where you are at this point? Also, don't waste time in favorably or unfavorably comparing your meditation, or anything about yourself with others. Meditation is not a competition or beauty pageant.
- *Don't seek to solve anything in meditation.* Problem-solving is a good activity, but not appropriate to formal mindfulness.

- *Don't expect or try to force anything.* Just relax; that's enough. Trust. The meditation will do the rest. There will be times when we are meditating that it will flow easily. Other times our meditation may seem flat empty. We may even be bored for a time. That's all right. As Zen teaches us, if you are bored for two minutes in meditation, then do it for four!
- *Don't cling.* Just breathe in good energy and breathe out peace, then let whatever comes up flow through you like a light wind. If some issue or theme repeatedly comes up just come back to your centering word or counting your breaths by counting from one to four again and again until you are settled. Remember letting your meditation move with your breathing in and out is an anchor in meditation.
- *Although you should be regular in meditation, allow for times of intense, longer meditative periods.* Taking at least a few moments each day to center yourself is essential. Being disciplined to meditate regularly is the spiritual backbone of a life well lived. However, if possible, there should be times when you extend your meditation for longer periods of time.

Include Everything

One of the most important elements of mindfulness meditation—serving as a tool to maintain or restore a healthy perspective—is to include everything in our practice. Jack Kornfield, once again in his Eastern spirituality work *A Path with Heart*, notes:

I had hoped for special effects from meditation—happiness, special states of rapture, extraordinary experiences. But that was not primarily what my teacher offered. He offered a way of life, a lifelong path of awakening, attention, surrender, and commitment. He offered a happiness that was not dependent on any of the changing conditions of the world but came out of one's own difficult and conscious inner transformation. In joining the monastery, I had hoped to leave behind the pain of my family life and the difficulties of the world, but of course they followed me. It took many years for me to realize that these difficulties were part of my practice. . . . The simple phrase, "This too, this too," was the main meditation instruction of [another of the spiritual masters] with whom I studied. Through these few words we were encouraged to soften and open to see whatever we encountered, accepting the truth with a wise and understanding heart.

What makes mindfulness rich is including all the specifics of life. When something joyful, puzzling, sad, or upsetting occurs—no matter how insignificant it may seem at first—remember to bring the attitude of "this too, this too" into your meditation and mindfulness practice. Viewing even what we consider distractions as sources of new knowledge can lead to great rewards. The goal of this approach is to transform all aspects of our life into a rich, mindful experience. In this way, instead of being tied down by so many other "voices"—culture, peer pressure, family fears, or neediness— we can respond to the truth's sometimes soft, inner voice that calls us toward newfound freedom and a fuller life, fostered by a healthy and clear perspective.

Going on Retreat: Periods of Dramatic Solitude

Philosopher Henry David Thoreau, as previously noted, is arguably one of the most well-known Americans who sought out significant periods of solitude. His explanation of why he did this remains compelling even today:

> I went to the woods because I wished to live deliberately, to confront only the essential facts of life, and see if I could not learn what it had to teach, and not, when I came to die, discover that I had not lived. I did not wish to live what was not life, living is so dear; nor did I wish to practice resignation, unless it was quite necessary. I wanted to live deep and suck out all the marrow of life, to live so sturdily and Spartan-like as to put to rout all that was not life, to cut a broad swath and shave close, to drive life into a corner, and reduce it to its lowest terms, and, if it proved to be mean, why then to get the whole and genuine meanness of it, and publish its meanness to the world; or if it were sublime, to know it by experience, and be able to give a true account of it in my next excursion.

More dramatic than Thoreau's retreat to the woods is the one described in *A Woman in the Polar Night* by Christiane Ritter. In the introduction, Lawrence Millman writes:

> Stuck in the hut by herself during an epic snowstorm, Christiane almost did go crazy. At the same time, she realized that, however tough the cir- cumstances, she could survive them. And from then on, she did not think of the Arctic as an enemy. Rather, it was a realm "where everything goes its

prescribed way...without man's intervention." Such was her transformation that she could even suggest that "in centuries to come, men will go to the Arctic as in biblical times they withdrew to the desert, to find the truth again." I can't imagine any polar explorer making a statement like this. . . .

Christiane left what she called "the Arctic wilderness" in June of 1935, never to return . . . she didn't really need to return . . . since she brought it home with her, or at least brought home a radically different way of looking at the world. A short while after she got back from Spitsbergen, the Ritter family estate burned to the ground. But rather than go into mourning over the loss of her home and virtually all of her possessions, Christiane was more or less grateful, according to her daughter Karin. For she could now live simply, without a surfeit of ballast, just as she lived in the hut in Grahuken.

Her own reactions to living alone in a very small hut for extended periods are intriguing to read about. The lessons she learned come through clearly in her published memoir of her experiences, which are filled with a gratitude that can only arise after deprivation—when one begins to appreciate what is often taken for granted.

Less dramatic than these accounts are the reflections of people who undertake a silent retreat, whether alone or with others who respect the need to step away from noise and even meaningful conversation for a time. Such retreats may last 30 days, a week, or—more commonly for most of us—an overnight or weekend. Many of the individuals I have interviewed describe a mix of what they interpret as both pleasant and disagreeable experiences, such as:

- "I recognized how much was swirling around in my mind just below the surface."
- "How I had forgotten what the simple truth really is because even conversations within myself often sounded like cocktail party discussions."
- "I realized I rarely challenged my shame but covered it over with intellectualizations (i.e., "I crossed those boundaries with someone I work with at the restaurant because she needed extra physical assurance of my interest in her.")

- "There were fears in me that if I saw how I needed to change and did it, others would shy away from me, I would see how I had not really lived up to this point in my life, or if I did see the truth I would have to do something about it."

Despite such descriptions of the experiences encountered in silence and possibly solitude, most people who have undertaken a retreat or extended period of alone-time find that, in the end, their feelings, thoughts, and experiences often prove to be highly informative and beneficial—ways of understanding themselves that would not have been possible had they only engaged in a few hours or a single day of solitude.

However, alone-time, like anger or other reactions, is not beneficial in and of itself. It is our approach to and perception of these experiences that makes all the difference. That is why the practice of informal and formal mindfulness—helping us to lean back from our busy schedules and the constant stream of thoughts and judgments—is so essential. It is also crucial to recognize the natural resistances we may have to spending time alone. By understanding these blocks, we can continue to cultivate and deepen our alone-time rather than succumb to our challenges in creating this space.

To conclude, I leave you with the words of the poet Rainer Maria Rilke:

For what (ask yourself) would solitude be that had no greatness; there is but *one* solitude, and that is great, and not easy to bear, and to almost everybody come hours when they would gladly exchange it for any sort of intercourse, however banal and cheap, for the semblance of some slight accord with the first comer, with the unworthiest. . . . But perhaps those are the very hours when solitude grows. . . . But that must not mislead you. The necessary thing is after all but this: solitude, great inner solitude. Going-into-oneself and for hours meeting no one—this one must be able to attain. To be solitary, the way one was solitary as a child, when the grownups went around involved with things that seemed important and big because they themselves looked so busy and because one comprehended nothing of their doings. . . . And you should not let yourself be confused in your solitude by the fact that there is something in you that wants to break out of it. This very wish will help you, if you use it quietly, and deliberately and like a tool, to spread out your solitude over wide country.

Final Comments on Reflection and Time Spent
in Silence and Solitude

Reflection sounds like a peaceful, renewing, and enlightening process—and it can indeed be such an experience. However, when we quiet our minds and our lives, it creates a psychological vacuum where bustling activities once were, opening up space within our daily routine. Often, this new space is filled with troubling "visitors"—what psycho-dynamically-oriented psychologists once referred to as the "preconscious." But when this occurs, if we can welcome these thoughts, feelings, or memories in the right way, they can serve as teachers. Then, instead of ruminating endlessly about them, we can gently show them the psychological door. Doing so reduces the ongoing inner commentary, making it possible to become more present, aware, and clear.

When we intentionally set aside time to sit in silence, relax, breathe deeply, and remain attentive to the present moment with a spirit of both kindness toward ourselves and clarity about what arises, thoughts will pass through like a train. If we do not suppress or cling to them, their presence can lead to new self-understanding, reduce feelings of regret or the projection of blame onto others, and create the psychological space necessary for greater creativity and compassion.

The goal is to be like curious children sitting gratefully before the mystery of life—our lives. When we do this intentionally each day, on a regular basis, it "positively contaminates" the rest of our day. We respect this time, and because of that, we experience more than those who simply rush through the miracle of life. Calmly spending time in silence and solitude can leave us in a new place, with greater sensitivity to our surroundings. We will move further and deeper into our contact with life as it truly is—or as it can be—rather than how we or others wish to portray it.

Claude Monet once said, "To see, we must forge the name of things we are looking at." Quiet time allows us to keep this spirit in our hearts as we meet the possibilities of life more mindfully—even with respect to who we are. In this regard, Austrian composer Franz Joseph Haydn experienced a period of being cut off from regular contact with broader society. Reflecting on this time, he shared that it forced him to be original. This is the attitude we should intentionally cultivate—becoming more attentive to possibility and directing our interest and "psychological ears" toward new awareness and wisdom, rather than simply being busy or bored, waiting for the next interesting thing to happen.

Time spent alone in quiet, reflective moments enables us to experience our own "inner life," which existentialist Søren Kierkegaard would see as a unique aspect of our ongoing reflective process—one that is not always visible to others. This dimension of ourselves is not something we are constantly in contact with. Therefore, ongoing mindfulness meditation or reflective time is essential. As Gosetti-Ferencei notes in her book *On Being and Becoming*:

> For most selves, memory is only inconsistently reliable. Some experiences are well remembered, but others are forever forgotten. What is foremost in our concerns right now may give way to other concerns or priorities, or may cease to concern us at all. We may feel very different now from the person we were at an earlier stage in life—at times we might scarcely recognize our earlier self. We may gradually change over many years, or, should we experience a traumatic or dramatic event, we may change radically overnight. Any self is subject to alteration, continuity, rupture, and change.

She further explains that "existential thinking concentrates on the world as it is experienced in us, and how it matters to us—from the human and personal point of view." From a psychological vantage point, this is why mental health professionals are so interested—and even intrigued at times—by an individual's unique perspective and how their personal history and style of thinking and believing impact their understanding of life. We should have the same sense of interest in our own way of viewing our own life.

As Bridges in *Transitions* notes, this awareness is especially crucial during periods of change and when considering possibilities. The book points out that "People who have discounted or blocked out the inner callings from the future have cut themselves off from the very signals that really vital people use to stay on the paths of their own development. It is no wonder that people who have silenced those inner signals find meaningful careers difficult to launch and maintain, or that when they encounter times of transition, they are so confused and distressed."

Unless we take time to turn off the internal commentary and judgmental mind for a while, we will remain inside a cognitive envelope of evaluations that may not be accurate, and we risk missing the life we truly wish for ourselves. Therefore, in pursuit of genuine self-awareness and meaning-ful connection with the world around us, we need to ask ourselves simple but essential questions such as:

- Where in your life does quiet time already exist?
- In what parts of your life is it realistic to create some new spaces where you can relax and practice mindful breathing?
- Imagine people in your life that you admire because they are more reflective and relaxed than you are. What are some basic ways to emulate them?
- In what ways can you create an environment in your home or office that is conducive to taking a brief period for sitting quietly and reflecting or meditating?
- How can you develop a list of triggers to help you become more mind-ful so you don't simply run to your grave thinking that once this task is done you will take time? (These reminders can and should include common daily triggers such as: the ring or vibration of a cellphone, unlocking your car to drive to work or on an errand, or your morning alarm.)
- In your own life, how would you describe the relationship between alone-time and the relationships you have at work and within your personal life?
- What has been your own array of experiences when you took time in silence and possibly solitude?
- If you have a formal mindfulness meditative practice, how do you handle distractions during meditation?
- What unique characteristics of mindfulness have you experienced and which ones noted in this chapter have you not and how do you understand this pattern?
- What are your favorite places of solitude?
- What are the most important approaches to meditation for you?
- If you use a diary to note your reflections after meditation or periods of alone-time, in what ways has this practice been helpful for you?
- If you don't record your impressions, do you think you might like to begin? What would it take for you to do this?

We need to take our own lives and the possibilities present at each stage more seriously, and as Zen Master Thich Nhat Hanh often shared with those who attended his teachings: "An entire sea of water can't sink a ship unless it gets inside the ship. Similarly, the negativity of the world can't put you down unless you allow it to get inside you." Quiet time helps to prevent sources of unnecessary psychological darkness and discouragement from taking root. It also opens us up to new possibilities, even amid the failures everyone encounters when seeking to fully engage with and make the most of life. Ultimately, we come to realize that the answers to what is possible at different turns in life depend more on our attunement to our inner life than on external circumstances. Therefore, a careful review of the following five lists in the section "For Review and Reflection . . ." on silence, solitude, mindfulness, and the dangers of mindlessness—is a very worthwhile step in uncovering and embracing the possibilities in our lives.

For Review and Reflection . . .

Experiencing the Gifts of Mindfulness

When we have periods of silence and possibly solitude or pay attention to what is going on around and within us without immediately judging, stopping, or overanalyzing our observations, we can experience such gifts as the following:

- Opportunities to relax, lean back from roles, and be able to be in the moment
- An ability to honor life's fragility and preciousness
- Taking walks to experience what is around us rather than being trapped in a cognitive envelope
- Experiencing an attitude of simplicity by being present to where we are, not where we want to be or running from where we have been
- Enjoying our relationship with ourselves more and needing the reinforcement of others less
- Seeing the thoughts and sense of anger, entitlement, grasping, cowardice, and fear that may be lying just below the surface and acting as invisible puppeteers during the day
- Time to recognize and embrace the natural changes that will always occur in one's life
- Unknotting complexities into manageable challenges that seem to get less burdensome or overwhelming in the process
- Becoming more intrigued about who we really are, what narrative we have been sold, and what sense of ordinary self can be explored further . . . and further
- A desire to unlearn and see things differently than others have claimed and we may in turn have embraced as part of enculturation
- More freedom to observe and receive life's smaller things as true gifts instead of submitting to the environment's advertisement that more is better
- Less desire to compare oneself with others but instead time to trace the paths of one's own development
- A greater ability to laugh at oneself
- The mindfulness needed to see life more clearly rather than inappropriately and rashly judging it to be unworthy of examining and providing new learning

- No longer wasting energy on trying to control the uncontrollable but instead more interested where and when we can make a good impact
- A greater willingness to face our own *koans* (life puzzles) that have no easy answers to them but require choices that will affect our lives … as well as those who count on us
- Surprising insights that lift us out of habitual thought patterns
- Freedom after a while from the anxieties and preoccupations that tend to represent the "white noise" of much of the day
- Recognizing more fully the value of leaning back from the constant activities and emotions of the normal routine
- Forgoing the comfort of denial for the true peace of having the courage to face and embrace what we must in life
- Recognizing new spaces in our life (in the shower, between phone calls, a short walk at lunch, just before we fall asleep or get out of bed, on the drive home, etc.) to take a breath instead of simply rushing to our grave and calling that practical
- Protecting our inner fire so when the time calls for it we can reach out without being pulled down
- A deeper appreciation for transparency, authenticity, simplicity, humility, and honesty as fruits of being open to new possibility each day and at each phase of life

What Mindfulness Is Not

- *Mindfulness is not trying to relax.* When we become aware of what's happening in our lives, it can sometimes feel anything but relaxing—especially if we're stuck in a difficult situation. However, as we learn more about ourselves, we become less surprised by the feelings that arise within us. We develop a less-reactive relationship to our inner experience, allowing us to recognize and let go of emotional storms more easily.
- *Mindfulness is not a religion.* Although mindfulness has been practiced by Buddhist nuns and monks for over 2,500 years, any purposeful activity that increases awareness of moment-to-moment experience is considered a mindfulness exercise. We can practice mindfulness within a religious context or independently of any religion. Modern scientific psychology recognizes mindfulness as a fundamental healing factor in psychotherapy.

- *Mindfulness is not about transcending ordinary life.* Instead, it involves making intimate contact with each moment, no matter how trivial or mundane. Simple things can become very special—extraordinarily ordinary—when we bring awareness to them. For example, the flavor of your food or the color of a rose becomes more vivid if you pay close attention. Mindfulness is also about experiencing ourselves more fully, not trying to bypass or ignore the mundane, rough edges of life.
- *Mindfulness is not about emptying the mind of thoughts.* The brain will always produce thoughts—that's its nature. Mindfulness helps us develop a more harmonious relationship with our thoughts and feelings through a deep understanding of how the mind operates. Sometimes, it may feel as if we have fewer thoughts, because we're not struggling against them so much.
- *Mindfulness is not difficult.* You shouldn't feel discouraged if you notice that your mind wanders incessantly; that's simply the nature of the mind. Ironically, it's in those very moments of despair, when you think you're failing at mindfulness, that awareness arises. It's impossible to practice perfectly or to fail altogether; that's why it's called a "practice."
- *Mindfulness is not about escaping pain.* This is one of the toughest concepts to accept, because we usually seek to avoid discomfort. Yet, with mindfulness and acceptance, we learn not to run from pain. Pain is like an angry bull: when confined to a small stall, it becomes wild and tries to escape. But when allowed to roam freely in a vast field, it calms down. Mindfulness creates the emotional space to hold and be present with pain.

Source: Germer, C. *The Mindful Path to Self-Compassion* (New York: Guilford Press, 2009).

The Red Flags of "Mindlessness"

When we live without a sense of mindfulness, we often miss and waste a considerable amount of energy. However, we can more quickly and mindfully return to "the now" with an open mind when we are able to recognize the red flags that indicate we are not truly aware of what is happening within and around us. Therefore, it is helpful to recognize and acknowledge our moments of mindlessness when:

- We get easily upset—often over the wrong things—and miss what life is offering us in all interactions and events.
- Interruptions are seen only as disruptive rather than informative or possibly, unexpected opportunities.
- Habits and rules continue to sap life's freshness for us.
- We spend too much time in the silver casket of nostalgia or rushing through precious moments of our lives under the impression that living this way is "only practical."
- We only fantasize about "the spirit of simplicity" and "letting go" rather than seeking to practice them more in our lives.
- Our promises to ourselves to adopt a healthier life-style don't translate into the necessary actions.
- We spend so much of the time in a cognitive cocoon of judgment, worry, preoccupation, resentment, fear, and regret that we miss life's daily gifts happening all around us.
- Our time in silence and solitude often ends up being boring and emotionally flat rather than renewing.
- We seem to ignore the spiritual gifts of laughter, a child's smile, or a good conversation and instead focus on increasing such trivial things as fame, power, security, and pleasure.
- A canceled get-together, a brief illness, or a delay in our schedule is not appreciated as a spontaneous period for spiritual mindfulness.
- Transitions make up much of our life but are not seen as being as valuable as our destinations.
- The "ghosts" of our past memories are not valued as the teachers they can be, but instead merely serve to pull us down or fill us with regret.
- A sense of intrigue or curiosity about ourselves—including both our gifts and growing edges—is overshadowed by our self-blame, discouragement, or projecting faults onto others.
- Too much of our life is spent running away from what we don't like or in "medicating" ourselves, seeking security, or grasping, rather than simply enjoying and being grateful for all that is around us.
- Sincerity, transparency, and being a person without guile seem absent even though we know we waste so much unnecessary energy on being defensive, wearing interpersonal masks, or seeking to manipulate others.
- We rush around like a gargoyle on roller skates while failing to notice people we have hurt, what we are eating, how we are feeling, or even

what we are really doing or supposed to be paying attention to (such as the road when we are driving a car or the person to whom we are supposed to be paying attention).

The Fruits of Mindfulness and a Healthy Perspective

When we are suffering or our lives feel "dark," mindfulness helps us to be more attuned to what life has to teach us, often in new and transformative ways. When we are fully present in "the now" and open, mindfulness can:

- Lift us out of stagnant, obsessive thought patterns
- Alert us to when we are not living the experience of life but merely wandering around in an envelope of thought, thinking we are alive
- Move us out of the thicket of preoccupations, fears, anxieties, and worries about the past or future by having us "simply" be where we are
- Help us appreciate that *all* things/people/situations change
- Give us the space to step back and get unglued from our desires, demands, and attachments so we can have the freedom to flow with what is
- Enable us to get in touch with the invisible bonds of shame, loneliness, secrets, addictions, hopes, and other places in our hearts where we have expended a great deal of energy in avoidance
- Help us forgo the comfort of denial and avoidance for the peace that allows us to fear nothing but instead welcome all of our emotions, cognitions (ways of thinking, perceiving, and understanding), and impulses with compassion and clarity
- Open up true space for others by opening it up in ourselves
- Help us imitate those we admire by reaching out to others who are in need
- Enable us to see our defenses, failures, and growing edges as opportunities for new wisdom and opening to life (because rather than judging, we are intrigued by them)
- Ask if we are relating to ourselves with kindness and clarity
- Awaken us to our habitual, possibly deadening styles of thinking, believing, and behaving

- Allow us especially to become freer by taking "the sacred pause" spiritual guide Tara Brach suggests when confronted with suffering (a pause made up of a desire to recognize what is happening, allowing it, and experiencing it rather than trying to just figure out or control it)
- Help us see that permanent problems are so because of the way we formulate them, thus teaching us that loosening our grip on such ways of seeing our world makes all the difference
- Set aside the way we have created meaning so all things can be made new
- Increase our appreciation of how little things can produce emotional peaks and valleys in our lives
- Develop our respect for both formal mindfulness (meditation) and informal approaches to mindfulness that increase our awareness of "the now" during the day
- Incorporate simple practices, such as taking a few moments to notice something enjoyable; appreciating our own small, beautiful acts; and slowing down when we are caught up in a sense of mindless, driven action
- Encourage us to wonder more about what thoughts, emotions, and events help us create peace rather than suffering
- Teach us that being spiritually aware is more natural when we don't seek it aggressively, or with expectations or fear that it won't produce dramatic results
- Have us welcome and learn from, rather than label and reject, so-called negative experiences such as boredom
- Help us be clear and sort things out as well as deepen ourselves
- Encourage humility, help us see our foibles, and over time increase the enjoyment we have in being alone with ourselves and relaxed with others
- Result in less dependence on reinforcement by others while at the same time setting the stage for taking a healthier part in community
- Protect our inner fire by helping us see when we need to withdraw for time alone and also uncover time within our daily activity where we can take a few breaths and center ourselves, rather than be disturbed that we are being delayed or postponed in our travels or activities
- Make us more in tune with the inner voice of a healthy perspective that is continually being drowned out by society and our own inner habitual self-talk

Illustrations of Positive Movements of Mindfulness in Our Life

- Peace, joy, understanding, and patience spontaneously begin to take the place of anger, resentment, and other negative emotions.
- We reflect and act in a helpful way when someone misbehaves, rather than merely reacting.
- Judging ourselves or others is often replaced by a helpful compassion that can lead to positive change.
- Crippling guilt, which pulls us into the past and leaves us there, diminishes; we become aware of our faults, but in a way that makes the present and future different.
- We recognize when we have become inordinately preoccupied with the future, and a greater appreciation of the present moment and the ability to stay in that moment develops.
- A more natural tendency to move away from useless worry. In its place we meet life's demands more often with a concern that involves recognizing the challenges, appreciating their source, planning what we can do, doing it, and then letting others take care of the rest. Trying to be a savior never works.
- Our awareness of ourselves and those around us is more frequently marked by acceptance, compassion, and understanding.
- A deeper appreciation for patience and vulnerability instead of a desire to control becomes evident.
- Surprising episodes of gratitude for people and things we used to take for granted show themselves more readily in our daily encounters.
- There is less interest in competition, less concern about what others may think of us.
- Experiences of collaboration and connectedness seem to spontaneously occur.
- A real sense of intrigue about our own thoughts, ways of understanding, perceptions, emotions, and behaviors begins to replace the old tendency toward self-blame, resentment, or fear.
- We don't automatically believe our thoughts—especially the negative ones—without checking them out.
- Self-awareness becomes more a gentle process of self-appreciation rather than a process of comparison of ourselves with others.
- We seek to be more inclusive rather than exclusive in the way we bring everything into our prayers and lives.

- A desire increases in us to use our speech to benefit others by being truthful, expressive of our own experiences, sensitive to the feelings of others, supportive, encouraging, accurate, and specific rather than vague, negative, and self-referential in an exaggerated way.

When we experience these positive shifts through mindfulness meditation, we discover why and how making alone-time part of our entire day—not just during formal meditation—leads to a more centered, full, and compassionate way of living. Truly, aspiring to live in such a meaningful way is a noble and rewarding goal.

6

What Missing the Mark Can Teach Us

Failure, Faithfulness, and Epiphanies During Periods of Change and Uncertainty

"The great virtue of mistakes, whether they occur accidentally or by design, is their ability to enlarge our range of experience, shrink our ego, and thereby increase the chance of discovery."

—*Brilliant Mistakes*
Author, Paul J. H. Schoemaker

"I finally found my rhythm when I realized even the steps backwards were part of the dance."

—*Self Love Poetry*
Author, Melody Godfred

Antoine de Saint-Exupéry, in his book *Night Flight*, wrote: "Victory, defeat—the words were meaningless. Life lies behind these symbols, and life is ever bringing new symbols into being. One nation is weakened by a victory; another finds new forces in defeat." A storm can be destructive and disruptive or... it can simply clear the air for us to breathe more deeply.

The attractiveness that modern society attributes to "success" is very alluring. But ancient and contemporary philosophers and spiritual guides have not always viewed these goals positively. For instance, in 424 BC, Aristophanes, an Athenian poet, listed three essentials for climbing the ladder of success: "to plunder, to lie... [and] to show your arse!"

How We View and Deal with Failure

Experiencing unnecessary suffering when you fail is unfortunate—especially when, instead of providing information to broaden your horizon, it causes you to pull back. Consequently, our perspective on failure is essential. This is not only important for those in "official" leadership or mentoring roles but also for those who rely on them to remain involved—especially when the odds are great against succeeding, as most people naturally wish to do. Our attitude is key in all of this. It will determine whether we can weather the storms of failure and a sense of loss when our goals are not achieved. In her memoir *Dakota*, author Kathleen Norris wrote that she was called to reflect on this when she came across a handwritten note by her grandmother inserted in an old family Bible. On it was written, "Keep me friendly to myself; keep me gentle in disappointment."

A Chan (Chinese Zen) master expressed this sense of self during failure even more pointedly when he shared, "I never regret anything I've done. I have made mistakes and will make more, but in response, I am clear, learn, and move on." Obviously, this is easier said than done for most of us. In addition to being clear about what can be learned when we don't succeed, sometimes we need friends around us to help us break through and discover what benefit failure might hold—even though no one likes to be seen in this light—especially when we feel like a failure as a person.

A classic example of this for me is an experience reported by William Sloane Coffin, the former chaplain at Yale University. During his tenure there, he experienced serious marital difficulties at a time when ministers might be expected to bow out of their work if they divorced. He became so distraught that he offered his resignation to Kingman Brewster, Yale's president. The temptation for Brewster to accept was there because Coffin was at times a troublesome activist. However, much to Coffin's surprise, Brewster responded by inviting him to move in with him and his wife for a while.

Coffin was still not sure whether he should resign or not, so he took it a step further by consulting a faculty colleague, Richard Sewall. Sewall also advised him not to resign but added a compelling reason: "Bill," he said, "if you have suffered from anything, it is an aura of too much success. A little failure can only improve your ministry."

Understanding the potential value of dealing with failure is scarce today. Educators teaching in schools with a strong value system—one that is not only expressed but also practiced—can relate to this. More often than not today, parents will seek out schools they respect because of the values they hold. Yet, a number of those very parents will come to the school to complain to teachers and administrators when their children's personal and educational failures are pointed out and the students are held accountable. A student's wonderful sense of self can become distorted when both parents and the students themselves view success as the ultimate (and only) goal.

People today often live their lives in front of a mental mirror. How different this philosophy is from that of an ancient Chinese sage, who presents the following lesson on success. It is conveyed to us in Thomas Merton's *The Way of Chuang Tzu*:

> When an archer is shooting for nothing
> He has all his skill.
> If he shoots for a brass buckle
> He is already nervous.
> If he shoots for a prize of gold
> He goes blind
> Or sees two targets—
> He is out of his mind!
> His skill has not changed. But the prize
> Divides him. He cares.
> He thinks more of winning
> Than of shooting—
> And the need to win
> Drains him of power.

In addressing surgical residents, I told them that before I discussed the principles and practices of resilience and maintaining a healthy perspective, I wanted to bring up something they would need to face in their delicate work—and that all of us need to be aware of no matter what we do or when we seek possibility. This was that during their tenure as surgeons, they were going to injure some people. Hopefully not through malpractice, but through mis-practice, because it is literally impossible for them to be at an "A level" 100% of the time. To a different degree, the same can be said for all of us who seek to truly embrace life.

Another reality for all of us today is that the more involved we are, the more we are going to fail. If we are to be "people of possibility" at the different turns in life, we must be able to put failure into perspective. Failure is part and parcel of involvement. Given the many demands and the inability to be perfectly "on" all the time, failure will occur. And while this is inevitable, failure can still provide helpful information. For instance, it can limit future mistakes and offer better insight into how we experience life's existing and potential gifts—as well as the challenges we must face in the process. In fact, if we look carefully at ourselves when we fall short of our own or other's goals, failure can actually teach us to:

- Recognize the dangers of pride and the need for openness
- Consider ways to avoid errors in the future
- Change factors that increase the possibility of failure
- Experiment with new interpersonal approaches
- Learn about ourselves
- Be sensitive to early warning signs of mistakes
- Consider the impact of negligence
- Uncover areas where further education, guidance, or support is required
- Appreciate unrealistic expectations of ourselves and others
- Improve pacing in one's life
- Acknowledge professional limitations that can be improved as well as become more aware of the personal limitations in ourselves

If failure is carefully considered as an appropriate source of helpful information—rather than solely as a source of self-condemnation or as an impetus to blame, deny, or distort the situation—then both we and the persons who cross our path will benefit immeasurably from the process of our self-examination. But to accomplish this, we must seek to be critical thinkers and recognize that, in the words of Swiss psychiatrist Carl Jung, our life—if it is to be seen as a true inner journey—is "not a career or success story. It is a series of small humiliations of the false self that become more and more profound."

Paul Schoemaker, founder and executive chairman of Decision Strategies International, Inc., and research director of the Mack Center for Technological Innovation at the Wharton School of the University of Pennsylvania, in his book *Brilliant Mistakes,* indicates that the errors we make are "not created equal. Some have high cost and offer little learning value, while others cost little and produce deep, valuable insight. These are the brilliant mistakes, the ones to embrace rather than to avoid."

He then offers the following key message to make the point that, in decision-making for many, "the problem is not that they make too many mistakes, but too few." He is keenly aware, in making such a statement, that the real issue often lies in the inability to recognize, understand, and embrace true possibility because of errors of omission rather than commission. He explains further that:

1. It is important to embrace the learning potential of mistakes—first, by overcoming shame and fear that lead us to overlook the covert messages they carry about how we think.

2. To learn from a mistake, it's critical to separate the decision process—the part that you own—from the outcomes, which are usually influenced by external factors.

3. There is a difference between silly errors and brilliant mistakes, and it all hinges on the relative costs and benefits of what is at stake. Designing for, and learning from, a mistake can make it brilliant.

4. In some cases, it's advisable to allow room for mistakes to be made. Just as random mutations have advanced evolution, clever, well-designed mistakes can further human progress by opening new vistas.

5. One of the important points he also makes in his creative and practical guide for current and aspiring leaders and groundbreaking visionaries is that focusing on preventing mistakes, rather than seeking how best to learn from them, is a common mistake that persons and organizations often make. Additionally, when making a decision, he points out that "had you evaluated your strengths, considered other options, assessed their benefits and risks, and selected according to your deepest preferences," mistakes made after such a process can only lead to much-needed additional knowledge about how to move forward. In such cases, mistakes that occur can produce value far beyond the short-term "failure" experienced. Being wrong can also create a sense of humility that results in a reassessment and opens up new knowledge, previously blocked by cognitive blind spots in how we were thinking and perceiving the situation. It can diminish overconfidence, minimize prejudice, lessen the fear of appropriate risk (as opposed to being rash), uncover faulty assumptions, and contradict what was previously seen as "evidence."

6. In *Brilliant Mistakes*, one of the overarching goals of Schoemaker is to encourage a more open and fertile mind. In pursuit of this, he poses a number of questions to help us see if we are ready for "deliberate mistakes." Although the wording is designed for business executives

and managers, we can all benefit from them, as well as from his book's more in-depth treatment of the topics:

- Do you think that many of your crucial beliefs about your business [and I would add yourself] might be wrong?
- Did you ever do something against your better judgment just to see what would happen?
- Have you ever given an award to someone who tried something new that did not work?
- When confronted with puzzling data, do you naturally insist on multiple explanations?
- Are you viewed as an innovator in your field—as someone who challenges received wisdom?
- Have you systematically tried to identify your implicit business assumptions?
- Are you tolerant of mavericks—that is, credible people who hold unusual or contrarian views?
- Do you value a learning culture in addition to a performance culture?
- Has your industry seen disruptive changes, with new business models arising?
- Has past success made you complacent or perhaps even arrogant; is there hubris?

These questions made me think more broadly and reflect on a quote from a very different source—Pope John XXIII—who said, "Consult not your fears but your hopes and dreams. Think not about your frustrations, but your unfulfilled potential. Concern yourself not with what you tried and failed in, but with what is still possible for you to do." Failure in others' eyes can lead us to simply feel upset, or it can, with an attitude of intrigue, ultimately lead us to mine new insights about who we are and who we can become.

As I write these words, I am reminded of an interaction I had many years ago with a quite famous and accomplished colleague. I had received a letter from him that I thought contained manipulative information. Instead of allowing myself time to let my emotions settle and consider how I would respond, I immediately called him and let him know what I thought. In response, he said we needed to sit down and discuss this. Obviously, I had hit a nerve with him—by the way, I presented my feelings in a very raw way.

When we did have a chance to meet, each time I would give him an illustration of why I was upset, he would respond with an answer that was less than satisfactory to me. Finally, I recognized that since I had hurt his feelings in the first place—what some in psychology would refer to as causing "narcissistic injury"—I was the last person to help him see how manipulative he could sometimes be. I also realized, as we discussed the events, that it wasn't the details of what he had done that were most problematic. It was the style—the "music"—of how he was behaving; to my mind, he was being "slick" in his approach to colleagues who had gone out of their way to work for him. So, I concluded that the best approach was to diffuse the emotion in the room, let go of my need to control, and try to ease out of the situation since I was obviously accomplishing nothing.

As I was trying to do this, he looked at me and said, "You know, when you called me to confront me about my actions, I called up several people and asked them about you." When he said this, I was caught completely off guard. At first, I thought he was simply being defensive—which was probably partly true. However, as he continued and my own defensiveness started to wane, the thought came to me that while I certainly no longer felt called to be prophetic about his behavior, he was truly awakening me to my own manipulative tendencies and defenses.

As I stepped back from the event later that day, I also began to realize a greater point to ponder: that everything critical said to me—no matter how poor the motivation of the person sharing it—still contained information that could be helpful if I approached it with a sense of intrigue rather than defensiveness or offensiveness. As a result, even today, when I recall that unpleasant event and feel anger, anxiety, or the temptation to be angry at someone else or myself for not meeting certain expectations, it helps me surface questions such as:

- What is *really* upsetting me about this unpleasant interaction or sense of failure?
- What am I being asked to let go of or what lesson I am be asked to wake up to that I want to resist for some reason?
- How is my ego or insecurity preventing me from seeking what I need to observe about myself?
- What new approaches can I put into place that can prevent or lessen such a negative sense of myself or others in the future as well as prevent unnecessary mistakes?

Most people run away from looking closely at their failures—even when they are sitting alone at the end of the day, attempting to learn from the events, experiences, feelings, and thoughts they have encountered. The reason is quite simple: it is often unpleasant and painful to reflect on how we have failed. However, as French philosopher Camus notes, "When a man has learned—and not on paper—how to remain alone with his sufferings, how to overcome his longing to flee, then he has little left to learn."

One of the ways people are encouraged not to run away from life's necessary darkness is to help them see the benefits of staying the course. Some of those advantages are:

- Increased motivation and determination to face what we experience as darkness or failure in ourselves and others
- Greater insight into one's own personality style, defenses, values, gifts, and areas of vulnerability
- Less dependence on the recognition and approval of others
- New skills and styles of behavior to complement our usual—possibly habitual—ways of interacting with others
- A sense of peace that is independent of external success, comfort, and security

I must confess that the above brief thoughts didn't all come to me at once after a failure or series of failures. I was too upset at the time for that to happen. Then, as now, each time I need to let the "psychological dust" settle by allowing the negative emotions I felt to come to the surface. This space is so important because those negative feelings often bring along dysfunctional black-and-white thinking or name-calling that produce such unwanted, unpleasant feelings.

Failure and less-satisfying interactions that push us to our limits and reveal our denials offer valuable information that can help us transform our lives in a positive way. I have long felt that when I get upset with people, these very individuals can be the guides I need. If I can see what they are teaching me instead of simply condemning them or myself, they can call me to shape my life in a new way—both facing my darkness and embracing my talents with a more complete, and thus healthier, sense of self. This can lead to a more responsible, honest style of relating. Once again, the lesson is: any negative comment about or to us, no matter how poor the motivation of the person saying it, is true to some extent. If we are able to mine these truths, we can become freer. Moreover, this is a gift that success rarely offers us in quite the same way.

However, at some level, this requires a willingness to risk seeing things differently and having the courage to take steps we might not normally take. Yet, one of the greatest human paradoxes is that we seem to complain the most about a lack of passion in life and compassion for others—at the very time when we are willing to risk the least. We are challenged, for example, in times of failure, crisis, and loss, to be open to seeing and acting on life differently and to receiving support from possibly different sources at different times.

Given this, the overall goal of resiliency awareness is not merely to bounce back but, in the process, also to go deeper. Yet, to do this, we need to truly embrace the risks that come with involvement. Paula McClain seems to reflect this in her novel *Circling the Sun*, when the adventurer and pilot Beryl Markham, the central character, says:

I have a chart that traces my route across the Atlantic, Abingdon to New York, every inch of icy water I'll pass over, but not the emptiness involved or the loneliness, or the fear. Those things are as real as anything else, though, and I'll have to fly through them. Straight through the sickening dips and air pockets, because you can't chart a course around anything you're afraid of. You can't run from any part of yourself, and it's better that you can't. Sometimes I've thought it's only our challenges that sharpen us, and change us, too—a mile-long runway and nineteen hundred pounds of fuel. Black squadrons of clouds muscling in from every corner of the sky and the light fading, minute by minute. There is no way I could do any of this and remain the same.

During the height of the sexual abuse crisis, I was asked by the Roman Catholic Archdiocese of Boston to speak to the priests about navigating psychological and spiritual darkness. The final group I was asked to address was a group of retired clergy. They were in an especially tough spot because, just prior to my arrival, someone they respected and trusted had also been accused of being an abuser. Knowing this, I aimed to be both informative and gentle. As with all the persons I treat or mentor, I wanted to balance kindness with clarity. Just as I was concluding the question-and-answer period and preparing to leave the stage, a kindly elderly priest whom I had a chance to chat with during one of the breaks raised his hand. Recognizing him, I asked, "Father, did you have a question or comment you wished to make??"

In response, he said, "I would like to divinize you for the moment." I replied, "That sounds dangerous," and there was a ripple of laughter in the room. However, he went on in a very serious vein. "Given all we have been through these past few years, can you predict when this will all end?" The room was suddenly very silent, and I, myself, paused at the poignancy and import of this question. Finally, after some time, I replied, "Father, even if I knew the answer to this question, I wouldn't answer it." "Why?" he asked in a puzzled voice. "Because it is the wrong question." Then, after waiting a few heartbeats, I added, "The question is not, 'When will it all end?' The question is, 'What can I learn from all of this?'"

With the proper awareness, like failure, distress, loss, and trauma can also lead us to even more generative actions for others rather than being only involved in ourselves to the point where we lose a healthy perspective. Examples are present in everyday people who are not psychotherapists or clinicians of some type.

In Ishinomaki, Japan, after the tsunami, a person who was relocated into a shelter shortly after his own house became uninhabitable almost immediately started sweeping out the shelter where he was crammed with others. When asked why he did this, he replied, "No one should live like this. I just do better when I am helping other people." The point? Compassion has a place in being resilient—not simply after the fact but during it.

In the Waldo Canyon disaster in Colorado, a resident first exclaimed upon looking at the rubble that stood in place of his house, "I have lost everything!" And then, after some time, he added, "No, I have lost my home of 30 years and all my physical possessions, and this makes me sad, but I have not lost my life." The point? Developing a healthy perspective is part of resilience.

In another case, a priest who was called to a hospital to meet with parents of twins—one of whom was born dead—said, "When we first went to the morgue to pray over the shrouded child who had died, we cried and prayed. Then we went up to the neonatal intensive care unit and prayed beside the twin that had survived. We cried and prayed again, but this time they were prayers of joy, which I don't think I could have done had I not first cried those tears of sadness." The point? We don't gain a new perspective or deeper sense of gratitude for what is truly important in life by avoiding sadness, trauma, or loss but by facing it directly with a sense of openness and possibility.

Examples like this then require that we simultaneously appreciate the dangers of involvement with others while recognizing the personal meaning and rewards of doing so. A key problem is that because we are naturally drawn to care for others—whether in a professional or personal capacity—we set ourselves up. The seeds of personal burnout and the seeds of compassion are, in reality, the same seeds. While we don't wish to be callous—and I am not recommending that (we have enough callous people in the world already!)—over-involvement with the emotions or expectations of others can prevent us from doing the very tasks we want to do for friends, family, or, in the case of professionals, clients or patients. The opposite of having some emotional distance from others is not compassion but seduction. We are pulled in by the tension or upset of the moment and then become of limited use to the person we are trying to help.

There is a Russian proverb that captures the situation being described here: "When you sleep next to the cemetery, you can't cry for everyone who dies." Leaning back from the emotions experienced by others under stress, after loss, or following trauma is part of a triad: we lean back, reappraise, and then renew ourselves so we can re-enter the fray with new energy and understanding.

In Jeffrey Kottler's classic work *On Being a Therapist*, he rightly recognizes that "The destructive energy dissipating from a patient or client pollutes the spirit of the healer. Most therapists understand they jeopardize their own emotional well-being when they intimately encounter the pain of another." He cautions those who care to appreciate that part of being compassionate includes being desensitized by human emotion, and that trying to insulate ourselves from the pain of others, our own desire to perform well, or the belief that we are "special" and able to effect change where others have not—or have not been able to over a long period of time—are all difficult yet essential aspects of helping. I would add that these dangers apply to everyone who cares—not simply professionals.

They also imbalance our own sense of what is right and what we should be doing. I am sure I am not the only helper whose attention wanders, who can't determine whether I am being too active or allowing things to take their course for too long in reaching out. Additionally, there are negative responses and efforts to destabilize our desire to reach out and help that can be painful. Two illustrations involving two persons in the healing and helping professions quickly come to mind: one with a Catholic nun and the other with a psychotherapist.

The nun was sent to me by her religious congregation for a psychotherapeutic evaluation. It seems there was great anger toward her from other members of her community. The cause was her own negative style of interacting, according to her local religious superior. When I went out into the waiting room to meet her for a first visit and to introduce myself, she saw me, looked up, and frowned. I smiled and said, "Sister, we haven't even begun the treatment, and you're giving me dirty looks." To which she responded, "That is why they sent me here." I smiled again and said, "Well, let's go into my office and chat because I can't charge you for what we are doing out here," finally eliciting laughter and a smile from her.

Once she was able to share her story, describe her angry interactions, and we explored what she had experienced over the past several years—dramatic, unwanted, and frightening changes that had never been understood by her or others—I could see what was really going on. She was not suffering from an angry heart; she was suffering from a broken heart. How often this occurs without a person understanding it or having someone make room for it to be explored, without reacting in kind to it.

A similar case occurred with a psychotherapist who was poorly treated by the organization she was in. I was asked to mentor her through what she was experiencing, and I must admit that, because of her anger and sarcasm, it wasn't easy. The emotional scene with her could change so quickly. On one occasion, she even came into the room and said to me that she had read my book *Riding the Dragon* and really loved it. I was surprised by this positive comment and thanked her. To which she quickly added, "Too bad you're not like what you've written." Within me two reactions quickly followed one another. The first was a natural negative reaction to hearing something like that. The second was to see how such responses in the past pushed people away or had them respond in kind. Knowing that in therapy and mentoring, the goal is not to react but to reflect within and then between the two of you, I said, "From your words and the tone in your voice it sounds like you feel I've let you down in some way. Maybe we can speak about that."

Anyone who reaches out to others—whether they are professionals or someone simply trying to be a good parent, caregiver for a spouse, sibling, or their own parent, or someone acting on the desire to help coworkers or those in need—must recognize that having a caring attitude can be dangerous to one's own sense of commitment to what we know is good. For instance, a number of years ago, a large search was undertaken for a chancellor of a major university system. After a long and arduous process, he was chosen, only to resign after less than a year in office. When asked about this, he said it wasn't anything major that overwhelmed him; it was the "gnats" that got to him. The constant bickering, complaints, obstructions, minor hostilities, hypersensitivity, and other stresses drained his energy and made him feel overwhelmed, under-appreciated, and creatively drained.

One of my own senior colleagues seemed to understand this, even though the patients he saw in his clinical practice were some of the most psychologically difficult you could treat. I once asked him what his secret was to not just surviving but actually thriving as a psychologist. He looked at me, smiled, and said, "Bob, there are really only five annoying, extremely needy patients in the whole country." When I gave him a quizzical look, he then laughingly added, "They just travel from practice to practice, and they're coming to yours next!"

His humor was one of the saving graces that helped him keep a healthy perspective. However, it was more than that, and I could sense it from what he quickly added—this time with a serious expression on his face: "Bob, when we see patients or clients who are very demanding, who quickly turn on us even when we have gone the extra mile and then some to help them, we must always remember that this is the best they can do, and not take it personally." He then added, "You are a very talented person, therapist, and mentor, but all of us fail at times, no matter how talented we may be."

I still remember what President Jimmy Carter's mother, who volunteered in India, once said when she was discouraged about the way one of her adult children was behaving: "There are times when I look around at my children and think, 'I should have remained a virgin!'"

My colleague's humor was precious and filled with enough insight for me to see that he wasn't just making fun of things or me, but helping me realize how tough it is to care for others and how important it is to do what we can— including using humor—to maintain a healthy perspective. But even more than that, he was reminding me not to personalize the negative responses from persons who were going through so much. With what they were experiencing, they were doing the best they could. The goal in being compassionate to others is: low expectations and high hopes.

People who are born helpers need to realize that they will never truly get used to failure, not simply because they wish to be successful— as enjoyable as that is— but because they hate to see people suffer, especially when it is unnecessary. The most they can be expected to do is develop the "psychological scar tissue" that comes from being in tough situations—sitting alongside those who are crying, angry, depressed, under great stress, or grieving over a profound loss. Yet, even then, the occupational hazard of being compassionate will sometimes catch up with us. When we care for others—whether as professionals or in our daily lives—we must recognize that "secondary stress" (the pressures we experience in reaching out to others) is a quiet, slow process rather than a cataclysmic event.

I remember coming home one day after a full day of clinical practice. When I walked in the door, my wife asked me, "How was your day?" In response, I said, "Terrible." She was surprised and asked, "Well, what happened today?" After sitting down and thinking about it, I replied, "Nothing awful." And when she asked, "Well, why did you respond that way?" I said, "Because when you asked that question, my response was that I wanted to cry." After reflecting on it for a while, I realized what was going on. It was nothing dramatic in the moment. Instead, over the day, week, month, and maybe the year, I had absorbed people's sadness, feelings of futility, sense of not being understood, depression, stress, and anxiety. What I needed at that moment was contemplative Thomas Merton's recommendation: "Courage comes and goes. Hold on for the next supply."

If we are willing to ride the waves of compassion, then we will be thrown off our normal game at times. This is to be expected—even if we are careful, alert, and seek to maintain the right balance in our lives. It is how we bounce back at these crucial points that makes the difference.

The following words of Reinhold Niebuhr I think help us put our efforts in perspective when we face failure, take risks, and address trauma experienced by others. He said, "Nothing we do, however virtuous, can be accomplished alone..." Knowing this will come about when we take the time to realize that faithfulness doesn't necessarily bring success—and that failure, when faced in the correct manner, teaches us so much. Yet, facing it is not a one-time action. It is also not something that will be possible without leaning back psychologically, creating refreshing emotional space within so we can gain a sense of a world that is freer and more spacious—no matter what is going on around us.

In an article titled "Learning to Fail," Jessica Bennett reported on programs being initiated at Smith College to help students—who were high achievers in high school—cope with the setbacks that come with now being part of a group of other outstanding minds. One of the creative approaches was projecting onto a large screen on campus during finals week the following admissions by peers and instructors about their own failures:

"I failed my first college writing exam," one student revealed.

"I failed out of college," a popular English professor wrote. "Sophomore year. "Flat-out, whole semester of F's on the transcript, bombed out, washed out, flunked out."

One of the goals in doing this was to teach those who are referred to at Harvard as "failure-deprived" individuals an appreciation of the reality that failure is part of learning. It is part of reaching for the highest levels. Such awareness helps destigmatize failure and thus enhances resiliency. The reality is that, statistically, the more you are involved, the higher the chance for failure. Therefore, we need to know how to deal with and benefit from it.

Once, when I presented a lecture on involvement, spontaneity, and being a gentle, ordinary presence in the world, during the question-and-answer period, one person ventured to say, "You make being a sensitive, ordinary person sound so positive. But I have this fearful question nagging me. What if I fail?" To which I responded, "Oh, don't worry about that. Let me assure you: you will fail!"

At this, her eyes widened, she made a face, and said, "Oh, great! Thanks!"—which brought laughter to all present, including the two of us. Yet, as Albert Einstein is once reported to have quipped, "Anyone who has never made a mistake has never tried anything new." This includes the way we view ourselves.

The reality is that simply attempting to be ourselves and to be more fully open to who we are at each stage of life brings with it a certain amount of failure. Part of this failure—which often hurts us the most—is the recognition (or resistance to such awareness) of personal limits, poor motivations, and personal inadequacies that we may have partially hidden from ourselves or feared confronting until now.

In my case, for example, I've always thought of myself as a generous person who has a hard time setting limits for others. But over the years, I have come increasingly to see that, instead of being true to myself and others, the reality is that at times I am a fake. One reason for this is that I like to look good, and because of this, I often promise more than I can realistically deliver. Then, when people call on me to follow through, I pull back and think to myself that they are asking too much.

However, if I were willing to know and embrace myself better, I could offer a more realistic welcome to others, prevent hurt on their part, and also head off the sadness I feel when people are angry or upset with me because I have let them down. And so, the questions I must continually face are: Am I willing to give up being a showman in the friendship I offer people but sometimes don't really mean? Am I also willing to recognize the hurt that bravado and false generosity (sometimes alcohol-induced) can produce?

As you can imagine, it's not so easy for me to have such truthful eyes. I guess it isn't for anyone who wants to be an honest person without guile, capable of loving in a concrete and real way. Abstract love never involves risk or failure—just good wishes and a rich imagination. Still, love in the concrete often isn't pretty, but its results are wonderful if we are willing to take the chance to confront ourselves honestly as we open ourselves to others in ways that reflect our ordinary selves.

Failure provides helpful information regarding uncovering egoism, the need for new approaches to ourselves and life, the importance of further mentoring in certain areas, and deepening our understanding of our expectations and sensitivities—especially regarding why certain things affect us so strongly. However, carefully mining our failures is often difficult because many of us tend toward self-condemnation or projecting blame outward as a way to avoid being pulled down by self-awareness of our mistakes or shortcomings.

One way we can face this—and strengthen our ability to readily appreciate our gifts and recognize our foibles—is when we can gently laugh at ourselves. When people enjoy themselves and can get in touch with their own natural inner beauty, they are in the strongest position to tease themselves in good ways. Humor frees us to be more open to others instead of being overly protective due to unnecessary concerns about our public image. As a result, when we are comfortable with—and knowledgeable about—both our gifts and our growth edges, we can relax with ourselves. When we feel this way, as has been previously emphasized, it's not just about us; we can even help those around us relax with themselves as well.

Honoring our ordinariness and having a sense of humor go well together. They set the stage for us to relax enough to see ourselves honestly, not to take ourselves too seriously, and to learn how we can best be a welcoming presence to others—without unduly carrying the burden of our pride. The joy of being at ease with oneself is a great and gentle gift. Without it, our presence to others becomes just another chore rather than a wonder to experience—even in the darkest of times.

Encountering Fear

Fear of what might happen if we let go and simply be ourselves is another reason why we may avoid exploring and experimenting in the search for the ordinary self. Pema Chödrön expresses this well in what has become a contemporary classic for many in the Buddhist tradition, *When Things Fall Apart,* when she addresses both the desire and fear one encounters in moving closer to the truth about aspects of oneself:

> Embarking on the spiritual journey is like getting into a very small boat and setting out on the ocean in search for unknown lands. With wholehearted practice comes inspiration, but sooner or later we will also encounter fear. For all we know, when we get to the horizon, we are going to drop off the edge of the world. Like all explorers, we are drawn to discover what's waiting out there without knowing yet if we have the courage to face it.

She goes on in this work to encourage us to "stay with the shakiness" that certain encounters leave us with. She aptly notes, "Curiously enough, if we primarily try to shield ourselves from discomfort, we suffer. Yet when we don't close off and we let our hearts break, we discover our kinship with all beings." The "advantages" of not being self-aware and viewing the process of fuller self-discovery as an ongoing, never-ending journey can be very costly to us. And so, in lieu of whatever remaining comfort we find in remaining oblivious to how we have given up our own selves and traded habit for personal dynamism out of fear, that must be confronted. As a matter of fact, staring our fears in the face may shock us with how easily they melt, and a new willingness to be grateful for the opportunity to change can arise. The interpersonal environment we experienced early in life—and are in now—often operates on fear. As highlighted earlier in this book, fear is frequently marketed to us when the actual danger is absent, being exported to us for other reasons.

Fear is often misplaced, even on a larger scale. We worry about things we needn't. In a chapter aptly titled "There's Never Been a Better Time to Be Alive," in his book *The Science of Fear,* Daniel Gardner writes:

> There are clouds on humanity's horizons, of course. If, for example, obesity turns out to be as damaging as many researchers believe it to be, and if obesity rates keep rising in rich countries, it could undermine a great

deal of progress. But potential problems like this have to be kept in perspective. "You can only start worrying about overeating when you stop worrying about undereating, and for most of our history we worried about undereating," [Economic Historian Robert] Fogel wryly observes. Whatever challenges we face, it remains indisputably true that those living in the developed world are the safest, healthiest, and richest humans who ever lived. We are still mortal and there are many things that can kill us. Sometimes we should worry. Sometimes we should even be afraid. But we should always remember how very lucky we are to be alive *now.*

Gardner then goes on to note that fear is a marketing tactic. People make money from enhancing our sense of insecurity and needs, even though we are living in a first-world nation where starvation is less of an issue than obesity is. The same can be said of the goals of advertising with respect to "ordinariness." We are lured to be more concerned with the niceties of life, as if they were true needs, than the true essentials—not only in the case of things, but in the case of our identity.

Knowing this, Thomas Merton wrote in the following passage from his novel *Argument with the Gestapo*: "If you want to identify me, ask me not where I live, or what I like to eat, or how I comb my hair, but ask me what I am living for, in detail, and ask me what is preventing me from living fully for the thing I want to live for." I think this is a question we need to be mindful of ourselves, especially when we can sense we are taking ourselves too seriously or becoming upset that others aren't honoring us as we feel they should. It is also a question worth exploring with mentors who model ordinariness for us in its fullest form. When we do this, we will be in a better position to receive good feedback and support. In addition, the learning and example provided will help us, in turn, to model it for others in our actions as well as in the feedback we give them when they request it.

Other Perspectives on Failure

Adam Grant, Wharton professor at the University of Pennsylvania, organizational psychologist, and author of *Hidden Potential: The Science of Achieving Great Things*, emphasizes the importance of taking even the smallest steps in seeking to grasp the true possibilities of life. Discomfort, for him, is a signal that rather than retreating, much can be gained by stepping out of our comfort zone. He notes:

> Becoming a creature of discomfort can unlock hidden potential in many different types of learning. Summoning the nerve to face discomfort is a character skill—an especially important form of determination. It takes three kinds of courage: to abandon your tried-and-true methods, to put yourself in the ring before you feel ready, and to make more mistakes than others make attempts. The best way to accelerate growth is to embrace, seek, and amplify discomfort.

In reflecting on his own life, he is candid about how personal limits, failures, and modest beginnings actually set the stage for further accomplishments. He shared that: "I care about unlocking hidden potential because I've lived it. My most meaningful accomplishments have come in areas where I started with serious shortages of talent. Thanks to stellar coaches, I went from being the worst diver in my school to ranking among the best in the country. . . . If I had judged my potential by my early failures, I would have given up. What I learned along the way helped me create my own scaffolding for future leaps. It left me determined to demystify how we surpass our supposed limits."

Worse than failures, according to Grant, is when, in an effort to be totally secure, you "bore out" due to chronic under-stimulation. In line with this, he feels that taking creative breaks as well as seeking helpful feedback from others allows us to hear out loud what works . . . and what doesn't. He also points out that courage, rather than constantly seeking security and comfort, can lead to greater skill development.

Another scholar who writes on dealing with failure and a lack of progress is Adam Alter, a professor of marketing at New York University's Stern School of Business. In his work *Anatomy of a Breakthrough*, he offers practical advice on how to get "unstuck" when it matters. Among the points I found especially helpful are:

- Be aware of a "lull in motivation" that comes in the middle of a long protracted project and deal with it by breaking down tasks into smaller segments so the goal doesn't seem so far away.
- When challenges become difficult, this is the very point where creativity can and should kick in. It is also a time when seeking mentoring

from people unlike you can prevent you from becoming entrenched in the same unhelpful approach.

- Know that a sense of isolation and loneliness experienced when you are stuck or failing is universal and inevitable for those who seek excellence.
- Be like inquisitive children who are always asking why something is the way it is. Common wisdom may be common . . . but not wise to follow at different turns in life. Be experimental to unlock *possibility*.
- Reframe threats as challenges so your emotions move you toward rather than away from seeking solutions.
- Seek to be outstanding, rather than "perfect," so you continue to be inspired to reach higher goals, rather than experience shame because you didn't achieve them.
- Ease up at periods of feeling stuck so you can relax with your thoughts in ways that creative ideas can be given the mental space to arise—an imaginative pause can provide more results than simply plodding on in the same way unproductively because you feel stopping is simply a waste of time.
- Tolerate error and setbacks—they are part of the process as long as they are not constantly occurring which indicates a radically new approach would be better.
- Honor the positive results that brought you to the point where success is elusive as a way of minimizing discouragement.
- Don't simply think yourself into taking good actions, but also take small actions/steps to help you discern what works . . . and what doesn't.
- Uncertainty is often a nudge to act at least to some degree in order not to get stuck in the first place but instead receive the next bit of information on how to perform better.

In reviewing Alter's work, I was reminded about a line in Rachel Corbett's book about the poet Rilke: "[He] felt like he was failing a test he shouldn't have been taking in the first place." Alter's insights are the very ones which can save energy that is often wasted on unhelpful attitudes which lead down psychological cul-de-sacs, rather than being made available to meet external change, necessary inner transitions, and seeking new possibilities personally, professionally, and in leading a more meaningful, energizing, and satisfying life.

To become more aware of these limiting factors, questioning ourselves with an attitude of both clarity and kindness can lead to the information we need to meet changing situations. Simple exploration of events, feelings, and cognitions (ways of thinking, perceiving, and understanding) can provide a wonderful resource of material for reflection, adjusting dysfunctional thinking, changing our perspective to a healthier one, and ultimately produce important changes in both our attitude and behavior. Asking ourselves questions that are driven by principles from critical thinking, cognitive-behavioral and schema therapy, as well as the classic spiritual discernment literature can be helpful in this regard.

This will assist in not simply telling ourselves we didn't try hard enough or are not smart enough or our luck is bad. Without the instructive information that arises when we question ourselves in the right way, we will remain at a dead end rather than arrive at a new beginning. In a similar way, when uncertainty about ourselves or the situation arises because of limited awareness of the situation or a lack of knowledge, this too is a time when creativity, rather than remaining stuck, can be the result.

Uncertainty

Rebecca Solnit writes in *Hope in the Dark*, "Leave the door open to the unknown, the door into the dark. That's where the most important things come from, where you yourself came from and where you will go." When we cross new personal, societal, family, and professional boundaries—when we seek possibility—we shall certainly meet the darkness of uncertainty. Many pull back at such points, but there are others who see such a psychological encounter as the doorway to creativity and the chance to see life anew.

Maggie Jackson, the author of *Uncertain*, fathoms the wisdom and wonder of being unsure at times. In her work, she encourages us to do something truly necessary if we are to uncover new possibilities during times of change in an unpredictable world. She encourages a re-evaluation of the concepts of uncertainty and a lack of familiarity with what we face. By not rejecting or avoiding unpredictability but reframing it as a stimulus to see life in broader, deeper ways, we can become more likely to accept and benefit from uncertainty in ways that point more readily to new directions. Moreover, flexibility in thinking and perceiving the unfamiliar, in a positive way, is a sign of greater psychological health and maturity. After all, once again, change is the one constant.

Uncertainty can open us up to seek many possibilities rather than one solution. Those who can't tolerate uncertainty, however, may feel relieved when they believe they have actually found "an answer" to their questions—but it might not be the best one. In the words again of Jackson: "The best thinking begins and ends with the wisdom of being unsure."

Uncertainty points to the incompleteness of our knowledge—which is always the case. However, it can do so in a way that helps us gain greater clarity on the limits of our present knowledge, in a way that encourages further search with humility that can lead to wisdom. We are called to pause, reflect, and slow the process down when necessary. When we only see uncertainty as solely a lack of confidence or information we should have, such positive outcomes are not possible.

Once more, the words of Jackson: "Most of thought and life itself is the pursuit of resolution. Yet along the way, it is uncertainty that equips us to envision the unimaginable, adjust to the unexpected, value a question as deeply as an answer, and find strength in difference and in difficulty. We need not fear the indefinite. For that is where we find the better solution and the path of hope. This is uncertainty's edge." She recognizes when "understanding is held lightly," and uncertainty is "wisdom in motion."

Final Comments About Failure, Uncertainty, and Creativity

People who fail don't necessarily learn from their setbacks. Also, many of us assume that attempting again will lead to success. However, reevaluating what happened and looking for additional support systems/resources that lead to uncovering and attempting new strategies are crucial. This is so we can determine what contributed to the failure or uncertainty in the first place and sets the stage for brainstorming and new approaches. It also will equip us to aid others who are struggling. As Shiv Sudhakar notes in *Health News*, though, research indicates that some often overestimate the possibilities of success after failure without taking into consideration the steps needed to benefit from a setback. This is magical thinking—and a mistake—when amazing progress can be achieved with the right effort.

One of the truly wondrous results of effectively dealing with failure is creativity. Novel solutions can be the product of efforts by persons who embrace both individual freedom and responsibility for their mistakes. Critical thinking and creativity go hand in hand when those who have failed honor complexity, conflict, and the need to be tolerant of ambiguity and flexibility of thought.

Creativity requires a longer attention span and alertness to different factors as they arise. Also, a sense of intrigue, sensitivity, and love of formulating questions broadens problem-solving skills and tolerance of mystery and abstract thinking.

Both failure and uncertainty can either discourage us or open us up so we can view situations, people, and ourselves in new, creative ways. Creativity encourages us to recognize the unexpected in life to be . . . well, expected! And so, we need to be prepared for it by mentally seeing surprise when it occurs as simply an impetus for our creativity. To accomplish this, it is important to appreciate that time and space for reflection and consultation with an array of "voices" different from ours are essential steps to maximizing the variety and usefulness of our responses.

To respond to the unexpected, it is also essential to expect the hidden inner voices of worry, hesitation, and criticism to announce their presence. They can hold back the production of original ideas if not spotted and "welcomed" with a teasing comment to yourself: "Are you back again? Why don't you go visit someone else for a while, because I plan on reflecting and seeking and acting with different responses that will lead to more information."

Imagining models of independent thinkers will also provide encouragement to seek new ways of approaching the unexpected and challenging ways of acting in the past. In addition, reframing surprises so they are seen as part of the mystery of life also casts new questions that catch us off guard in a favorable light. This is especially the case when we need to employ critical thinking, applications of cognitive psychotherapy for daily life, and the psychological literature on post-traumatic growth when facing severe stress, dramatic challenges, personal darkness, trauma, and loss.

For Review and Reflection . . .

Careful Self-Questioning with Respect to Failure

When I fail, do I:

- Ask myself what I feel most badly about for not succeeding?
- Catch myself when I am tempted to see everything as a failure instead of this one event?
- Give myself the alone-time necessary to be upset, understand, and move on?
- See how my own ego is preventing me from being open to all the agendas and learning possible?
- Appreciate what I can learn about myself that would not have been possible had I succeeded?
- Learn what contributed to this failure both in myself and in the situation surrounding it?
- Appreciate how to avoid or minimize failures like this in the future without feeling I must totally withdraw from the scene as a way of dealing with this lack of success in this instance?
- See the role of unrealistic expectations and how my own thinking may have contributed to my having them?
- See how failure and the pacing of efforts in my life are possibly related because I was moving too fast, slow, or precipitously?
- Acknowledge personal and professional limitations in my life that can be improved?
- Miss early warning signs that if addressed could have averted this result?
- See this as an impetus to initiate new interpersonal approaches to the challenge in question?
- Truly recognize that failure is part and parcel of involvement and that the more I am involved, statistically, the more I will fail?

Do I emulate cognitive behavioral and schema therapists, as well as critical thinkers and spiritual discerners, by seeking the wisdom, intellectual power, and healthier perspective that can result from more carefully:

- Examining comfortable, but unsatisfying patterns with an eye to practicing a step-by-step approach to undo and replace them?

- Recognizing my own gifts, growing edges, agendas, negative emotions, attitudes, motivations, beliefs, and ways of thinking, perceiving, and understanding when a feeling or reaction arises?
- Seeing "the grays" of life rather than simply shunning ambiguities and seeking only so-called right or wrong answers to the questions of life?
- Entertaining both the possible and probable as I reflect on a challenge, problem, or question?
- Appreciating (and then enjoying more fully) the positive elements already present in my interpersonal circle?
- Uncovering when I over-predict worrisome events and challenge them so even little potentially beautiful encounters in life aren't missed?
- Appreciating those times when I tend to exaggerate, catastrophize, minimize, "awfulize," or can't see the humor or nuance in events or interpersonal encounters?
- Dealing with disagreement, rejection, or change?
- Searching for what I can understand and let go of when I encounter personal emotional hot-button issues?
- Picking up "self-talk" that is defeating in nature such as: minimizing or disqualifying the positive, if I feel it, it must be true, if I don't succeed at something then I am a total failure, etc.?
- Balancing the way I am looking at an event by exploring alternative possibilities/interpretations?
- Recognizing an inclination to see negative and self-defeating behaviors as being a "natural" part of one's life rather than a schema/belief to be uncovered, challenged, and replaced with a healthier perspective/life pattern?

Do I seek further clarity in examining something during my daily debriefing by discovering:

- What emotions are elicited by this particular topic, event, or area and what is the thinking behind them?
- What mature and immature agendas do/did I have in this interaction?
- On what am I basing my conclusions/interpretations regarding this and what might be some other possible ones that I might see now that I have stepped back a bit from the interaction/event?
- What makes this challenge possibly a more difficult or emotional one for me?

- What might be some other ways to look at this that I haven't yet considered?
- Are there additional details or input I could obtain which might help me broaden or deepen my understanding?
- Why might I resist changing my opinion on this? (i.e., What consequences or vulnerabilities are in play here?)
- What was unexpected and surprising in what I am now examining?
- What is the first thing that comes to mind when I think of this topic/event/person and what can this reaction teach me about *myself*?
- Am I giving enough time for reflection and consideration of the issues at hand?
- Am I picking up the "voices" of self/other blame, discouragement, and unhelpful labeling of people and events and responding to them so they don't prevent critical thinking?
- What factors do parental/family/corporate/religious/other values and notable past events in my life play in preventing me from thinking more openly about this issue?
- What would it take for me to replace hypersensitivity with a sense of intrigue about these events or occurrences?
- How I can use this particular issue as an opportunity for practicing building resilience and strengthening a healthier perspective by (1) leaning back emotionally from the event, (2) reappraising it, and (3) renewing myself by gaining new wisdom through humility and new learning?
- This as an opportunity to increase my sense of intrigue about where I am spending my energy and learning what the emotional centers of gravity are in my life?
- New abilities in: asking myself questions; developing logic and abstract reasoning; clarifying my values and collecting as much information as possible in ways that my self-knowledge and enjoyment of all of life (both what is perceived as bad as well as good) is accomplished?
- Innovative approaches to: track dysfunctional styles; enhance life-giving activities and approaches; and become fascinated with learning more and more ways to loosen the grasp of ongoing unproductive habits?
- Possibly opposing views to mine which may balance or enrich my understanding?

- The unfamiliar as well as the familiar in how I understand my actions?
- Where immediate self-interest blinds me to new information that may lead to a broader, healthier perspective for me in the long run?

Source: This is an adapted, updated version of material from my book *Perspective: The Calm Within the Storm* (New York: Oxford University Press, 2014). Used with permission.

Self-Questioning Regarding Uncertainty

- Do I value uncertainty as a gateway to new knowledge or simply see it as upsetting to my normal sense of assurance?
- Am I able to entertain uncertainty as a preventive process to continuing a distortion of the present or future based on how I have viewed the world in the past?
- Have I the sense that there is a true connection between being intrigued about situations and greater satisfaction with life, *my* life, going forward?
- Do I see surprise as an impetus to learn more deeply and broadly about something I thought I had mastered and not simply as proof that I am "behind the times" or as a prompt to ignore/deny the new evidence before me?
- Are there times when I put what I know about a person/situation aside so I can seek to see them as if for the first time as a way of gaining a knowledge of them from a different perspective?
- Do I set aside time to simply let my mind wander and free associate to enhance my mental flexibility?
- When faced with uncertainty, do I mentally lean back, relax, and see what new knowledge is missing or do I become discouraged and rigid?
- Do I recognize and prize the connection between uncertainty and creativity going forward?

7

Let's Be Clear About This

Basics in Critical Thinking and Developing More Accurate Ways of Perceiving and Understanding

"Unlike the brain, the stomach alerts you when it's empty."

—African proverb

"Being at ease with not knowing is crucial for answers to come to you."

—Eckhart Tolle
Author, *The Power of Now*

In a question-and-answer session on September 4, 1980, Indian philosopher, writer, and spiritual sage Jiddu Krishnamurti said something that seems so countercultural today: "Doubt is very cleansing, it purifies the mind. If you doubt your experiences, your opinions, you are free to observe clearly." He felt that beliefs and conclusions burden us in ways that prevent thinking critically and clearly. This is explained from a psychological vantage point as cognitive dissonance. When this occurs, people reject any evidence that a core belief they are holding may be incorrect because to consider new data as possible makes them uncomfortable.

Whereas when we are open, reflective, and mindful, we can gain, regain, and maintain a healthy perspective because such an outlook encourages us to:

- Be more nonjudgmental and aware, or psychologically "mindful"
- Expand the narrative we have of ourselves or the ones that have been imposed on us
- Understand how to personally debrief ourselves and use structured reflection and journaling to see the heretofore unrecognized schemas

(beliefs) that may be serving as invisible "psychological or cultural puppeteers" in our lives
- Make "friends" with the resistances to openness so that they can atrophy and make room for new possibilities
- Introduce ourselves to the especially helpful aspects of a contemporary psychology and the ancient wisdom of gratefulness and happiness
- See that significant stress that all of us experience at times need not be the end of the story or the final word, but actually may turn into a source of new meaning-making in life

Awareness of All Our Agendas

Thinking that we do things for only one reason is naive. In most cases, there are a number of reasons we do things—some immature, others mature. Since the ones we don't like to acknowledge tend to remain beyond our awareness, clarity calls on us to uncover and make creative efforts to embrace all of them. Through this awareness, chances will increase that the defensive motivations will atrophy while the healthy outlook is given the "psychological space" to grow and deepen. To accomplish this goal, though, we must first accept that we are all defensive in some unique way. Such an admission is an excellent beginning because it doesn't put us in the position of asking, "Are we or aren't we?" Instead, it moves it out of the black-and-white situation and into the gray areas where most of us live psychologically. When we look at all the reasons why we react to situations in the way we do, we can begin to appreciate why people react to us in the way that they do. Otherwise, we will remain puzzled, consider ourselves misunderstood, and project most of the blame outward so as never to learn what the dynamics of our behavior are and how to unravel them in any given situation.

If colleagues don't like to work with us in stressful situations, it would be helpful for us to know our part in the problem so that we can work on decreasing the incidence of it. For instance, once a candidate applying for a position as my assistant when I was chair of a counseling program asked me, "Do you know how the human resources department is billing the main challenge of working with you?" Surprised—after all, how could there be *any* challenge in working with me—I responded, "No, I don't." To which she replied with a shy smile, "They are billing you as a perfectionist who gives vague instructions and gets upset when they are not followed exactly." Imagine!

Impatience, anger, and other negative reactions on our part decrease our effectiveness when we are working with colleagues in a difficult situation or emergency. Blaming our reactions solely on other people's incompetence provides very limited information for improving the situation or changing our own behavior. We contribute to the problem rather than the solution.

Clarity calls on us to recognize our agendas, face our own fears, understand the games we play with others, lessen our defensiveness, develop new coping skills, and create alternative ways to deal with stressful situations. Yet to do this, we have to be honest. We also have to appreciate that this can have a positive domino effect on our life because by moving through the resistances we have, we create more opportunity for growth and change. Moreover, when we start focusing on understanding individual interactions, larger questions open up as to whether we are getting enough rest or leisure, the right balance of time alone and with good friends, and whether we are setting appropriate limits in all aspects of our life. It is important to recognize that *the self is a limited entity* that can be depleted if we don't involve ourselves seriously in a process of self-care that includes self-knowledge.

Through simple, periodic self-questioning (contained in the closing chapter of this book), we can better see our motivations, fears, and interpersonal style. The more this is accomplished, the more we will almost automatically withdraw our projections, take control of our lives, and—in the process—reduce unnecessary chronic and acute stress. The problem is that, as aware adults, we take for granted that we do this as a matter of course. Unfortunately, with busy schedules, such time for structured self-awareness often isn't undertaken as often and regularly as it should be. This can develop into a real problem—especially when we are confronted with failures and uncertainty, as we surely will be.

Critical Thinking

Critical thinking helps us to not only grasp what is going on around us, but also to recognize our own agendas, negative emotions, attitudes, motivations, talents, and growing edges. This greater grasp of reality also stops the drain of psychological energy it takes to be defensive or protect our image.

Since critical thinking is not always natural (although we may think it is), it takes discipline—a willingness to face the unpleasant, and a stamina that sustains us when we don't grow or gain insight as quickly as we'd like.

Essentially, critical thinking is *a life long process*—especially now when we encounter so much online that we may not be consciously aware of its subtle influence on our thinking and positions. Once I saw a cartoon picturing a little girl coming home from her first day at school. Her mother looks at her and asks, "Did you learn a lot in class today?" To which the little girl nods and says, "Yes, but they still want me to come back tomorrow."

The willingness to be a critical thinker (and face questions like the ones above) also takes not only motivation to be a continuous learner but also involves an appreciation of how resistant to change most of us are much of the time without knowing it. To accomplish this, we must be a continuous *un*-learner to make space for what is relevant *now*. As a result, to face the above questions, we must also, de facto, face our natural resistance to "unlearn," be open, and change as well.

In *On Being and Becoming*, Jennifer Anna Gosetti-Ferencei pointed out that Greek philosopher Socrates indicated that "human beings, even in the best of circumstances, often go wrong. [He] found the problem to lie in our tendency to be misled by appearances, mistaking mere opinion for knowledge. We often confuse the object of our strivings—what we take to be the good—for what is good in itself. Socrates thought that our view of the good, influenced by opinion and habit, must be subjected to critical reflection."

In a similar vein, Lewis Vaughn, in his instructive *Concise Guide to Critical Thinking*, recognizes the simple reality for all of us is that "Some of your beliefs truly inform you and some blind you, some are true, some are not. But the question is *which ones are which?*—a question about the quality of your beliefs—the fundamental concern of critical thinking . . . is not about *what* you think, but *how* you think."

Nathan King, in his book *The Excellent Mind*, also points out that there are different types of thinkers. His book is a treasure trove of information that enables us to value such factors as character, open-mindedness, and fair-mindedness, as well as reasonable skepticism of our past beliefs/opinions, the need to make connections between seemingly different findings/conclusions, the value of imagination and humility, and—as in the case of Maggie Jackson in her book on uncertainty—the appreciation of curiosity for knowing the truth.

In one of my classes, I would challenge my students with the following question and statement: "What do you want written on your tombstone about you after you die? . . . Now remember, it's a small stone!" King also shared that he conducts a similar exercise with some of his students and found, "Except jokingly, no one has ever listed wealth, fame, fashion sense, good looks, or good grades. Without fail, the discussion always reaches the same conclusion: in the end, character matters—a lot."

And so, when we speak of possibility, we must also consider meaning-making, joy, peace, and compassion. We need to be aware of the impact of the possibilities we pursue and must understand how these may affect our family, friends, and society. This requires humility, allowing knowledge to evolve into wisdom, with our sagacity, in turn, leading to generative behavior. This is certainly in opposition to the arrogance of those who always assume they are right—even when they know little about the topic (the Dunning–Kruger effect). As Nathan King affirms in his book *The Excellent Mind*, "[O]ur intellectual character expresses a lot about who we are *as persons* . . . whether or not we care about truth and understanding."

Improving Self-Talk and Cognitive Clarity

Just as there is much to learn about improving clarity from the literature on critical thinking, information from the cognitive therapy school of thought can be quite helpful as well. Rarely do we sense that our ways of thinking, perceiving, and understanding are imperfect—or irrational and possibly harmful—but too readily, we think otherwise. In more cases than most of us would recognize, we unknowingly are filled with "oughts" . . . "shoulds" . . . "musts" and labels for people and situations that rarely get examined fully enough to determine whether they are wrong or need to be revised.

One of the main contributions of cognitive behavioral psychological theory is its ability to help us better appreciate how our beliefs (schemata) and cognitions (ways of thinking, perceiving, and understanding) can impact the way we feel and behave. It also guides us to improve our self-talk. To achieve this, we learn that dysfunctional or incorrect ways of perceiving ourselves and the world are common and often left unchallenged. Such inattention is psychologically dangerous—especially if you are involved in stressful situations in your family life or at your workplace.

A number of years ago, in line with the work of seminal thinker Aaron Beck, psychiatrist David Burns, in his popular book *Feeling Good*, illustrated how people fall prey to cognitive errors that may lead to depression or an overall sense of discouragement. Perfectionistic individuals are in particular danger of such irrational thinking if they are not aware of it. Some of the well-known categories of cognitive errors include the following:

- *All or nothing thinking*: You see things in black-and-white categories. If your performance falls short of perfect, you see yourself as a total failure.
- *Overgeneralization*: You see a single negative event as a never-ending pattern of defeat.
- *Mental filter*: You pick out a single negative detail and dwell on it exclusively so that your vision of all reality becomes darkened, like the drop of ink that discolors the entire beaker of water.
- *Disqualify the positive*: You reject positive experiences by insisting that they "don't count" for some reason or other. In this way, you can maintain a negative belief that is contradicted by your everyday experiences.
- *Emotional reasoning*: You assume that your negative emotions necessarily reflect the way things are: "I feel it, therefore it must be true."
- *"Should" statements*: You try to motivate yourself with "should" and "shouldn't." The emotional consequence is guilt. When you direct "should" statements toward others, you feel anger, frustration, and resentment.
- *Personalization*: You see yourself as the cause of some negative external event that, in fact, you were not primarily responsible for.

For me, the core of the issue here is that negative thinking is quite common. For some reason, all of us seem to give more credence to the negative than to the positive. We can hear numerous positive things but still somehow allow a few negative things to discolor and disqualify the previously affirming feedback we received. Therefore, we need to (1) recognize and acknowledge our negative thinking so that we can (2) link the negative thoughts we have to the negative feeling we experience, so that (3) our negative self-talk can be replaced with a more realistic thought or belief. In this way, we can begin to change our negative thinking and thus our negative beliefs can eventually be modified as well.

We can always—and, unfortunately, frequently do—find a negative comparison to make when we are reflecting on our thoughts, actions, and motivations. Making negative comparisons between our situations and those of others is never a problem. Maintaining perspective is the difficulty!

We may say we already know this but just can't seem to put it into practice. When I hear this statement, I think of Mark Twain's comment: "The difference between the right word and the almost right word is the difference between lightning and the lightning bug." We may say we know it, but unless we can truly recognize and short-circuit the negativity that causes insecurity and increases defensiveness, then we really don't know it.

As Rainer Maria Rilke wrote in his classic work *Letters to a Young Poet*:

> Only someone who is ready for everything, who excludes nothing, not even the most enigmatical, will live the relation to another as something alive and will himself draw exhaustively from his own existence. For if we think of this existence of the individual as a larger or smaller room, it appears evident that most people learn to know only one corner of their room, a place by the window, a strip of floor on which they will walk up and down. Thus they have a certain security. And yet that dangerous insecurity is so much more human which drives the prisoner in Poe's stories to feel out the shapes of their horrible dungeons and not be strangers to the unspeakable terror of their abode. We, however, are not prisoners. No traps or snares are set about us, and there is nothing which should intimidate or worry us. . . . We have no reason to mistrust *our* world, for it is not against us. Has it terrors, they are our terrors; has it abysses, those abysses belong to us; are dangers at hand, we must try to love them.

The issue once again is this: The *way* we perceive something is just as relevant as what we perceive. Only when we realize this can we see that both successes and failures can be used to increase self-understanding and self-appreciation. This is so much more life-giving than seeing our successes and failures only as a constant seesaw of ups and downs. When we recognize this, how we look at or question ourselves changes dramatically, as do our overall results. Additionally, cognitive clarity helps us maintain enthusiasm for possibility by preventing us from falling prey to one of the leading wastes of mental energy: *worrying*.

Wasteful Worrying

In greeting possibility, we need to think critically, examine our ways of understanding and perceiving carefully, and not waste the energy needed for openness and reasonable risk. In his book *Why Are You Worrying?*, psychologist and former colleague Joseph Ciarrocchi cautions that overly paying attention to what he refers to as "internal noise" decreases effective performance and can—in the extreme—lead to stress disorders and self-defeating/limiting strategies. This is so because, with worrying, the delicate balance between too much and too little concern is upset. He also notes that it can interfere with relationships because it leads to extreme self-consciousness as to how you are coming across.

And so, it is important to understand the difference between normal concern, which is good, and abnormal worrying. If you have been diagnosed with a physical ailment, concern about how to proceed is natural and necessary. However, when people become anxious about events that have little chance of happening, this is a waste of energy.

Although they appear similar, worry and concern are as different as preoccupation and planning. Concern and planning are realistic and productive, whereas worry and preoccupation are like the proverbial "psychological rocking chairs." They are activities for sure, but they lead nowhere and yet can be even more exhausting than their useful counterparts.

Concern allows our mental apparatus to work toward a healthy response or solution. Worry is fueled by fear, which stymies problem-solving. As Ciarrocchi noted in his book, "When you focus only on the potential threats and dangers, worry spirals out of control . . . catastrophizing [and also] subverts the natural problem-solving component in the worry cycle . . . anxiety fuels up when your brain and body take your negative view of the situation and run with it. . . . Worry and the fear that accompanies it makes you forget for the moment the hundreds of times you managed difficulties, overcame crises, or coped with stressors. This 'selective amnesia' fuels your view that the situation is unmanageable."

Concern, in contrast, seeks to determine what can be changed and plans for it. It also determines what is a negative given (past trauma, illness, and death) and faces it in ways (as discussed in the next chapter) that recognize it is unalterable but that it can still have positive results that heretofore could not have been imagined.

Changing worry to concern begins when we feel the emotion and are able to look at the dysfunctional thinking that gave rise to it so that it can be changed to a helpful outlook given the situation. We see the situation as new and challenging but are motivated to see what can be done and what really can't be done. In the process, we see what can be learned going forward.

Challenging catastrophic thinking is a cornerstone of altering unhelpful assumptions that have negatively blanketed our thought processes. Also, when we do this, we put ourselves in a better position to prompt greater creativity in our approach, to recall past experiences when we successfully faced difficult situations, and to remember the signature strengths we have and the courage we have already demonstrated.

In addition, concern is built on an approach that describes in greater detail what we are facing, which in itself causes worry and danger to lessen. This approach lists the types and extent of potential negative outcomes while highlighting the talents and resources available to deal with them, as well as what additional assistance or actions would be helpful. A process like this needs the time and space to enable it to be productive. Obviously, for instance, the period just before we are trying to fall asleep is not the best time to do this!

After identifying a challenge, recalling how we faced similar situations in the past, and assembling a repertoire of possible responses, we are then ready to evaluate each option, choose the one we believe is best, and both try it and see what information comes from acting on it. This process allows us to deal specifically with what we are facing. As American psychologist, educator, and author Martin Seligman once noted, "Finding temporary and specific causes for misfortune is the art of hope. . . . Finding permanent and universal causes for misfortune is the practice of despair."

Final Comments

Clarity enables us to face the truth and honor impermanence, allowing us to enjoy our brief life more fully. It helps us embrace our gifts, recognize our growing edges, and identify the situations in which we "psychologically trip over" rather than effectively use our talents. This awareness reduces defensiveness and allows us to see the truth more clearly. Clarity also breeds an attitude of well-being and flexibility based on the wisdom that arises from the humility of knowing who we truly are … and who we are not. It enables us to see the disturbing emotions as simply gateways to greater self-knowledge, rather than merely a disruption to our sense of inner peace. Goals of critical thinking and uncovering unhelpful ways of perceiving and understanding include the following:

- Valuing spending time in silence and solitude, with a spirit of intrigue and gratitude, to learn more fully about ourselves and the world around us without being tyrannized by our and society's sometimes negative or misplaced values
- Familiarizing ourselves with our past views and how they are helpful and unhelpful now
- Recognizing negative emotions and understanding what is producing them, with the goal of seeing more clearly so that we can flourish as human beings and help others to do so as well
- Honoring the need for patience with ourselves and the process of unfolding greater clarity in the search for meaning
- Identifying which egotistical desires, "dressed up" as benefits and rights, are actually psychologically seducing us, even though in the long run they are self-defeating and reveal entitlement and competitiveness rather than gratitude for life and a genuine desire to be the best for ourselves and others

As we consider the above points and reflect on what was previously discussed in this chapter, we might feel these are romantic and unrealistic goals in a sometimes dark, competitive, and ugly world. Yet, while the selflessness and compassion contained in them and our desire to live a beautiful, meaningful life might seem elusive, there are role models present that teach us that this is not so. To the contrary, wisdom that arises from combining humility with knowledge can open our eyes to this and transform inordinate fear and self-involvement into a self-interest that motivates us to be all we can be by cultivating a more positive appreciation for ourselves and life, rather than merely focusing on the negatives.

For Review and Reflection . . .

The Types of Questions Asked by Critical Thinkers

As persons with full lives requiring many decisions, we must, as critical thinkers, ask ourselves questions like these:

- Am I willing to avoid seeing things simply in black and white and to entertain ambiguity in life?
- Can I appreciate that the "answer" or "diagnosis" I have now in my life is always tentative?
- Am I able to entertain the possible as well as the probable without undue discomfort?
- Do I need to come to a quick solution or take one side of an issue because I lack the intellectual stamina that encourages an open mind to see both sides?
- Am I so uncomfortable with personal rejection, a tarnished image, or failure that I capitulate when others disagree with me?
- Do I realize the obvious and less noticeable ways that I resist change? Am I open to seeing my emotions and extreme reactions as red flags that can often indicate that I am holding on because of fear, stubbornness, or some other defensive reason?
- How might I confirm the accuracy of my conclusions?
- What are some other perspectives from which I can view what has happened, how I felt, or how I behaved?
- Am I willing to entertain views that differ from mine?
- What is the logic behind my actions, emotions, and thoughts regarding this event?
- What is the most significant "takeaway" from my reflections on this matter?
- How can I develop and pace a process of change that involves entertaining new behavior, preparing for it, acting in new ways, and maintaining healthier behavior based on my findings from critical thinking?
- How can I move from the familiar—what I already know—to doubting it, so as to welcome new perspectives on both specific situations and on my ethical understanding of how life should be and how I should live it?

- How do I distinguish between fine traditions I have followed and being chained to traditionalism?
- Am I willing to "unlearn" what I have learned that is not useful anymore and be open to new techniques and approaches?
- Do I recognize that a lot that psychologically weighs me down is really not mine to carry?
- Do I only respect the views of people with "credentials"?
- What are the signals for me to verify alleged facts?
- What is the ethical aspect of an issue I am examining?
- In what ways do I find myself "getting emotional or personal" about an issue at hand that I am examining?
- Am I reasonably skeptical of all sources—including ones that parallel or support my way of thinking?

Questioning Ourselves to Gain Greater Clarity and a Healthier Perspective

In what ways do I . . .

Examine comfortable but unsatisfying patterns with an eye to practicing a step-by-step approach to undo and replace them?

Recognize my own gifts, growing edges, agendas, negative emotions, attitudes, motivations, beliefs and ways of thinking, perceiving, and understanding when a feeling or reaction arises?

See "the grays" of life rather than simply shunning ambiguities and seeking only so-called right or wrong answers to questions at different turns and phases in life?

Entertain both the possible and probable as I reflect on challenges, questions, uncertainties, or problems?

Appreciate (and then enjoy more fully) the positive elements *already* present in my interpersonal circle?

Uncover when I over-predict worrisome events and challenge them so even little potentially beautiful encounters are not missed?

Acknowledge when I tend to exaggerate, catastrophize, minimize, "awfulize," or can't see the humor or nuance in events or interpersonal encounters?

Deal with disagreement, rejection, change, transition, or uncertainty?

Search for what I can understand and let go of when I encounter personal emotional "hot button" issues?

Pick up "self-talk" that is defeating in nature, such as minimizing or disqualifying the positive or seeing a mistake as a total failure on my part?

Balance the way I am looking at an event by exploring alternative possibilities/resources/alternatives?

Recognize an inclination to see negative and self-defeating behavior as being a "natural" part of my life rather than a style or belief that needs to be challenged and replaced with a healthier perspective or life pattern?

....

During my daily self-debriefings at the end of the day, do I seek further clarity about something significant that recently happened by exploring questions such as ...

What emotions does this particular topic, event, or area elicit, and what is the thinking behind them?

What mature and immature agendas do/did I have in this interaction?

On what am I basing my conclusions/interpretations regarding this, and what might be some other possible ones that I might see now that I have stepped back a bit from the interaction or event?

What makes this challenge potentially more difficult for me?

What might be some other ways to look at this that I haven't considered yet, and should I consult with a friend or colleague to broaden my view of it?

Why might I resist changing my opinion on this? (i.e., What consequences or vulnerabilities are in play here?)

What was unexpected and surprising in what I am examining now?

What is the first thing that comes to mind when I think of this topic/event/person, and what can this reaction teach me *about myself*?

Am I giving enough time for reflection and consideration of the issues at hand?

Am I picking up the "voices" of blame, discouragement, and unhelpful labeling of people and events and responding to them in ways that prevent critical thinking?

What role do parental/family/corporate/religious/political/societal values and notable past events in my life play in preventing me from thinking more openly about this issue?

What would it take for me to replace possible hypersensitivity with a sense of intrigue about these events/occurrences?

How can I use this particular issue as an opportunity to practice building resilience and strengthening a healthier perspective by (1) leaning back emotionally from the event, (2) reappraising it, and (3) renewing myself by gaining new wisdom through humility and new learning?

How might an examination of this interaction help me learn more about the emotional centers of gravity in my life so that I can better understand where and why I spend my energy?

What innovative approaches can I use to track dysfunctional styles, enhance life-giving activities, and become more fascinated with learning more and more about ways to loosen the grasp of ongoing unproductive habits or routines?

How do I welcome more openly opposing or unfamiliar views than mine as a way to balance or enrich my own understanding?

What is it about this situation that is raising fear, anxiety, or fear of loss?

What is the worst thing that could happen if I fail in this situation?

8

Darkness and Gaining Previously Unattainable Wisdom

Applying the Principles of Post-Traumatic *Growth*

"Experience is the hardest kind of teacher. It gives you the test first and the lesson afterwards."

—Oscar Wilde

"In the depths of winter, I finally learned that within me lay an invincible summer."

—Albert Camus

Sometimes lessons learned from extremely dark situations contain information that is extremely helpful to all of us at different turns in life. Mary Beth Werdel, in her book *The Paradox of Trauma and Growth in Pastoral and Spiritual Care*, notes that there are some, who upon having a "night experience," come to find that "a part of themselves starts to bloom. They have come to see themselves, others, or the world in a way that is stronger, wiser, deeper, or more brilliant than they had known before." Their perspective has altered. They don't romanticize, minimize, ignore, or deny the tough or traumatic times. Instead, their aim is not only to bounce back from what they have experienced but also to accept new wisdom, joy, and healthy relationships back into their life in an even deeper way.

Many in society focus only on the sadness and other negative aspects of failure, defeat, trauma, and loss. However, there are those who, while not denying the tragedies of life ("the night"), are also open to the possibilities within the darkness that would normally be missed if we were not alert to their mysterious presence. In the words of martyred Bishop Oscar Romero, "There are many things that can only be seen through eyes that have cried." One such thing for me is the reality of hope and the importance of trust in who and what are good.

Just prior to their 1993 elections, I was invited into Cambodia to do a workshop on resilience for English-speaking nongovernmental officials) from the international community. Professionals constantly working with persons suffering from stress, psychological and physical trauma, anxiety, sexual/physical abuse, and depression are prone to difficulties themselves, and this was a chance to help these healing and helping professionals keep their emotional flame alive while extending their warmth to others.

They were from the United States, Canada, France, Malta, Japan, Thailand, and several other countries, as well as from Cambodia itself. These persons were working closely with the Khmer people to help them rebuild their nation after a long period of terror during the reign of Pol Pot. They included professionals in psychiatry, ministry, education, relief work, psychology, nursing, and general medicine. When I got to know them, I found them to be really amazing people.

In Cambodia, I expected that "vicarious post-traumatic stress," a specific form of secondary stress (the pressures experienced in reaching out to others), would especially be a problem among these professionals because so many people in Cambodia had undergone terror, anxiety, and trauma at the hands of the Khmer Rouge regime. And so, I expected that those who worked with them had to be affected in a similar way as well.

As is my custom when visiting a new setting, I try to experience in some small but symbolic way what the people are going through who help there. In this case, to get a sense of the terror of the recent times and to get a feeling as to what had gone on in Cambodia, I arranged to visit both "the Killing Fields," where many Khmers were buried, and Tuol Sleng (a high school that had been turned into a torture chamber by the Khmer Rouge).

In visiting the Killing Fields, I was stunned by the monument that contained rows and rows of skulls of some of the one and a half million victims who died during the totalitarian rule. I walked on the bits of bones and pieces of shirts and pants that still littered the ground and witnessed the leg and arm bones that protruded from places in the ground. They were left there in gaping holes that marked the exhumation of at least some of the torture victims.

Following the visit in the Killing Fields, I then went to see Tuol Sleng, a large makeshift prison that had its second floor balcony covered with barbed wire mesh so that those held captive there could not jump and commit suicide during their excruciatingly painful interrogations. Tuol Sleng was an especially horrible place, to say the least. (One of the drivers could not even enter the grounds because he once was a student there when it was originally a high school. After it became a prison, both his parents had been tortured and killed there.)

As I walked the cramped dark corridors and visited the torture rooms that were still stained with blood, I could not help but take in the horror of what had happened. I wondered, "How could the people who hadn't died during this period go on? How could those who had to witness all of this terror and torture continue to survive psychologically and spiritually to meet the possibilities of a new day?

After leaving both settings, I knew that there was something in the visit to these two sites that would give special meaning to my trip and that these two "highlights" would mark me for the future. However, as poignant as they were, two other "side trips in wisdom" raised my sensitivity to a lesson that may have been even more important yet possibly missed if I hadn't been open at the time to receiving it.

The first was in my own hotel. During my stay in a little place operated by Khmers (the name of the people of Cambodia) who had returned from France after the downfall of the Khmer Rouge government, I had the pleasure of interacting with the staff each day.

One of them frequently served as receptionist at the desk and also as supervisor for others who were working on the main floor. She was impressive not only because of her mastery of several languages but also because of her outgoing, warm, cheerful attitude.

On one occasion early in my stay, I had wanted to ask her a question about one of the services in the hotel, and so I approached the desk. Since the area surrounding it was carpeted and she was busy working on some administrative task, she didn't hear or see me coming. When she finally looked up, she was startled. The startle reaction was not a normal gasp of surprise but a sharp intake of air and an expression on her face of real fear and horror. It was a typical startle reaction for someone who was suffering from post-traumatic stress disorder. It was not unusual since so many people were threatened, raped, tortured, and terrorized during the Pol Pot regime and she was just old enough to have been a small, impressionable child during that time.

Although I knew this and should have expected the possibility of it, I was taken aback by the look on her face. Even though I am a psychologist, worked in hospitals, had a private clinical practice for a long time with a specialty of working with helpers and healers on their secondary stress, as well as having served as an officer in the U.S. Marine Corps, the pure look of terror on her face had a deep impact on me. It reminded me personally of the look on my mother's face when I told her that my father had just died and she tried to comprehend that she would never see him again.

There was a basic lesson here for me. The pain some people must endure in living their simple lives is beyond belief. Their courage can add meaning not only to their lives but to ours if we have the eyes to see it, the ears to hear it, and the heart to embrace it. However, too often we want to run away from the necessary pain in our own lives and in the lives of others. The results in a life of denial and hidden anxiety. We live in the constant fear of losing comfort, security, one's image in the eyes of others, or the illusory control we believe we have over life. At such times, peace is beyond our reach, and what we may mistake for pure joy is a fleeting sense of happiness that in its absence leaves us lonely, bored, and adrift, waiting for the next "fix" of fun … rather than the dawning of new true possibility and meaning in our lives.

The second encounter was on my first Sunday in Cambodia. On that day, I was invited to drive outside the city of Phnom Penh to visit a village of ethnic Vietnamese who had lived peacefully with the Khmers in Cambodia for generations along the Mekong River. When we arrived, we were given a choice to stay on one side of the river or to take a small boat across to visit a village on the other side, where we could also meet with the people living there. The village recently had a series of mysterious house burnings that were tentatively attributed to the Khmer Rouge, who, although situated now in the north, tended to make incursions throughout the country to disrupt the elections which were scheduled to happen shortly.

I chose to go across the river. Upon my arrival I met a man who had been a victim of the house burnings. He had only the clothes he was wearing. *All else had been lost.*

As he showed us the remnants of his house and the ashes of some of the others that had been burned, I looked around and saw that many of his fellow Vietnamese, because of their fear, had literally picked up their houses, loaded them into boats, piece by piece, and left to return to Vietnam—a "home" some of them had never lived in or even seen before this trip. Of the original 570 homes, only 70 remained. And this man and his family were among them.

In walking through the village, the anguish on his face struck me. Still, as we moved through the village, I noticed someone else as well. As I walked along, a young girl of about eight kept bumping into me. Finally I realized (people like me can be really dense!) that she wanted me to take her hand. I finally did, and we walked together until we reached the center of town.

After a short lunch with the village elders there, we proceeded back to the boat to cross the river again. This time both the man whose house had been burned and the little girl (who turned out to be his daughter) came with us. She sat next to me in the boat, holding onto my hand, and we shared the time in silence with her father and the others while re-crossing the river back to the other side.

I hope I'll never forget the experience of their presence with me in the boat. The man's face showed anguish yet commitment. The young girl's expression showed hope in possibility for the future. Being with the both of them at one time and feeling the emotions of a special day (as well as the emotions engendered by the encounter with the previously traumatized young hotel clerk) broke through the psychological and social crust of my understanding of life in a way that even the Killing Fields and Tuol Sleng— as important and dramatic as these experiences were—could not. Maybe the difference was the personal contact with "living examples of possibility."

They taught me that even in the darkness or when one feels totally lost, one must also remember the important reality of hope. Hope isn't simply believing that things will go well because one is a good person who deserves such rewards. Instead, hope is an attitude of living that makes one seek and find new possibilities because of an attitude of trust. As Vaclav Havel, the once creative leader of the Czech Republic, recognizes: "Hope is an orientation of the spirit, an orientation of the heart. It is not the conviction that something will turn out well, but the certainty that something makes sense, regardless of how it turns out."

I guess a good example of this can be seen in some of the people who are involved in relief work in places like Gaza throughout the world. In an interview on public radio, Dr. Collins, a physician in Somalia during the height of the starvation there, commented on our reaction to seeing and hearing the news about their plight. He said that while people who saw them on television felt despair, those who met them, those who knew them as more than anonymous faces, had a different experience. Like those who saw the horror of starvation on TV, they also felt the pain—maybe they even experienced more pain—but they also felt something else, something very significant. It was reflected in one comment he made during the interview when he said, "You can't lose hope when you are making friends."

At a very basic level, the young girl I traveled with across the Mekong River had a sense of trust. She had inherited the deep inner strength and enduring hope of her family and the community of Vietnamese people who had faced adversity generation after generation. The question for me in my contact with them was: Could I learn from them? Would I have the eyes to see possibility even amid, especially within, dark, uncertain times? When challenged, would I be able to persevere and maintain a healthy perspective in my life as well? Would I see that it is good to be lost once in a while? Knowledge of the concept of post-traumatic growth (PTG) would certainly help in this regard.

Post-Traumatic Growth

Fairly recently, the mental health profession has explored the possibility of what Tedeschi and Calhoun termed post-traumatic growth. With PTG, there is a possibility of changes in perception of self, relating to others, and the philosophical changes in our philosophy, priorities, sense of meaning-making, and appreciation of life. Its tenet is that if we remain honest as to the horror of the trauma or loss, on the one hand, and are open to where it may take us, on the other, something amazing might happen. We may grow and deepen in ways that would not have happened *had the trauma, serious stress, or dramatic loss not happened in the first place.*

The reality remains that most persons would trade any PTG for the event not having happened. Yet, since it did occur, the chance for something good (new personal depth as a person) should be honored. To increase the possibility of this happening, the gift of psychological knowledge about the process of PTG can help us navigate the perils involved.

Initially, an array of negative emotions occur as part of truly acknowledging what has happened. This is also part of the grieving process and includes sadness, loneliness, guilt, shame, regret, anxiety, anger, depression, and even despair. There is a sense of permanency about a change and irrevocable loss that has happened in one's life. What makes the person feel worse is also a sense of helplessness and even panic that may cause regression. In response, there may be a temptation in some to excuse, minimize, deny, or spiritually romanticize what has happened.

The seeds of such grief and negative emotions may also be the seeds of a new life that doesn't deny the loss or trauma but offers portals to new understanding and possibilities that couldn't have arisen before. The shock to one's previous sense of meaning and structure of life and outlook leads to a total re-evaluation of how and why one has lived in a particular way up to this point. The basic assumptions about life are shattered.

From a psychological perspective, the person begins to realize more profoundly what has happened, and in accepting the reality at some point, the person appreciates that while the trauma is real, it doesn't represent their whole past, present, or future life. This acceptance begins to break up what was a complete psychologically dark sky into a series of "emotional clouds" that are real but no longer completely overwhelming.

From a spiritual vantage point, the previous religious sense of a divine power and life is crushed, or at least goes through a significant disassembling that opens up the possibility of an even deeper, more mature, and compassionate sense of faith and the divine. For instance, having a more sensitive awareness of and appreciation of God walking *alongside*, the religious person may report a sense of a divine presence that is different, more powerful, and vivid. Compassion for others' suffering and feeling a greater solidarity with others in ways they couldn't in the past or were more intellectual, rather than heartfelt, may also be reported.

Psychologically, the ability is there to care for oneself and others in new nurturing ways. Simple encounters with music, nature, and comforting events may also evolve and be honored in a vastly vibrant way. In turn, the ability to honor others' rage and depression as well as one's own often increases. A person at this point in the healing process and road to PTG may remark how freeing it is now to express negative emotions they didn't feel comfortable sharing in the past. They also begin to have greater insight into how far they have come in the time since the trauma or significant stressful event.

To enable this, both therapists and spiritual guides alike must be patient and provide an accepting and safe environment so the person coming to them can express any emotion—even if the "religious person" now can express anger at God without fearing they are doing something wrong. With the modeling of acceptance by mentors and counselors, the person can then feel more open with themselves and with what some would refer to as "a greater power."

Also, with the assumptions one may have lived by being shattered, an appreciation for life, others, and the appearance of new coping skills that are more creative than in the past may occur. And so, self-view may change, interpersonal style may alter, and priorities may be shuffled. If this doesn't happen, rumination may occur about why the event happened until they are able to revise their perspective on life. In addition, all of this alters how one meets difficulties in themselves and others in the future.

Those who deal with personal darkness—others as well as their own—recognize what is now termed post-traumatic *growth*. This refers to new psychological depth that would not have been possible had the extreme stress, failure, loss, or trauma not happened in the first place.

Most of us, for a good portion of our lives, are guided by a set of basic assumptions. As Mary Beth Werdel and I pointed out in *A Primer on Post-traumatic Growth*, we walk through our days thinking: "The world is safe; bad things do not happen to good people; young people are not supposed to die. However, extremely stressful and traumatic life events can violate and even shatter these basic assumptions, resulting in experiences of distress as well as a sense of loss of control, meaning, and predictability. . . . Even though trauma and extreme stress are arguably rare, everyone experiences internally framed negative events that have the capacity to challenge basic life assumptions in various forms at different times: rejection, illness, caring for an aging parent, unwanted dramatic change at work, and divorce."

However, with the right attitude, the darkness we experience in life need not be the final word. . . . Instead, it can actually be the first word in living a more centered life with greater meaning. Stress can soften us psychologically. Suffering can enable us to see the true value of love as never before. As we entertain new possibility after a loss, significant change, or trauma, even such actions as the sarcasm and bitterness of others, paradoxically, can instill in us even greater compassion. In the words of Anne Frank, a young holocaust martyr, "You can always give something. Even if it is only kindness."

Yet, as we see in the world, this is not the automatic or easy response when experiencing darkness. Philosopher Frederick Nietzsche recognized this a long time ago and warned, "Whoever fights monsters should see to it he does not become a monster." However, when trouble experienced is met with openness and support from others, the possibility of change for the better increases significantly. Traversing tough times opens up the chance to get more in touch with what is important, builds our sense of confidence and resilience, and enhances our belief that we can meet the difficulties all of us must traverse in the future. We begin to see more clearly how adversity and resilience go hand in hand.

Survival may be all that is possible for some and for all of us at the moment after confronting unexpected challenges. However, if PTG is possible, people can heal and build on it by living in ways that were previously unimaginable. Negative feelings when one is betrayed, abused, belittled or rejected, scapegoated, manipulated, silenced, victimized, oppressed, or experience psychological toxicity in other ways are, unfortunately, more or less part of everyone's life. And, while it isn't easy, processing difficult encounters is definitely worth the work to get to "the other side" of the experience. As we think about situations and begin to see them as not being dangerous, but informative, true learning about handling them and others going forward is the reward.

Patience, Timing, Perseverance

Key elements occurring in PTG are patience, timing, and perseverance. In ourselves and others, we need to be open to the possibilities dark times bring us but not push ourselves or people who turn to us after a trauma. Otherwise, guilt and pressure to "get better," "let go," or "deepen" may inadvertently result. However, not to have an openness to positive change, new possibilities might be missed. As in meditation and contemplation, a sense of intrigue is the middle ground, so if and when something happens that is surprisingly positive amid the sadness, anger, and grief, it is honored. In summary, in the words of French existentialist Albert Camus, "In the depths of winter, I finally learned that within me lay an invincible summer" is the outcome that all must be open to but not forced. The words of Camus also acknowledge that not only do trauma and stress lead to negative results but that they also can produce awe-filled positive change as well. *Suffering and loss need not be the final words both psychologically and in the spiritual life.* Instead, they may be a dramatic beginning for good. In the words of Viktor Frankl once again, "To live is to suffer, to survive is to find meaning in the suffering."

Part of the healing process is to understand what went wrong. But just as important, the culmination of the healing process for many is to ask what am I learning about life that is, paradoxically, life-giving to me and others because of this horrible event? In an interview with Alex Banayan, author

Maya Angelou, who had herself been abused, shared a line that Alex said he would never forget: "Every storm runs out of rain."

Much will be determined by the personality of the person, details of the negative event(s), how and to whom the person is able to self-disclose, religious-cultural-familial influences, and how the distress is handled. All of this will impact the assumptions and beliefs about the world—what they were and what might they develop into now. In essence, meaning-making from both the past and going into the future will grow, be shattered, and leave the person helpless, or at the very least force the person into a state of constant confusion and disillusionment.

Much has now been written on PTG for both psychotherapists and a general audience. In one of these books by Werdel and Wicks, a summative statement made is:

When we fall, do we get up? And if we get up, do we get to an up experience that is cognitively and emotionally different than where we were before we and our physical and assumptive worlds fell down? And within this sense of newness is there anything positive? Or is it merely negative or neutral? These are the fundamental questions of the work of stress and growth.

Post-traumatic growth advocates do not presume in any way that new and different experiences, understandings, or perspectives are always positive, but sometimes pieces of them are. Accordingly, the study of post-traumatic growth is not a comparison of pre- and post-lives in the sense that one is better or worse. Instead, it is the study of coming to terms and accepting what is different and about questioning the piece or pieces that are different and determining if they have intrinsically positive qualities that are worthy of being honored for what they are. When these qualities are honored, amazing results become truly possible.

Welcoming a New Perspective and Growth

The world is a stage . . . how we walk, or even dance, on it is dramatically different for each person. Stories continue to abound with helpers as they seek to keep afloat while they stand with others suffering and dying. Yet, once again, it can't be overemphasized: Darkness need not be the final word—and knowing this is important for *all* of us because no one is exempt from stress, some form of trauma, and the knowledge of everyone's inevitable death. Suffering is a part of human experience and development. The question is: Do such dark experiences hold the possibility of changing us, and if so, then how?

A counseling student who was known for her good spirit and optimism in her graduate program wrote a final paper that included her biography. Knowing her to be a person of great hope and resilience, the professor admitted that he was dumbfounded after reading it. He was astounded so much so that he actually approached her and asked, "Is what you wrote about your life true?" She was caught off-guard by the question, as one might expect, and replied, "Why, *of course!*"

He then said, "I read that your husband died early in the marriage, leaving you with two sons to raise. The older of the two died in a car crash, and the younger committed suicide years later, and yet I don't exaggerate that despite the multiple tragedies you have experienced, you are a beacon of hope for the other students. I also expect you will be that for those you counsel and your colleagues as well going forward. How did this happen given all you have been through?"

She responded, "Well, it was all horrible, tragic, and very hard. *Very* hard. However, I eventually realized that I had a choice. I could let it psychologically bury me or I could let it soften my soul and help me honor the rest of my life and aid others who have been through so much to do the same."

Knowing some additional basics of resilience from a positive psychology perspective and reflecting on some key themes would help position us to be more open to receive new knowledge and make better decisions going forward after having experienced serious stress, life disruption, and even trauma. In a sense, they set out positive horizons for us to follow by seeding our attitude with hope. Techniques are important, but having a wonderfully healthy and optimistic spirit may even be more crucial.

As Antoine de Saint-Exupéry, the world famous French author of such books as *The Little Prince* and *Wind, Sand and Stars* once recommended, "If you want to build a ship, don't drum up the men to gather wood, divide the work, and give orders. Instead, teach them to yearn for the vast and endless sea."

As I also indicated in a previous work (*Perspective: The Calm Within the Storm)* when we are mindful (in the now, aware, and open), the stage is set for increasing the possibility of growth by taking the more beneficial path following trauma and stress. So, when we are in this place, and are wise (and therefore well aware of personal limitations—i.e., have a degree of true humility), we can then appreciate the need to be realistic, honest, and open to set the stage for new meaning-making.

New Meaning-Making

With such fruits of personal maturity as these (and the many others that may come from a sense of mindfulness and personal awareness), we can even more completely take to heart what researchers have uncovered for us with respect to enhancing the process of PTG when its seeds start to blossom and appear in our life. We also can see more clearly, and so we can, in turn, guide others who have experienced trauma and serious stress to appreciate the key aspects of PTG—if and when we and they might be open to these life realities.

Understanding PTG is all about choices and the support we need to make the best ones in—even in, *especially* in—the darkness. Viktor Frankl, an Austrian neurologist, psychiatrist, philosopher, author, and Holocaust survivor, expressed that resilience in the face of tremendous odds and dehumanizing experiences was centered in the acquisition of new meaning. In his classic work *Man's Search for Meaning*, he wrote:

> We who lived in concentration camps can remember the men who walked through the huts comforting others, giving away their last piece of bread. They may have been few in number, but they offer sufficient proof that everything can be taken from a man but one thing: the last of the human freedoms—to choose one's attitude in any given set of circumstances, to choose one's own way.

Given all of these guides, at the heart of an openness to PTG is an understanding of the reality that after the jolt to our psychological system that trauma, serious loss, or significant stress causes, new meaning-making must occur as well. The groundbreaking work of such researchers as Park and Neimeyer has helped us immeasurably in understanding this process.

Psychological research on coping articulates that when a person experiences a trauma, the usual approaches to problem-solving are not sufficient to decrease the person's sense of distress. (You can't "solve" a rape, the death of a child, or a sudden unwanted, unexpected job loss or divorce.) What is needed is assistance in the search for new meaning in life now that a tragedy or great stress has occurred.

Meaning-making is more than putting a positive cast on something. It involves global meaning (the way we view life)—what we consider fair (young people do not die), what we thought we had control over, how we predict things. It also involves situational meaning—the meaning we assign to specific life events.

What often happens is that the two processes collide after a tragic event and then the task is left for the person to deal with the disparity and dissonance between the two. For instance, an innocent child may die in a terrible storm, and our global meaning may tell us that bad things shouldn't happen to little children—whereas, our situational meaning process may tell us that these things happen in nature.

After this happens, some people remain upset because they cannot reconcile the two (global and situational) types of meaning. Others change their situational or global meaning to accommodate the other so that they can reach a new, possibly deeper place in life. When this happens, the person views themselves, events, others, their values, sense of meaning, and relationships differently. They also may develop new ways of living, coping, and relating, as well as a more satisfying attitude toward life that allows them to value the moment, people, and the little things in life as never before.

The way this occurs is that people often tentatively entertain new beliefs as a bridge to a healthier perspective on life. This is especially true if these new assumptions aren't avoiding or denying something unpleasant, or merely providing a positive reframe for the trauma, significant stress, or psychological darkness, but instead serve as a way to be open in new ways that weren't present—or even possible—in the past.

The initial steps in trying to make sense of life in new ways is like being handed life's menu again. The hope is that we won't simply lament that our former favorites are no longer there. Instead, it urges us to try new selections with an openness that doesn't deny the absence/loss of something/one we loved before, but does tentatively explore potentially new joys and a new context for experiencing life's positive aspects.

At times, finding new meaning/assumptions about our life will be difficult or impossible. This isn't terrible. It just is for some of us under certain circumstances. The process of meaning-making, though, as indicated earlier, helps us and others adopt new assumptions about life, which eventually provide enough closure after the trauma or loss so that new ways of seeing and experiencing life, *our* life, become possible.

PTG occurs when a new perspective emerges—one that helps us realize something previously unencountered in the way we view life. This often arises after an experience of trauma, great stress, or personal darkness, when we haven't denied the sadness or personal horror of it, but still—perhaps eventually—become open to seeing something new. The new sense is that "I thought my life was a dark house in which I was locked. Now I see it was only a dark hallway and I have opened the door now to a new series of healthy perspectives on the present and future which gives me a life I could have never dreamed of before."

Abraham Harold Maslow, an American psychologist who was best known for creating Maslow's hierarchy of needs, a theory of psychological health predicated on fulfilling innate human needs in priority, culminating in self-actualization, echoed this theme from a slightly different angle. He noted that "In any given moment we have two options: to step forward into growth or to step back into safety." And so, with a sense of honesty about the darkness being faced (romanticizing it does no good), on the one hand, and an openness to the discovery of new possibilities, an appreciation of yet unfound or unused strengths, honoring of healthy relationships, and a development of new meaning-making, on the other, unheard of personal depth may be possible. With PTG, our perspective changes, which is a profound psychological movement in how we understand and embrace life. As naturalist and author Henry David Thoreau once noted: "The question is not what you look at but what you see."

Yet, to do so, as was noted previously, we need to honor the psychological resistances we have in facing and embracing new wisdom. It is not easy to be clear—especially in a world that often pulls us in directions that are unhelpful, and toward attitudes that certainly do not connect compassion for others with self-compassion. And so, knowing how to (1) *debrief ourselves* so we may gain greater clarity so as to become a true critical thinker with respect to our lives and (2) *becoming more mindful* by taking out time in silence and, on occasion, solitude are essential approaches worth considering. Yet, before we address these topics, let's just take a moment or two to reflect on the following questions on enhancing a healthier perspective. It is this goal that is at the source of not only PTG but also facing stress and becoming more resilient in general.

In looking at a difficult situation, Sheila A. M. Rauch and Barbara Olasov Rothbaum, in their book *Making Meaning of Difficult Experiences*, also offer the following simple components of the process that is referred to as "natural recovery":

1. You must allow yourself to think about the event and be around people, places, and situations that remind you of the event, and experience the feelings that come up without pushing them away.
2. When you think about what happened and approach/engage with event-related situations, you have the opportunity to learn that *thinking* about the event is not dangerous and also that event-related situations, people, and places are not dangerous either. You will learn that you can do what you need to do in life and that you can handle negative emotions.

I see these two steps, when one is ready, as being key not simply to traumatic events but also more importantly for the purpose of this book as being essential when we have any setback with persons in our family, circle of friends, acquaintances, or people/situations at work. They give us a chance to take what I would refer to as "side trips to wisdom." They help us embrace *possibility*—especially when we feel lost.

Anomie

A patient came in to see me for the first time. I motioned for him to sit in the chair opposite me. In response, he sat down, and then using both hands on the arms of the chair lifted himself in the air, leaving his wooden clogs on the floor while simultaneously crossing his legs under him as he sat back down. When I asked him how I could be of help, he said, "I am suffering from anomie."

Émile Durkheim, founder of modern sociology, described "anomie" as a psychological sense of worthlessness, frustration, a lack of purpose, and despair. Although I had heard the term used before, it was not one commonly used except perhaps in undergraduate textbooks. In response, I said, as I would have if he had said he was anxious, under stress, or depressed, "Why don't you describe when it began and how you have responded to it."

When he told his story, what became evident was that he was a very sensitive person who experienced life uniquely and intently but that for a while such experiences were not rewarding but disorienting. The individual sounds in his psychological orchestra were blaring, so he was unable to enjoy the meaningful overall symphony of his life. It had become simultaneously "too much" and "not enough." He was lost.

Today, following a pandemic that seemed to last forever, many feel as though they have lost their way. The media doesn't have to exaggerate or focus on the negative to overwhelm us with natural disasters, political upheaval, divisiveness, and modern medical challenges that never seem to end. Persons thrown off their normal schedule find themselves multitasking or bored, alone, and encompassed by periods of silence and solitude for which they are ill prepared. They have gone from mindlessness to emptiness because they don't know how to be mindful, reflective.

With the patient I just mentioned, I responded to his expression of anomie with a request to embark on a journey to find new meaning. I wanted him to use his sensitivity to open himself up to appreciate portals in purpose that he didn't know were there or how to open them. In today's society, the same call is now present for all of us. Many will go down the psychological and spiritual dead ends of projection, anger, and blame, or guilt and discouragement. However, today's disorientation can also open the door to intrigue about how they can live their life going forward, moment by moment. This is ideally done with:

- A new set of greater values
- Awareness—rather than denial—of personal vulnerability
- A greater understanding of the breadth and depth of true friendship
- An appreciation of how being compassionate is a "circle of grace" that helps us proceed even when, maybe *especially* when, we may be feeling completely lost

Consequently, this relationship with a new sense of meaning-making can move an individual to become a deeper and better person. A more beautiful psychological and spiritual symphony is possible when we entertain such a possibility and look for it with hope and some guidance.

Today people are more than simply physically tired. Rest can relieve that. Instead, many of us—at least at times—are psychologically and spiritually exhausted, and this requires something different in our approach. It needs a route to inner peace and wisdom that is actually dependent on the darkness we are going through in different ways now both personally and as a community—especially when one has experienced trauma or severe stress.

In contemporary society, Covid-19, for example, introduced more people to unavoidable psychological and spiritual exhaustion than ever before. The question all of us were left with is: How can we best face it and other stresses in our lives? Whereas there are many responses to this question, one of the key approaches is to have a realistic sense of the pressures you are under while being open to where it might psychologically take you. Such an approach will not only be new, but also be beneficial in ways that previously you might have considered impossible.

This attitude of openness will not lessen the pain. However, it can trim unnecessary suffering and also put us in a position to grow personally in ways that wouldn't have been possible before. In addition, with openness, honesty, and hope, there is a greater possibility that one can gain a new sense of meaning-making in life (i.e., valuing more deeply alone-time as well as unexpected greater time with family), and—in the end—allow us to enjoy the other simple gifts of life in ways we may not have before.

French Jesuit priest, scientist, theologian, philosopher, and teacher Pierre Teilhard de Chardin once quipped, "It doesn't matter if the water is hot or cold if you have to walk through it anyway." Walk through the tough times we must. However, what we learn and experience for the better, as a result of this very journey, is entirely another matter.

One of the greatest psychological and spiritual *koans* (puzzles) in life is trauma. When persons are physically attacked in war or sexually assaulted, they are certainly emotionally and spiritually violated as well. The death of a loved one and the loss of one's means of financial support can also produce a deep sense of loss and disrupt how we view the world—affecting the way we make meaning and understand, from our own vantage point, how we believe life works.

When people experience great trauma and loss in life, this must be respected as both significant and unique. However, all of us must encounter some level of trauma and loss at different points in life, and it may cause all types of difficulties. They can range from problems in intimacy and trust to self-destructive behavior, weight problems (anorexia or obesity), and even drug and alcohol abuse.

For Review and Reflection . . .

Key Themes and Questions in Welcoming Forms of Post-Traumatic Growth

- How do I honor life's fragility?
- In what ways am I mindful so less in life is missed or judged to be unworthy of examining and providing new learning?
- Do I know when to let go of the "whys" so experience of "the now"—and not just cognitively—becomes a more possible outcome?
- Have I developed a personal good self-care regimen and healing rituals in life so compassion toward myself is not simply a psychological duty but a natural expression and valuing of the full self?
- Do I recognize that we surprisingly make war with ourselves at times because of a desire to control the uncontrollable both in ourselves and our interactions with others in unrealistic ways?
- How do I appreciate the value of simplicity in the ways I view and live life, while having an intentional approach to seeking periods of silence and solitude for reflection and mindfulness?
- Do I have a willingness to face my own *koans* (life puzzles) that have no easy answers to them but require choices that will affect my life and those I interact with?
- Do I see to see the differences between "pain" (what happens to me) and "suffering" (the negative results that arise from the perspective I either unconsciously or consciously have toward this painful event)?
- Am I patient with myself and others who have gone through trauma or serious stress/loss?
- Do I remind myself that worry transforms itself into helpful concern and saves me from wasting energy when I realize what I can control . . . and what I can't!
- Do I keep in mind that letting go of what was hurtful, *when one is able to*, is beneficial. (One of Nelson Mandela's famous quotes is: "As I walked out the door toward my freedom I knew that if I did not leave all the anger, hatred, and bitterness behind, that I would still be in prison.")
- When trauma or darkness occur, which I would obviously avoid given the opportunity, and when I or others feel ready, entertaining the following question is worthwhile: How might this undesirable event open the door to profound positive change that might not have ever been considered before?

- What simple joys are appreciated even more now that I have stepped back from what has happened that was terrible and draining?
- Once my life has been changed forever because of encountering significant darkness, what psychological and spiritual detours and changes have opened me to new meaning-making as to how I see the world and myself since life was originally shattered?
- Do I appreciate the new courage that has arisen in me to entertain new possibilities in my physical, social, moral, emotional, intellectual, psychological, and spiritual approaches to life? (People describe such courage as "I can be myself, more readily go against the tide now when I feel it is wrong, embrace my emotions more freely, be willing to *un*learn what is not helpful any longer and know more deeply what it means to live a more compassionate life that includes healthy *self*-compassion.)
- Am I able to balance being both optimistic and realistic simultaneously so that I don't close my eyes to darkness and hurt but also don't inordinately focus on it to the degree that it leaves me psychologically frozen?
- Do I realize that I can't do it alone, don't feel impotent because of that, but instead feel a greater sensitivity to the value of community and my part in it so that I see the connection between altruism and resilience by appreciating the importance of *both* being selfless and the need for self-care and interpersonal support?

Tenets of New Meaning-Making

- A current basic set of assumptions will not always work; life changes, and so must our outlook.
- Loss of control, meaning, and predictability will occur at times; how we perceive this and respond accordingly is the key to personal growth and depth.
- No one wants trauma, serious stress, and sadness, but they can teach us in the long run new lifelong lessons . . . *if* we are able to let them.
- Perspective and priorities that change in response to experiencing trauma can alter one's philosophy of life in previously unforeseen, rewarding ways (i.e., a richer narrative about one's own personal life).
- Openness to and awareness of the process of growth by and in others with no preconceived expectations of need for them to undergo the

experience is essential for PTG to occur in a timely fashion. (Note that one of the best ways for us to prepare for this is to use the same reflective approach to growth in ourselves during periods of "alone-time" in silence, solitude, and mindful meditation.)

- Welcome the appearance of new positive meaning-making after trauma as something filled with potential, rather than simply a form of resistance or denial. This is especially true when there is a full recognition of the adverse nature of the event; positive meaning-making is not genuine if it involves denying or downplaying the reality that something terrible has, in fact, happened to us.

- Appreciate the value of sometimes underrated personality traits of "curiosity" and "openness" that play a significant role in determining whether PTG will be possible in ourselves.

- Explore the role of openness to forgiveness and compassion (as distinct from reconciliation or forgetting) when the timing is right.

- Appreciate that psychological researchers have offered studies on growth after trauma, but that there is much nonempirical "wisdom literature" that predates this (such as works by Frankl and Yalom, as well as on mindfulness and spiritual approaches to suffering that are both theistic and nontheistic such as Buddhism) that in the spirit of learning widely and deeply about PTG would benefit us personally, and the way we walk with others who are currently not able to access or understand this literature.

- Appreciate that PTG is *not* based simply on a positive reframing of a negative event but a *simultaneous* honoring of the undesirability/horror of it while being open to possibly unforeseeable growth that might not have occurred had the significant stress or traumatic event not happened.

- Discern between the perception of the distress experienced by us (or people we interact with) and the severity of the trauma itself since the *former* is actually of greater import in terms of impact. Our perspective on trauma or serious stress is the key.

- Fathom the importance of our perspective when we become upset at the possibility that we seem to have lost our way in life. (Daniel Boone was once reported to retort to a question as to whether given his tracking skills that he had ever gotten lost: "No. But I was bewildered once for three days.")

- Acknowledge the subtle yet crucial roles that patience and pacing play in supporting others on the journey toward PTG (as well as on our own life journey, since great stress is part of everyone's life). The lesson? Be gentle and give yourself and others plenty of time to adjust, heal, and deepen.
- Appreciate the potential place that faith, religious community, image of God, spiritual strength, and other related religious themes might have if and when they arise in your own or other people's journey after great stress has occurred because they can be either a deterrent or enhancement to the growth process.
- Discern the difference between ruminations that are constructive (i.e., help us adjust to realizing and incorporating what has happened) and deliberate and negative ones that are intrusive, as well as ones that are positive or negative, because they can have an important impact on PTG. (If our own or other's ruminations appear immediately after the trauma, this often is a natural occurrence that may eventually lead to PTG, whereas rumination that continues long after the trauma may not).

Source: Wicks, R. J., *Perspective: The Calm Within the Storm* (New York: Oxford University Press, 2014).

Questions for Consideration to Enhance a Healthier Perspective

- Do we believe when things get very tough that we may not be able to remake the world that gave birth to them, but we can remake ourselves and the way we view it in time?
- Do we see that while asking why things have occurred is natural after something terrible has happened, we will only begin to feel better once we become involved in a new meaning-making process that changes the way we see ourselves and the world we live in?
- Do we realize at a deep level that PTG isn't simply thinking positive thoughts but is instead the willingness to face fully the negative aspects of what has happened while simultaneously being open to any new ideas and signs that we are enduring the stress in different ways and even growing/deepening in a previously unimaginable fashion?

- After a trauma, loss, or significantly stressful time, are we able to express either in writing or verbally what "pops into our mind" and intrudes in ways that has us ruminating about the event since this process is often a prelude to growth and a healthy transition?
- Do we appreciate that as we try to make new sense of life (given our own worldview as to how life should be now that what we did believe has been shattered) and that this process is often an important prelude to new meaning-making and part of both coping and being open to the PTG process?
- Are we sensitive to, and do we honor the presence of, positive emotions when we are in the midst of a negative experience so that their presence isn't clouded over by the also valid negative feelings we are having?
- Do we encourage ourselves to be mindful and stay in the present with what we are experiencing, if it is possible to do so, rather than giving in all the time to the natural temptation to deny, avoid, or minimize?
- Can we simultaneously have low expectations and high hopes as to what may come of what we are going through even though it is very unpleasant and discouraging now?
- Do we seek out affirming, faithful, and wise relationships that help us in our pursuit of acceptance and arriving at new meaning in our lives after a traumatic event has happened to us by being with people whom we feel free to talk openly and process our losses, fears, angers, and confusion?
- If we are persons described as "persons of faith" or "spiritual persons," are we able to search for support from these aspects of our life and seek guides who can help us do so during such a sensitive period of transition and vulnerability?
- Do we realize from the vantage point of both the mindfulness and PTG literature that *what* has happened (the painful/traumatic event) is not as important as *how* we see it (perspective)?

Source: Wicks, R., *Perspective: The Calm Within the Storm* (New York: Oxford University Press, 2014).

Epilogue

What Can I Do Most Beautifully with My Life?

"There's no greater agony than bearing an untold story inside you."
—Maya Angelou
Author, *I Know Why the Caged Bird Sings*

"You are always one decision away from a totally different life."
—Robert Petterson
Author, *The Book of Amazing Stories*

"Compassion, tolerance, forgiveness and a sense of self-discipline
are qualities that help us lead our daily lives with a calm mind."
—Dalai Lama

It's Good to Be Lost Once in a While has explored the possibilities of living a full life by being open to new experiences. Spending our limited time on earth confined in a cognitive bubble—merely thinking about life or following the dreams of others—results in merely existing rather than truly living. To keenly experience life and embrace possibilities at different turns, we must understand the contributions that increased awareness can bring in the areas of discernment, friendship, resistance to change, letting go, mindfulness, failure and uncertainty, critical thinking and cognitive clarity, and post-traumatic growth.

Discernment . . . "That's Where the Beauty Is"

Such discernment also involves appreciating the elements of meaning-making and holding values that call us to develop ourselves fully. At the core of this spirit is a real and ongoing sense of openness. Viktor Frankl, author of *Man's Search for Meaning*, noted this value in a way only he could by proclaiming, "Live as if you were living a second time, and as though you had acted wrongly the first time."

To accomplish this, we need to avoid the three psychological dead ends: arrogance (where we project the blame on others), ignorance (where we condemn ourselves for failure and hesitation to act), and discouragement (which is the final home of egotism). Instead, we need to have a spirit of *intrigue* about ourselves and the world around us so that we can:

- See the value of learning about ourselves and becoming more and more like our true selves.
- Affirm the belief that each person—including ourselves—has a unique voice to discover and develop through reflection, discussion with a supportive circle of friends, and by focusing on talents, fears, or past training that may be holding us back from growth.
- Take risks that explore potential gifts we may not feel we possess, but which guides have reflected they see in us.
- Honor the discipline and patience necessary to build courage for experimenting with new ideas and innovative behaviors, rather than only contemplating them.
- Expand our tolerance for failure and looking foolish, recognizing that this process involves understanding ourselves, our talents, as well as our unnecessary fears and anxieties. (After all, it's silly to grimly hold onto the side of the pool when we could swim a few laps—smiling along the way.)

Giorgia Ori once told aspiring photographers, "The truth is to look where no one else is looking. That's where the beauty is." Discernment and spending time with an attitude of curiosity help us do the same with our lives. Additionally, a circle of healthy friends, with a diverse array of insightful, supportive, and inspirational voices, helps us gain and maintain a perspective on life that better uncovers and embraces possibility.

Friendship

Buddhist and former scientist Mattieu Ricard noted in his book *Happiness* that happiness doesn't simply come to those who are fortunate; instead, he emphasized that "training the mind takes time . . . a sound road map based on cultivating the conditions for genuine well-being" is necessary. However, he also added, "Everything changed when I met a few remarkable human beings who exemplified what a fulfilled human life can be." Once we have the motivation in place, one of the true conditions for learning and achievement is the support of friends, coaches, mentors, and teachers who respond to that motivation with a desire to help what is dormant inside us come alive.

For our part, we need to become more aware of those who can teach us. Some enter our lives as encouraging presences—a cheerleader. Others offer prophetic lessons, and still others help us maintain a healthy perspective by teaching us to laugh at ourselves. Finally, we need inspirational and mentoring voices to call us to be all we can be, even though we are where we are in life at this moment. These people guide us to listen carefully to ourselves so that we do not accept the "manifest content" (what we think, say, and do at the moment) as the "total content" (our potential life, as well as what we have already achieved in knowledge and accomplishment). Instead, they help us seek out nuances in what we share with them to uncover some of the "voices" guiding our lives unconsciously—especially those that make us hesitant, anxious, fearful, or willful. A reporter interviewing a 104-year-old woman asked, "And what do you think is the best thing about being 104?" She replied, "No peer pressure." Hopefully, with good friends, we won't need to wait that long!

Each true friend helps us see that our journey may not be the same as theirs. However, the music of their friendship is one of encouragement, allowing us to appreciate ourselves and, in turn, honor their gifts—even if they are different from ours. Finally, what we must realize deeply is that sages can make all the difference in our lives—if we notice their presence. Since graduating from Hahnemann Medical College in Philadelphia with my doctorate in psychology, I have been tasked with working with physicians, nurses, psychologists, psychiatrists, counselors, and social workers to help them stay psychologically afloat and prevent secondary stress. As a former U.S. Marine Corps captain, I also found myself working with members of the military because they believed I understood what they were going through and trusted me to help them take care of themselves as well.

As a result of all this, I have tried to use my experiences and insights gained from my books and presentations to help all people, so that their daily lives as helpers and healers can be more peaceful and joyous as they reach out to others in need. However, in doing this—sometimes for what seem like silly reasons—I've been pulled down. For example, once while making hospital rounds, I met a brilliant psychiatrist I knew. When she looked into my eyes, she said, "My, my, you look like you've been through a traumatic event." In response, I told her I hadn't, and I was embarrassed because I felt affected by a hurtful note from someone I didn't know, which impacted me more than I expected.

Unlike a male colleague who might have laughed off such a comment, she smiled gently and said, "This happens to all of us. We deal with terrible things—and I know you've been in Haiti, Cambodia, and even dealt with helpers from Aleppo, Syria—so you would think you and I would be immune to all of the little criticisms. However, people who negatively respond the way you indicate a person recently did to you, can sometimes catch us off-guard or push us over the psychological edge when we are feeling vulnerable from the dark times we must face with trauma victims. What we must realize, though, is that such persons are also in a tough spot themselves . . . otherwise, they wouldn't take the time to communicate such negative things. Instead, do as I do and feel sad for them as a way of helping to let the message go. They need to be helped by someone else that they trust and respect—whereas other people who are open to the help you offer really do count on you. And so, you can't afford to waste energy because your ego gets hurt. Instead, silently wish them well in your mind and feel sad that they wouldn't be grateful to you for what you try to do for them in this world filled with war and hunger. Remember what the Sufi mystic Rumi once said, 'Those who don't want to change, let them sleep.'"

As I reflect on this interaction, I believe that almost every day, we encounter sages like the psychiatrist—even if they do not have her credentials. The question is: will we have the humility to notice and learn from them?

Relationships are vital from the very first moments of our lives. The attachment literature in psychology speaks to the fundamental need for positive social relationships in our early development. Our early relationships help shape the ways we relate to others in adulthood. If we have developed successful relationship skills and are fortunate to have supportive people in our inner circles as adults, these relationships can help us feel good, safe, and complete both physically and psychologically.

Healthy relationships can benefit us in many ways—including helping us perceive the world in innovative and transformative ways. They can weaken outdated ways of thinking about ourselves and situations as we face new challenges in life. Through the information they share, the support they provide, and the meaningful encounters we experience with them, life can become more beautiful.

Having people with whom we can "simply be ourselves," process what is happening in our lives, feel a sense of worth, and receive suggestions for coping with difficulties, uncertainty, and failure—while also celebrating our successes—makes a profound difference.

Embracing possibility involves having nurturing, challenging, humorous, and inspiring forces in our lives. While encountering life anew at different stages certainly involves effort on our part, human beings are inherently interconnected. We need each other. Good friends help us discover what resiliency expert Robert Brooks calls "islands of competence." He encourages us to move from a deficit-based approach to a strength-based perspective, especially when we feel lost or struggle. As the well-known TV personality Oprah Winfrey puts it, "Lots of people want to ride with you in the limo, but what you want is someone who will take the bus with you when the limo breaks down."

Another TV personality, Mr. Rogers, put it this way:

When I was a boy and I would see scary things in the news, my mother would say to me, "Look for the helpers. You will always find people who are helping." To this day, especially in times of "disaster," I remember my mother's words and I am always comforted by realizing that there are still so many helpers—so many caring people in this world.

Overcoming Resistance to Change

In the conclusion of Adam Alter's *Anatomy of a Breakthrough*, he offers "100 Ways to Get Unstuck." (It is worth the price of the book in itself!) He introduces this material with a line that touched me deeply: "I hope you find yourself stuck only rarely and that when you do, breakthroughs aren't too far behind." I share the same feeling, which is why I chose the hopeful—and, I believe, honest—title of the book you have just read: *It's Good to Be Lost Once in a While*. All of us get lost at different times in our lives. If you never do, there may be something wrong—either you have settled for too little or you're refusing to admit to yourself the things that challenge you.

We must recognize that, for all of us who wish to live a beautiful and meaningful life now, there will be resistances and external barriers at times. In fact, the simple reality is that the more we seek to challenge ourselves, the more subtle resistances to growth and change we will uncover—resistances that others might easily overlook. Additionally, when we experience a lack of motivation or feel "stuck," if we regard these moments as challenges rather than merely obstacles, we create a natural training ground for creativity and trying new approaches. Such hindrances become signals that we need to break down the tasks at hand and understand that quitting at that point is not a sign of failure but a matter of simple common sense!

Letting Go and Mindful Reflection

In the book *Transitions*, Bridges refers to the letting-go process as "dismantling":

> Getting unplugged from your old place in the interpersonal and social world that gave you an identity is where the transition process starts, but disengagement only stops the old signals and cues from being received. It leaves untouched the life infrastructure that you've constructed in response to those signals. The disengagement can take place in a moment: "I'm leaving! We're finished! Good-bye!" But the old habits and behaviors and practices that made you feel like yourself can only be dismantled. They have to be taken apart a piece at a time.

He also recognizes that during periods of outward change and inner transition, people often find themselves in a kind of "limbo"—between what was and what might be. This state may include or be caused by disenchantment with present realities and a need to alter one's outlook. The purpose of this is to take advantage of being disoriented, so that the past is not simply repeated in different psychological or occupational disguises as a way of avoiding or quickly replacing a loss or significant change. Endings represent a form of death that, as we have previously discussed, requires a process of grieving. Because of this, such periods call for true moments of mindful reflection.

When conducted productively, reflective periods can help uncover our lesser-known signature strengths. Embracing possibility involves not only recognizing opportunities around us but, more importantly, developing untapped possibilities within our personality. Consequently, surfacing all of our talents positions us to deepen our self-awareness and be in a better place to maximize our interpersonal style. In light of this, there are questions we would do well to ask ourselves—and even journal about—to better keep a record. Some of these questions include:

- What gifts do people praise you for possessing that you may not be paying enough attention to?
- What talents are you surprised to hear others credit you with?
- Which aspects of your signature strengths bring you the most joy to express and share?
- When the following virtues or strengths are mentioned, how do you live them out in your everyday life?

> Humility reflected in a willingness to embrace *both* your gifts and growing edges
>
> Fascination in learning new things about yourself and your situation
>
> Intrigue about how to determine a healthy perspective about life
>
> Honesty and appropriate transparency with others
>
> Gentleness and generosity with others
>
> Leadership and collaborative efforts that lead to generativity in yourself and others
>
> Flexibility and the ability to laugh at yourself
>
> An interest in meaning-making and developing a rich philosophy or spirituality of life
>
> Hopefulness and optimism
>
> Self-control or self-regulation so that urges and impulses can be examined before acting upon them

In reflective periods, by taking an honest inventory of yourself—without a defensive or overly critical self-view—and remaining curious about how you are living and reacting to others and situations, it is possible to gain more fruitful insights more clearly than if we do not take the time to sit in silence and solitude. During such moments, we can understand why some gifts are not being used or are underused, and work to correct these patterns. Silent periods also allow us to see where our talents are imbalanced, revealing if we are spending too much time modeling only a few of our gifts. For example, while being a good listener is a wonderful trait, it is equally important to reflect upon and share what we have learned with others.

For this to happen, a plan to rebalance our gifts is necessary. In the example of listening, deciding when and how to act or share our knowledge, observations, and responses with specific people can be very helpful. After taking these steps, it's also important to set aside time for self-reflection and to share what we have done—along with our perspective on the results—with those we trust. This process can help solidify new wisdom and gains. By doing so, we can view both blocks and achievements in a new light, recognizing that the external and internal factors that influenced the outcomes are not overlooked.

Space and rest from an active life not only lead to greater wisdom but also provide an opportunity to renew ourselves physically, emotionally, spiritually, and intellectually. This renewal can be achieved through activities such as:

- Physically taking breaks during the day, ensuring enough hours for rest and sleep, and going for walks
- Psychologically and spiritually renewing oneself by regularly spending time in silence and solitude, and having friends or family with whom you can share your emotions so they don't remain bottled up
- Mentally engaging in reading books, underlining or writing down important points that resonate with you—this includes novels and poetry, which can often evoke feelings and insights that might not be triggered by nonfiction works
- Detaching from technology for periods during the day to create space for reflection and presence

Vietnamese Zen Master Thich Nhat Hanh, in the journals he wrote between 1962 and 1966 (*Fragrant Palm Leaves*), recognizes the value of silence and solitude as means to "heal our wounds and enjoy life deeply." He encourages us to let nature's sounds "deepen the sense of [inner] silence," to appreciate the value of "simplicity and harmony," and to uncover our "deepest longing." He emphasizes the importance of continual growth and the role we must play in the present moment, stating, "We must sew our own clothes and not just accept society's ready-made suits." He urges us to face our wrong or incomplete assumptions, open "the dark curtains of our narrow views and selfish desires," and practice mindfulness so that we can welcome moments of insight—those ambassadors of truth and messengers of reality. Nhat Hanh sees reflection, truth, healthy friendships, and compassion as vital ways to soften our own sense of self. If we do not adopt such mindful approaches to life, he warns, "We are like an artist who is frightened by her own drawings of a ghost."

We must remember, as we navigate the corners of life, that the mindful person who takes time in silence and solitude to explore the peace, joy, and meaning of this brief life—moving so quickly—is truly worth listening to. Especially when that person is ourselves. Mindfulness dissolves the life support of entrenched and often erroneous beliefs, giving us the chance to breathe in the possibility of a richer, more meaningful life—so it doesn't remain an untold story. Furthermore, the process of mindfulness is not selfish self-involvement; if practiced authentically, it will lead to sharing yourself with others in ways that are more genuine and generative than ever before, simply because you are continually becoming more of who you truly are.

And so, as the poet Rilke suggests to a novice in his *Letters to a Young Poet*:

Allow your judgments their own silent, undisturbed development, which, like all progress, must come from deep within and cannot be forced or hastened. Everything is gestation and then birthing. To let each impression and each embryo of a feeling come to completion, entirely in itself, in the dark, in the unsayable, the unconscious, beyond the reach of one's own understanding, and with deep humility and patience to wait for the hour when a new clarity is born: this alone is what it means to live as an artist: in understanding as in creating.

Mindfulness and quiet time are not meant to make us into "trainee gurus," but rather to provide the space and opportunity to truly understand the lessons of failure and uncertainty, to think critically, and even to open the door to new growth and meaning amid the darkness that everyone faces at times. In other words, time in silence and solitude, wrapped in gratitude, serves as a nourishing place that gives us direction and strength to embrace possibility—including at life's final turn.

A recently retired friend once shared with me an experience from a retreat: "There, we were invited to reflect on the people, experiences, and things in our life that give us joy. Knowing that we most likely have fewer days in front of us than are behind us, we were invited to consider how we will grieve the loss of those things we love when we step through the veil into eternity. . . . We were [also] invited to reflect on our disappointments, failings, and shame, and consider how to grieve those things . . . to imagine my father and mother standing behind me with their hands on my shoulders, and their parents and grandparents of many generations standing behind them, too. The prompt invited me to enter into a conversation with my ancestors about my life and our relationships." The great calling for him was to reflect, understand, let go, and reframe both failure and uncertainty so that they can develop us, rather than tear us down.

Failure and Uncertainty

Failure provides valuable information for uncovering egoism, discovering the need for new approaches to ourselves and life, identifying areas where we require further mentoring, understanding our expectations, and gaining insight into what makes us especially sensitive—and why. However, carefully examining our failures can be difficult because many of us tend toward self-condemnation or projecting blame onto others as a way to avoid being pulled down by self-awareness of our mistakes or shortcomings.

One way to face this challenge and strengthen our ability to appreciate our gifts and recognize our foibles is to gently laugh at ourselves. When people enjoy themselves and connect with their own natural inner beauty, they are in a strong position to tease themselves in good humor. Humor frees us to be more open with others instead of being overly protective of our public image due to unnecessary worries. When we are comfortable with—and knowledgeable about—both our gifts and our growing edges, we can relax with ourselves. As previously emphasized, when we reach this state, it's not just about us; we can also help those around us relax with themselves as well.

It's wonderful to be able to laugh at ourselves, our dark side, and our foibles. Without this capacity, there's a tendency to bury our negative traits through denial or bravado. Doing so diminishes our sensitivity to our whole self—our self-awareness and ordinariness—and, in turn, increases defensiveness toward others, enveloping us in a cognitive shell of egoism.

Honoring our ordinariness and maintaining a sense of humor go hand in hand. They create the environment needed to see ourselves honestly, without taking ourselves too seriously, and to learn how to be a welcoming presence to others without burdening ourselves with pride. The joy of being at ease with oneself is a profound and gentle gift. Without it, our interactions with others become mere chores rather than opportunities to experience wonder—even in the darkest times.

Encountering Fear

Fear of what might happen if we let go and simply embrace who we are is another reason why we may avoid exploring and experimenting in the search for our authentic, ordinary self. Pema Chödrön articulates this well in her book *When Things Fall Apart*, which has become a contemporary classic for many in the Buddhist tradition. She addresses both the desire to be true to ourselves and the fear that often arises when we move closer to the truth about different aspects of ourselves:

> Embarking on the spiritual journey is like getting into a very small boat and setting out on the ocean in search for unknown lands. With wholehearted practice comes inspiration, but sooner or later we will also encounter fear. For all we known, when we get to the horizon, we are going to drop off the edge of the world. Like all explorers, we are drawn to discover what's waiting out there without knowing yet if we have the courage to face it.

In this work, she encourages us to "stay with the shakiness" that certain encounters leave us with. She aptly notes, "Curiously enough, if we primarily try to shield ourselves from discomfort, we suffer. Yet when we don't close off and we let our hearts break, we discover our kinship with all beings." The "advantages" or "secondary gain" of avoiding self-awareness, along with resisting the understanding that full self-discovery is an ongoing, never-ending process, can be extremely costly. Conversely, when we confront our personal shortcomings and the uncertainties in life directly, we may be surprised at how easily they begin to melt away—and a new openness to gratitude for the opportunity to change can emerge. The interpersonal environments we experienced early in life and those we are in now often operate out of fear. As highlighted elsewhere in this book, fear is often presented to us when the actual danger is absent—when it is exported to us for reasons other than a real threat.

Fear is often misplaced even on a larger screen. We worry about things we needn't. In a chapter aptly titled "There's Never Been a Better Time to Be Alive" in his book *The Science of Fear*, Daniel Gardner writes:

> There are clouds on humanity's horizons, of course. If, for example, obesity turns out to be as damaging as many researchers believe it to be, and if obesity rates keep rising in rich countries, it could undermine a great deal of progress. But potential problems like this have to be kept in perspective. "You can only start worrying about overeating when you stop worrying about undereating, and for most of our history we worried about undereating," [economic historian Robert] Fogel wryly observes. Whatever challenges we face, it remains indisputably true that those living in the developed world are the safest, healthiest, and richest humans who ever lived. We are still mortal and there are many things that can kill us. Sometimes we should worry. Sometimes we should even be afraid. But we should always remember how very lucky we are to be alive *now*.

Gardner notes that fear is often a marketing tactic. Companies profit by amplifying our sense of insecurity and need, even though we live in a first-world nation where starvation is less of an issue compared to obesity. The same applies to the goals of advertising when it comes to "ordinariness" and living with a sense of simplicity. We are often lured into focusing on the superficial niceties of life, as if they were genuine needs, rather than attending to what is truly essential—both in terms of material possessions and in our identity and how others perceive us.

We need to be mindful of ourselves, especially when we sense we are taking ourselves too seriously or becoming upset that others aren't honoring us as we believe they should. It is also valuable to explore this with mentors who model ordinariness in its fullest form. When we do this, we will be better positioned to receive constructive feedback and support. Furthermore, the lessons and examples provided will help us, in turn, to model these qualities for others through our actions and in the feedback we offer when they seek it.

Today, with all the terrible events happening and the pervasive divisiveness, it often seems impossible to be well-informed, think critically, and remain clear and at peace simultaneously. Yet, when we are judicious about the relevance and amount of information we consume—and when we discern what is within our control and what isn't—it becomes possible to stay aware and maintain our sanity. But this requires a conscious effort on our part, by setting aside time and space for reflection.

Enhancing Clarity Through Critical Thinking and from Cognitive Therapy and Positive Psychology Principles

Scottish-born, British author Alain de Botton, in *A Therapeutic Journey*, offers numerous valuable lessons on the importance of clarity "from the school of life." His goal is to demonstrate philosophy's relevance to everyday life. In this volume, he highlights some of the fascinating and often overlooked factors involved in maintaining an optimally functioning mind. For example, he notes that we are constantly editing our thoughts to discern how to live a meaningful life. To do this effectively, we need to be honest with ourselves without being overly harsh in our judgments. Additionally, how we compare ourselves to others should resemble the perspective of a true friend—differentiating between unnecessary worry, which drains our energy, and reasonable concern that helps us marshal resources to deal with life's challenges, whether they involve events or people.

De Botton also commends us for being able to bracket past regrets, temper negative thinking, and recognize the value of maintaining a healthy perspective. Our view of life and the surrounding realities largely determines how we mentally color our experience. He indicates that critical thinking is helped by "an atmosphere of kindness"—one that doesn't varnish clarity but knows, after all, that we are "only human."

Humility is another key trait he underscores, as "one of the great impediments to understanding our lives properly is our automatic assumption that we already do so." This is one reason an entire chapter in *It's Good to Be Lost Once in a While* is devoted to exploring ways to more carefully examine our perceptions, understanding, and judgments. Doing so allows us to gain a clearer cognitive sense of our attitudes and positions regarding inner transitions and outer change. Appreciating how and what we think about events, challenges, and people is an ongoing process. Questioning ourselves about what is truly happening for us helps prevent our assumptions from going unchallenged—an exercise especially vital at various turning points in life—so that our thinking can continue to develop and mature. Also, that the past occurred in a specific way for us is one reality that requires examination going forward so that it can be a springboard for new, possibly enabling additional knowledge. Rather than being tethered to an old and possibly static curriculum of life developed by others, we need to seek to gain more insight to what would help us flourish. Help in this pursuit is provided by the positive psychology movement today.

Positive Psychology

Practitioners of positive psychology aim to help people rebalance their lives when they feel dissatisfied. In doing so, they assist individuals in recognizing which goals may be truly unrealistic. Setting reasonable target attitudes and behaviors does not mean settling for less. Instead, it involves clarifying the next step to enhance personal well-being from the perspective of goal-setting.

We can emulate their approach by seeking to identify the values and beliefs that motivate how we live and love. To do this, we need to be critical thinkers who elucidate the alternatives available to us; choose, of our own accord, the paths we wish to follow; and discern our choices and ethical way of living in consultation with those we trust—something emphasized in the chapter on friendship.

When interacting with others we respect, questions can then arise regarding why we value or choose to live in a certain way. Many people take their approach to life for granted without examining whether it truly reflects how they want to spend their brief time on earth. In this reflective process, both immediate actions and long-term goals can become clearer. For example, an ultimate aim might be: "I want to become more educated." To achieve this, concrete decisions could include: "I will read for twenty minutes each night" or "I will take a formal course at a local university."

When steps are taken, it becomes easier to assess how important or meaningful the overall goal truly is. Moreover, as progress is made, we gain insight into how motivated, structured, and realistic our efforts are—rather than leaving these aims as mere fantasies.

Therefore, the strength of positive psychology's orientation helps us to face change and formulate desired possibilities in ways that enable us to grow and thrive in alignment with our true potential:

- Seeking what is better and possible, rather than remaining stuck or fleeing from what is seen as undesirable

- Being realistic by formulating and taking small, specific steps toward achieving our overall goal
- Recognizing the value—such as creativity or compassion—underlying our individual, incremental progress
- Reflecting on our dominant and less-known talents, examined beliefs, progressive actions, and available resources, all of which contribute to a sense of efficacy ("I can do it!") and overall well-being
- Demonstrating a positive attitude and determination not only to navigate dark or challenging times but also to deepen our growth because of those difficulties—understanding that facing adversity can lead to new possibilities that wouldn't have been realized otherwise
- Being interested in discovering activities that are fulfilling, energizing, enjoyable, absorbing, exciting, and interesting
- Remaining attentive to cultivating a mindset of possibility and growth, rather than allowing others' fears, needs, or limited perspectives to set our perceived "glass ceiling"

Applying the Principles of Post-Traumatic Growth

During Your Own Challenging and Dark Times

The final topic discussed in this book is post-traumatic growth. This concept highlights that, even in the darkest times and most difficult moments—especially during unwanted negative experiences—possibility is seen as not only achievable but also as potentially very beneficial. As Mary Beth Werdel writes in *Night Bloomers*, "The examination of the paradox of suffering brings into focus the potential for a wiser way of moving through life, a fuller and more complex sense of well-being, and a hope of a more resilient world." Her point, like those made in the seminal work of Calhoun and Tedeschi, is that through night experiences, individuals can gain new understanding of their personal strengths, discover possibilities they never knew before, and develop a deeper sense of meaning. Post-traumatic growth helps us welcome possibility and change as never before.

Furthermore, possibility comes about more frequently and naturally when we think more clearly, forgive ourselves and others more readily, and know when to be patient or take decisive action. Cultivating these attributes allows us to learn from others and to take appropriate risks—leaving our present "magical circle" to create a world where our inner environment can thrive and deepen each day.

We also recognize that such an innovative approach to life will inevitably face resistance both internally and externally. Even when we confront these obstacles, we may find external forces working against us at times. As American author and social critic Ursula Le Guin observed: "The exercise of imagination is dangerous to those who profit from the way things are because it has the power to show that the way things are is not permanent, not universal, not necessary."

When our rich narrative is lived out authentically, it can also profoundly impact others in ways we could never have imagined. Jim Cummings, the voice of Winnie the Pooh—famous from children's literature that continues to touch us as adults—would visit sick children in this beloved voice, either in person or over the phone. On one occasion, when he visited a dying child facing cancer, the result was extraordinary. The child's mother later said, "It was the first time I saw my daughter smile in six months."

Even when we feel we have failed, our quiet impact can still be meaningful. Once, I sent copies of one of my books to a group in India, but they got lost. I felt disappointed. When I shared this feeling with the organizer there, she simply replied, "Your goodness will not be lost."

In contemplating possibilities for ourselves, it's vital to live passionately and generously. Self-interest and self-protection may bring short-term success, but they won't lead to the richness of life that only blossoms when kindness, service, justice, and fairness are present. With that spirit, the gifts and defenses in others—and ourselves—will be approached with curiosity, honesty, and openness. In doing so, the potential for a larger, more meaningful life at every stage—including the final, mysterious one—becomes clearer, bringing us greater insight and peace in the present moment as we meet our ongoing journey with hope.

By envisioning it this way, possibilities come naturally because we are always walking with them, psychologically and spiritually. Yet, this journey requires a willingness to take time for renewal, vulnerability, failure, and dealing with uncertainty. It is through these experiences that we can hear the gentle call of new and different possibilities.

It's Good to Be Lost Once in a While offers guidance from a variety of perspectives, wisdom figures, and settings. This diversity helps us to make the most of change—whether driven by external circumstances or internal developmental stages—even when everything seems dark. I am accustomed to feeling lost at times. My work and travels across the globe for my whole life have placed me among helpers and healers facing seemingly impossible situations.

I have listened to NGOs and relief workers in the midst of genocide in Rwanda, and adults in Cambodia share their stories of family members committing suicide rather than enduring continued torture under the Khmer Rouge. It surprised me, then, when I learned about children in Gaza being operated on without anesthesia, or the innocent souls in Israel haunted by memories of the Holocaust, and the ongoing violence in Africa and Ukraine—where neither Putin nor Zelensky seem eager to negotiate an end. These tragedies moved me to my emotional knees. After all, this is what I do for a living: I help helpers in the most challenging circumstances imaginable.

However, I realized that it was not just these dramatic horrors. It was also watching right-wing political and religious leaders strut around while people suffer. It seemed that kindness and acceptance of those who are different from them had been lost. Then, I leaned back mentally and suddenly thought: *Am I any better?* No. I need to start with myself, to do more to soften my attitude, and to be helpful in new ways. Will I convince my friends, family, and neighbors to change their views? Probably not. Instead, I must focus on letting negative situations soften my own attitude so that I can develop greater understanding and forgiveness, while continuing to do what I can in my corner of the world.

Final Thoughts on *Possibility*

All the material in this brief work is intended to be useful when you feel lost and want to take advantage of the possibilities present at the various turns life asks of us. However, as Nietzsche reminds us, "No one but you can build the bridge upon which you alone must cross the stream of life, no one but you alone."

Each person's choices, resistances, bold moves, and rash actions are uniquely their own. This book prompts the questions: Why not act? Why stay put? How do you face the issues of internal transitions—or choose to ignore them? As the controversial Turkish figure Harun Yahya put it: "I always wonder why birds stay in the same place when they can fly anywhere on the earth. Then I ask myself the same question."

Emphasis is placed on the daily necessity of quiet time—even if only for a few minutes. This time is not only for reflection with a spirit of curiosity but also so we don't feel compelled to quit when we simply need renewal or a fresh perspective. Restful times include changing the pace so we don't feel rushed, practicing patience so we don't act impulsively just to feel like we've done something, surrounding ourselves with friends who can verbally walk us through our options, and—most importantly—taking care of ourselves throughout the process.

The goal, of course, is to do the best thing at the right time, guided by what we discern will help us *lead a meaningful life.* As mentioned earlier, this often requires asking ourselves the right questions, such as: What would give me fulfillment right now? Why am I questioning my judgment at this moment? How am I really doing emotionally? What do I need to take the next step? What is causing my self-doubt?

If life is to be full, shifts are inevitable at various points along the way. As Virginia Woolf noted, "A self that goes on changing is a self that goes on living." Consequently, an ongoing series of small and significant acts of letting go is essential for growth. Yet, feeling that we are abandoning life or failing because we move from one phase to another is common and can hold us back.

Personal development involves more than recognizing external possibilities; it requires an openness to self-revision—one that may mean embracing uncertainty as a starting point. Imagination and creative acts are necessary if we are to fly instead of remaining perched in the cage of the status quo. External change might open the door to new journeys beyond where we are, *but* if we feel confined and must stay put, we will never seize the opportunities before us.

As the author of this book, I have written it as much for myself as for you. Every time I have walked alongside others as they humbly climbed the mountain of knowledge to meet possibility and grasp more of life's truth, joy, peace, happiness, and meaning, I realized that when we reached the summit of wisdom, I was there with them. May you find that same truth—that as you face yourself and life wholeheartedly, and approach the journey with compassion for yourself and others, you will deepen your understanding and experience of life's richness.

For Review and Reflection . . .

Questions and Activities on Friendship

And so, since friendship is so essential to meeting possibility and finding ourselves—especially when we are lost—the following questions/activities are worth reflecting upon:

- Do I have friends with whom I can simply be myself?
- What type of friends do I value most? Why do I think that is so?
- What do I feel are the main qualities of friendship?
- List and briefly describe the friends who are now in my life.
- Describe ones who are no longer alive or present to me now but who have made a positive impact on my life. Why do I think they made such a difference?
- Among my circle of friends, who are my personal heroes or role models?
- Who are the prophets in my life? In other words, who confronts me with this question: To what voices am I responding to in life?
- Who helps me to see my relationships, mission in life, and self-image more clearly? How do they accomplish this?
- Who encourages me in a genuine way through praise and a nurturing spirit?
- Who teases me into gaining a new perspective when I am too preoccupied or involved in myself?
- When I am lonely or worried, whom do I turn to for support?
- Who in my circle of friends is the best problem solver?
- Who do I know with a similar history to mine, someone who best understands what I am experiencing in my search for a meaningful life?
- Who do I most enjoy meeting with, calling, texting, or emailing?
- When and with whom do I play different (prophetic, supportive, etc.) roles as a friend? How do people receive such interactions?
- With whom do I feel I can share *absolutely everything*?

Things to Remind Yourself When Feeling Frozen or Lost

- Recognize that those you admire also faced many internal resistances to change that you may not see.
- Conserve your energy by taking time to discern what is within your control and what isn't.
- Set intermediary goals or next steps while also envisioning and drawing inspiration from a distant, broader objective.
- Understand that time spent in planning and reviewing alternatives—whether alone or in consultation with others—can actually save you time in the long run.
- Accept that not every goal is worth pursuing—sometimes, we eventually realize that a particular aim in life was simply not worth it.
- At different moments in life, take the time to note your progress and victories.
- Be aware of the tendency to hear praise softly and criticism as thunder—maintain balance and perspective.
- Recognize that obstacles to a goal can serve as opportunities for greater creativity—if you allow them to.
- When reading books (nonfiction, poetry, fiction, or works specifically about resistance to change, like *Anatomy of a Breakthrough*), take notes and review them periodically.
- Consult with members of your circle of friends—whether they are prophets, cheerleaders, critics, or inspirations—as well as outside experts, to ensure you receive fresh insights you might not consider on your own.
- In reflection, be aware of "mental cul-de-sacs," such as blaming others, condemning yourself for failure, or dwelling in disappointment—these are often the last refuge of ego. Instead, cultivate a spirit of curiosity and intrigue, a trait so natural to children but often lost with age.
- While discernment is important, sometimes it's more effective to act your way into a new perspective rather than overthinking. Taking action can transform your understanding of the task, yourself, and your life as a whole.

Key Points from *It's Good to Be Lost Once in a While*

- Uncover your own signature strengths more fully—including "quiet ones" that are rarely used or noticed.
- Understand that discomfort, failure, and uncertainty are common emotions experienced during inner transitions and external changes.
- Take time to reflect on your day, week, and year with an attitude of curiosity that avoids blaming yourself or others.
- Ensure your circle of friends includes the voices of the prophet, the cheerleader, the teaser/harasser, and the inspirational friend—all of whom encourage you to be your best self without making you feel ashamed of where you are now.
- Recognize that the more you enjoy sharing and developing your gifts with others, the more you will be inspired to discover new possibilities for improvement and practice.
- Don't hesitate to "run away" for a while to avoid burnout or turning your efforts into mere drudgery.
- Note that the quickest route isn't always a straight path; sometimes, detours teach us lessons that we wouldn't learn along our usual, "direct" psychological and behavioral journeys.
- If the opportunity arises, mentor others. It benefits them and also helps you see what you've learned about yourself and the challenges you've faced.
- Understand that every meaningful life involves mystery and ambiguity, and periods of silence and solitude are essential to let creative ideas surface within the psychological vacuum they create.
- Just like nature, honor the different turns in your day and the seasons of your life, which will sometimes require you to let go and unlearn so you can blossom through new awareness and embrace the previously unimaginable.
- Welcome the chance to change your mind as an invitation to new freedom of thought and action. People afraid to admit "I don't know" miss opportunities to learn from others and from life's lessons, especially at critical junctures.
- Seek personal meaning in what you do. Ask yourself: What would give your life a sense of worth and purpose? Society may promote power, success, and approval—or even envy—but true fulfillment comes from being generous, creating, and grateful.

- Remember that living with a sense of possibility is a reward in itself, even though moments of specific successes tend to pass quickly.
- Cultivate high, inspiring goals rather than ones that threaten or depress you—this leads to an enthusiastic, passionate life.
- Discern the difference between healthy self-awareness and concern, versus being overly preoccupied with yourself and others' reactions.
- Regularly express gratitude to those who love you—and do so often.
- Continue seeking education or personal growth in some form—whether informal or structured.
- Uncover your core principles and ensure you live according to them.
- Value tolerance, kindness, and the friendships you have.
- Appreciate the power of your perspective, ways of thinking, and understanding of life. As noted, possibility doesn't simply come to us; we must have the vision to see and approach it.
- Never stop asking questions. An inquiring mind will help you discover portals to possibilities that others might overlook.
- Maintain your physical and mental health by staying as fit as possible, including taking at least a short walk each day to enjoy exercise and fresh air.
- Value teamwork, which can help you achieve things beyond your individual capacity, and seek to learn from different styles and attitudes.
- At the end of each day or week, reflect by first examining the objective events that occurred (what happened) and then analyzing your subjective experience—how you interpreted those events and interactions cognitively, which influenced your emotional responses.

Sources

Alter, Adam. *Anatomy of a Breakthrough* (New York: Simon and Schuster, 2023).

Angelou, Maya. *I Know Why the Caged Bird Sings* (New York: Ballantine Books, 2009).

Attenborough, Richard (Ed.). *The Words of Gandhi* (New York: Morrow, 2001).

Bennet, Jessica. "Learning to Fail." *New York Times*, June 24, 2017.

Beresford, Thomas P. *Psychological Adaptive Mechanisms* (New York: Oxford University Press, 2012).

Berger, John. *Ways of Seeing* (New York: Penguin, 1990).

Berman, Jax (Compiler). *Friends: The Family We Choose* (Rye Brook, New York: Peter Pauper Press, 2015).

Braisby, Nick and Gellatly, Angus (Eds.). *Cognitive Psychology*, Second Edition (New York: Oxford University Press, 2012).

Braza, Jerry. *Moment by Moment* (Tokyo: Tuttle, 1997).

Brazier, David. *Zen Therapy* (New York: John Wiley and Sons, 1954/1995).

Bridges, William. *The Way of Transition: Embracing Life's Most Difficult Moments* (Cambridge, Massachusetts: Da Capo, 2001).

Bridges, William (with Susan Bridges). *Transitions: Making Sense of Life's Changes* (New York: Hachette, 2019).

Burns, David. *Feeling Good* (New York: New American Library, 1980).

Busch, Akiko. *Patience: Taking Time in an Age of Acceleration* (New York: Sterling, 2010).

Byrd, William. *Alone* (New York: Kodansha, 1995).

Calhoun, Lawrence G. and Tedeschi, Richard G. *Posttraumatic Growth in Clinical Practice* (New York: Routledge/Taylor Francis, 2013).

Camus, Albert. *Albert Camus' Little Book of Selected Quotes* (Independently published, 2021).

Carr, Alan. *Positive Psychology: The Science of Happiness and Human Strengths* (New York: Routledge, 2004).

Chadwick, David. *The Crooked Cucumber* (New York: Broadway, 1999).

Chodrön, Pema. *When Things Fall Apart* (Boulder, Colorado: Shambala, 2016).

Ciarrocchi, Joseph. *Why Are You Worrying?* (Mahwah, New Jersey: Paulist Press, 1995).

Conroy, Pat. *My Reading Life* (New York: Doubleday, 2010).

Corbett, Rachel. *You Must Change Your Life: The Story of Rainer Maria Rilke and Auguste Rodin* (New York: Norton, 2016).

Cousineau, Phil. *The Art of Pilgrimage* (Berkeley, California: 1998).

Cummings, e. e. *A Miscellany*, edited by George James Firmage (London: Owen, 1965).

Dalai Lama and Tutu, Desmond with Douglas Abrams. *The Book of Joy* (New York: Avery, 2016).

De Botton, Alain. *A Therapeutic Journey* (London: The School of Life, 2023).

De Mello, Anthony. *Awareness* (New York: Doubleday, 1990).

De Mello, Anthony. *One Minute Wisdom* (New York: Doubleday, 1986).

Dillard, Annie. *The Writing Life* (New York: Harper and Row, 1989).

Du Boulay, Shirley. *Beyond the Darkness* (New York: Doubleday, 1998).

Elgar, Frank J. and McGrath, Patrick J. "Self-Help Therapies for Childhood Disorders," in: Patti. L. Watkins and George. A. Clum (Eds.), *Handbook of Self-Help Therapies*, pp. 129–161 (New York: Taylor & Francis/Routledge, 2016).

Evans, Ian M. *How and Why People Change* (New York: Oxford University Press, 2013).

Farnham, Suzanne G., Gill, Joseph P., Mclean, R. Taylor, and Ward, Susan M. *Listening Hearts* (Harrisburg, Pennsylvania: Morehouse Publishing Company, 1991).

Fernández, Jordi. *Transparent Minds: A Study of Self-Knowledge* (Oxford: Oxford University Press, 2013).

Flinders, Tim (Ed.). *Henry David Thoreau: Spiritual and Prophetic Writings* (Maryknoll, New York: Orbis, 2015).

France, Peter. *Patmos* (New York: Atlantic Monthly Press, 2002).

Frankl, Viktor E. *Man's Search for Meaning* (Boston: Beacon, 2009).

Frankl, Viktor E. *Yes to Life: In Spite of Everything* (Boston: Beacon Press, 2019).

Gallagher, Winnie. *Rapt* (New York: Plume, 2009).

Gardner, Daniel. *The Science of Fear* (New York: Plume, 2009).

Georgiou, Steve Theodore. *The Way of the Dreamcatcher* (Ottawa: Novalis, 2002).

Germer, Christopher, Siegel, Ronald, and Fulton, Paul (Eds.). *Mindfulness and Psychotherapy* (New York: Guilford Press, 2005).

Godfred, Melody. *Self-Love Poetry* (Kansas City, Missouri: Andrews McMeel Publishing, 2021).

Goodhill, Ruth Marcus (Ed.). *The Wisdom of Heschel* (New York: Farrar, Straus and Giroux, 1970).

Gosetti-Ferencei, Jennifer A. *On Being and Becoming: An Existential Approach to Life* (New York: Oxford University Press, 2021).

Grant, Adam. *Hidden Potential: The Science of Achieving Greater Things* (New York: Viking, 2023).

Grumbach, Doris. *Fifty Days of Solitude* (Boston: Beacon, 1999).

Hanh, Thich Nhat. *Fragrant Palm Leaves* (New York: Paradox Press, 2020).

Harris, Judith (Ed.). *The Quotable Jung* (Princeton: Princeton University Press, 2016).

Harvey, Andrew. *Journey in Ladakh* (Boston: Houghton Mifflin Company, 1983).

Hershey, Terry. *The Power of Pause* (Chicago: Loyola Press, 2009).

Housden, Roger. *10 Poems to Change Your Life* (New York: Harmony, 2001).

Jackson, Maggie. "*How to Thrive in an Uncertain World*," Guest Essay. *New York Times*, January 13, 2024.

Jackson, Maggie. *Uncertain: The Wisdom and Wonder of Being Unsure* (Buffalo, New York: Prometheus, 2023).

James, William. *The Big Book of William James Quotes* (Independently published, 2023).

Johnson, Sandy. *The Book of Tibetan Elders* (New York: Riverhead, 1996).

Jouard, Sidney. *The Transparent Soul*, Revised Edition (New York: Van Nostrand Reinhold, 1971).

Kagge, Erling. *Silence* (New York: Pantheon Books, 2017).

Kinast, Robert L. *Let Ministry Teach: A Handbook for Theological Reflection* (Madeira Beach, Florida: Center for Theological Reflection, Undated).

King, Nathan L. *The Excellent Mind: Intellectual Virtues for Everyday Life* (New York: Oxford University Press, 2021).

Kornfield, Jack. *A Path with Heart* (New York: Bantam, 1993).

Kornfield, Jack. *The Wise Heart* (New York: Bantam, 2009).

Kottler, Jeffrey. *Change* (New York: Oxford University Press, 2014).

Kottler, Jeffrey. *On Being a Therapist*, Sixth Edition (New York: Oxford University Press, 2022).

Krishnamurti. *Life Ahead* (New York: New World Library, 1901/2005).

Langley, Kim. *Send My Roots Rain* (Brewster, Massachusetts: Paraclete Press, 2019).

Leahy, Robert. *If Only… Finding Freedom from Regret* (New York: Guilford Press, 2022).

Madigan, Steven. *Narrative Therapy* (Washington, DC: American Psychological Association Press, 2011).

Maitland, Sara. *A Book of Silence* (Berkeley, California: Counterpoint, 2008).

Matthiessen, Peter. *Nine Headed Dragon* (Boston: Shambhala, 1986).

McClain, Paula. *Circling the Sun* (New York: Ballantine, 2016).

Merton, Thomas. *Argument with the Gestapo* (New York: New Directions, 1975).

Merton, Thomas. *A Vow of Conversation* (New York: Farrar, Straus and Giroux, 1988).

Merton, Thomas. *Seven Storey Mountain* (New York: Harper One, 1999).

Merton, Thomas. *The Way of Chuang Tzu* (Boulder, Colorado: Shambala, 2004).

Merton, Thomas. *Wisdom of the Desert* (New York: New Directions, 1970).

Milne, A. A. *The Complete Tales of Winnie the Pooh* (New York: Dutton, 1996).

Mott, Michael. *The Seven Mountains of Thomas Merton* (Boston: Houghton-Mifflin, 1984).

Neff, Kristin. *Self-Compassion* (New York: Morrow, 2015).

Norris, Kathleen. *Dakota* (New York: Harper One, 2001).

Nouwen, Henri. *The Genesee Diary* (New York: Doubleday, 1975).

Nouwen, Henri. *Way of the Heart* (New York: Seabury, 1981).

Palmer, Parker. *On the Brink of Everything: Grace, Gravity and Getting Old* (Oakland, California: Berrett-Koehler, 2018).

Petterson, Robert. *The Book of Amazing Stories* (Carol Stream, Illinois: Tyndale House, 2018).

Prochnick, George. *In Pursuit of Silence* (New York: Knopf, 2011).

Rauch, Sheila A. M. and Rothbaum, Barbara O. *Making Meaning of Difficult Experiences: A Self-Guided Program* (New York: Oxford University Press, 2023).

Ricard, Matthieu. *Happiness* (New York: Little Brown/Hachette, 2006).

Rilke, Ranier Maria. *Letters to a Young Poet* (New York: Norton, 1934).

Ritter, Christiane. *A Woman in the Polar Night* (Fairbanks: University of Alaska, 2010).

Russell, Bertrand. *Bertrand Russell Quotes* (Scotts Valley, California: CreatSpace Independent Publishing Platform, 2016).

Rumi. *The Big Book of Rumi Quotes* (Independently published, 2023).

Saint-Exupéry, Antoine de. *The Little Prince* (New York: Harcourt Brace and Company, 1943).

Saint-Exupéry, Antone de. *Night Flight* (New York: Mariner Book Classics/Harper Collins, 1974).

Saint-Exupéry, Antoine de. *Wind, Sands, and Stars* (Boston: Mariner Books, 2012).

Sanford, John. *Healing and Wholeness* (Mahwah, New Jersey: Paulist Press, 1977).

Schneider, Pat. *Writing Alone and with Others* (New York: Oxford University Press, 2003).

Schoemaker, Paul. *Brilliant Mistakes* (Philadelphia: Wharton Digital Press, 2011).

Seligman, Martin. *Flourish* (New York: Atria, 2012).

Sharma, Robin. *The Monk Who Sold His Ferrari* (San Francisco: Harper San Francisco, 1999).

Solnit, Rebecca. *Hope in the Dark*, Second Edition (Chicago: Haymarket, 2016).

Steindl-Rast, David. *Gratefulness, the Heart of Prayer* (Mahwah, New Jersey: Paulist Press, 1984).

Stokes, Gillian. *Contentment* (Newburyport, Massachusetts: Red Wheel, 2002).

Storr, Anthony. *Solitude* (New York: Ballantine, 1988).

Strand, Clark. *The Wooden Bowl* (New York: Hyperion, 1998).

Sudhakar, Shiv. "People Often Overestimate Their Resilience Following Failure, Research Suggests" (New York: NBC Health News, June 10, 2024).

Tedeschi, Richard G. and Calhoun, Lawrence G. "The Posttraumatic Inventory: Measuring the Legacy of Trauma." *Journal of Traumatic Stress*, 9, 455–472, 1996.

Tedeschi, Richard G. and Calhoun, Lawrence G. *Trauma and Transformation* (Thousand Oaks, California: Sage, 1995).

Terrell, John E. *A Talent for Friendship: Rediscovery of a Remarkable Trait* (New York: Oxford University Press, 2015).

Teushkin, Joseph. *Rebbe* (New York: Harper Wave, 2014).

Turnbull, Colin. *The Forest People* (New York: Touchstone, 1987).

Vaughn, Lewis. *A Concise Guide to Critical Thinking*, Second Edition (New York: Oxford University Press, 2021).

Vonnegut, Kurt. *Piano Player* (New York: Dial, 1999).

Ware, Bonnie. *The Top Five Regrets of the Dying* (New York: Hay House, 2019).

Weiss, Andrew. *Beginning Mindfulness* (Novato, California: New World Library, 2004).

Weller, Francis. *Entering the Healing Ground* (Santa Rosa, California: Wisdom Bridge Press, 2012).

Werdel, Mary Beth. *The Paradox of Trauma and Growth in Pastoral and Spiritual Care: Night Blooming* (Lanham, Maryland: Lexington Books, 2023).

Werdel, Mary Beth and Wicks, Robert J. *Primer on Posttraumatic Growth* (Hoboken, New Jersey: Wiley, 2012).

White, Michael and Epstein, David. *Narrative Means to Therapeutic Ends* (New York: Norton, 1990).

Wicks, Robert. *Bounce: Living the Resilient Life*, Second Edition (New York: Oxford University Press, 2023).

Wicks, Robert. *Living Simply in an Anxious World* (Mahwah, New Jersey: Paulist Press, 1988).

Wicks, Robert. *Riding the Dragon* (Notre Dame, Indiana: AMP, 2022).

Wicks, Robert J. *Perspective: The Calm within the Storm* (New York: Oxford University Press, 2014).

Wicks, Robert J. *The Simple Care of a Hopeful Heart* (New York: Oxford University Press, 2021).

Wicks, Robert J. *Simple Changes* (Notre Dame, Indiana: Sorin Books, 2000).

Wicks, Robert J. *The Tao of Ordinariness: Humility and Simplicity in a Narcissistic Age* (New York: Oxford University Press, 2019).

Wicks, Robert J. *Touching the Holy: Ordinariness, Self-Esteem, and Friendship* (Notre Dame, Indiana: Sorin Books, 1992).

Williams, Redford. *Life Skills* (New York: Crown, 1998).

Yen, Sheng. *Footprints in the Snow* (New York: Harmony, 2008).

Permissions

I am grateful for the following permissions from Oxford University Press to excerpt, adapt, and update previously copyrighted material from:

Wicks, Robert J. *Bounce*, Second Edition (New York: Oxford University Press, 2023).
Wicks, Robert J. *The Simple Care of a Hopeful Heart* (New York: Oxford University Press, 2021).
Wicks, Robert J. *The Tao of Ordinariness* (New York: Oxford University Press, 2019).
Wicks, Robert J. *Night Call: Embracing Compassion and Hope in a Troubled World* (New York: Oxford University Press, 2018).
Wicks, Robert J. *Perspective: The Calm Within the Storm* (New York: Oxford University Press, 2014).

Cartoon in the front of the book is included with the permission of: Robert Leighton/The New Yorker Collection/The Cartoon Bank

About the Author

Dr. Robert Wicks has spoken on his major areas of expertise—resilience, self-care, the prevention of *secondary* stress (the pressures encountered in reaching out to others), and the integration of psychology and classic spirituality—on Capitol Hill to members of Congress and their chiefs of staff, led a course in resilience in Beirut for relief workers brought there from Aleppo, Syria, for a conference with him, and has spoken at Johns Hopkins School of Medicine, the U.S. Air Force Academy, the Mayo Clinic, and the North American Aerospace Defense Command, the Defense Intelligence Agency, Boston's Children's Hospital, Harvard Divinity School, Yale School of Nursing, Princeton Theological Seminary, and to members of the NATO Intelligence Fusion Center in England. He has also spoken at the Boston Public Library's commemoration of the Boston Marathon bombing, addressed 10,000 educators in the Air Canada Arena in Toronto, and spoken to the U.S. Army Medical Command. Additionally, he was the opening keynote speaker to 1,500 physicians for the American Medical Directors Association, and he has spoken at the FBI and New York City Police academies, and he has addressed caregivers in 20 different countries, including China, Vietnam, India, Thailand, Haiti, Northern Ireland, Hungary, Guatemala, Malta, New Zealand, Australia, France, England, and South Africa.

For over 45 years, he has been called upon by individuals and groups experiencing great stress, anxiety, and confusion to speak calm into chaos. Dr. Wicks received his doctorate in psychology from Hahnemann Medical College, is professor emeritus at Loyola University Maryland, and was on the faculty of Bryn Mawr College's Graduate School of Social Work and Social Research. He has taught in universities and professional schools of psychology, medicine, nursing, theology, education, and social work. In 2003, he was the commencement speaker for Wright State School of Medicine in Dayton, Ohio, and in 2005, was both visiting scholar and the commencement speaker at Stritch School of Medicine in Chicago. He was also the commencement speaker at, and the recipient of honorary doctorates from, Georgian Court, Caldwell, and Marywood universities.

In 1994, he was responsible for the psychological debriefing of NGOs and relief workers evacuated from Rwanda during the genocide there. In 1993 and again in 2001, he worked in Cambodia with professionals from the English-speaking community who were there supporting the Khmer people in rebuilding their nation following years of terror and torture. In 2006, he also delivered presentations on self-care at the National Naval Medical Center in Bethesda, Maryland, and Walter Reed Army Hospital to healthcare professionals responsible for Iraq and Afghan war veterans. More recently, he addressed U.S. Army healthcare professionals returning from Africa after assisting during the Ebola crisis.

Dr. Wicks has published over 50 books for both professionals and the general public, including the bestselling *Riding the Dragon*. His latest two books from Oxford University Press for the general public are *The Simple Care of a Hopeful Heart: Mentoring Yourself in Difficult Times* and the second edition of *Bounce: Living the Resilient Life*. His books for professionals include *Overcoming Secondary Stress in Medical and Nursing Practice* (second edition, with Gloria Donnelly) and *The Resilient Clinician* (second edition, with Mary Beth Werdel). He is also a coauthor of *A Primer on Posttraumatic Growth* and senior co-editor of *Clinician's Guide to Self-Renewal*. Dr. Wicks has received the first annual Alumni Award for Excellence in Professional Psychology from Widener University and is also the recipient of the Humanitarian of the Year Award from the American Counseling Association's Division on Spirituality, Ethics, and Religious Values in Counseling.

Index

For the benefit of digital users, indexed terms that span two pages (e.g., 52–53) may, on occasion, appear on only one of those pages.

A Chan, 166
Ackerman, Diane, 116
action
  concern over, 19
  discernment and, 8, 24–25, 27, 29, 33, 40–41, 183
  failure and, 118
  mindfulness and, 6, 139, 140
  negative, 80–81
  nonviolence and, 46
  for others, 174, 182, 240
  possibility and, 8, 47
  resistance to change, 64, 67–70, 72–73, 80–81
  self-questioning of, 92–93
Alain (French philosopher), 113
all or nothing thinking, 198
alone time, 128–139
Alter, Adam, 31–32, 43, 183–184, 233
Anatomy of a Breakthrough (Alter), 183, 233
The Anatomy of a Breakthrough (Alter), 31–32, 43
Angelou, Maya, 215–216, 229
anomie, 221–223
arrogance, 78–79, 168–169, 197, 230
authentic selves, 16–17, 128–129
awakening, 2–3, 8, 106, 110, 131, 141, 148, 160, 171
awareness. *see also* self-awareness
  of agendas, 194–195
  discernment and, 25
  failure and, 179, 184–185
  of feelings, 24
  of friendship, 39–40, 44
  mindfulness and, 139–143, 147–148, 152–156, 160
  of mortality, 56
  perseverance and, 29, 32
  of possibility, 80–81, 103, 105, 167–169, 173
  post-traumatic growth and, 213, 217–218, 222

  prophets and, 47
  resistance to change, 130
  self-questioning of, 23, 93, 94
  of talent, 22
Awareness (DeMello), 5

Baez, Joan, 50
Baldwin, James, 10
Banayan, Alex, 215–216
Beginning Mindfulness (Weiss), 132
Bennett, Jessica, 178
Berger, John, 107
Beyond the Darkness (du Boulay), 87
blame
  friends and, 42, 48
  resistance to change, 64, 67–68, 71, 77–81, 83–84, 92, 94
  self-blame, 71, 78
The Book of Amazing Stories (Peterson), 11
The Book of Joy (Dalai Lama and Tutu and Abrams), 53
A Book of Silence (Maitland), 126–127, 144
Braza, Jerry, 139
Bridges, William, 65–66, 119, 234
Brooks, Robert, 18, 52, 233
Buddha/Buddhism
  failure and, 181
  fear and, 239
  friendship and, 53, 230–231
  introduction to, 11
  mindfulness in, 124, 128, 130–131, 138–139, 145
  possibility and, 98–100, 106, 116
  resistance to change, 76, 78, 79, 84, 86
Burns, David, 198
Busch, Akiko, 30
Byrd, William, 129

Camus, Albert, 1–2, 172, 207, 215
careful discernment. *see* discernment
Chadwick, David, 127

Chah, Achaan, 143
change in life. *see also* resistance to change
    friendship and, 46–47
    introduction to, 4–6
    openness to, 4–7
    positive, 66, 215
    psychological seeds of, 6–10
    self-change, 76
    welcoming, 101–104
Change (Kottler), 66
Chardin, Pierre Teilhard de, 223
the cheerleader in friendship, 47–50
Chödrön, Pema, 181, 239
Christianity, 86, 99, 108
Ciarrocchi, Joseph, 200
Circling the Sun (McClain), 173
clarity
    awareness of agendas, 194–195, 201–202
    cognitive, 58, 197–199, 229
    compassion and, 197, 202
    concern and, 200–201
    critical thinking and, 58, 195–197, 201–202,
        229, 241–242
    discernment and, 9, 90–91
    fear and, 195
    humility and, 186
    introduction to, 193
    mindfulness and, 193
    motivation and, 195–196, 198–199, 201, 202
    positive psychology and, 241–242
    possibility and, 103, 113, 115, 118
    resilience and, 92
    resistance to change, 79–81, 90–93
    self-questioning and, 204–205
    self-talk and, 197–199
    talent and, 201–202
    willingness and, 195–196, 203
    worrying and, 200–201
Coelho, Paul, 69
Coffin, William Sloane, 166
cognitive clarity, 58, 197–199, 229. *see also*
        clarity
cognitive dissonance, 193
compassion
    clarity and, 197, 202
    discernment and, 15–16, 33
    failure and, 173–175, 177–178
    friendship and, 46, 49, 56–59
    meaning in life, 10–11
    mindfulness and, 126, 134, 140, 152,
        160–163, 229, 236–237
    possibility and, 102, 104, 118

post-traumatic growth and, 213–214, 220,
    222–223
resistance and, 81–82, 85
Concise Guide to Critical Thinking
        (Vaughn), 196
Confucius, 63
Conroy, Pat, 52
Contentment: Wisdom from Around the World
        (Stokes), 145
Corbett, Rachel, 184
Cousineau, Phil, 98–99
creativity, 186–187
critical thinking
    clarity and, 58, 195–197, 201–202, 229,
        241–242
    failure and, 186–187
    goals of, 201–202
    introduction to, 7, 11
    overview of, 195–197
    self-questioning and, 90–92, 184–185, 189,
        203, 205
    talent and, 195–196
cummings, e. e., 16–17
Cummings, Jim, 244

Dakota (Norris), 165–166
Dalai Lama (14th), 53–54, 229
De Botton, Alain, 241–242
decision-making in friendship, 41–43
defensiveness in resistance to change, 64, 71,
        74–75, 77–78, 80–81
DeMello, Anthony, 5, 44, 64, 110
despair, 113, 156, 201, 211, 212, 221
Dillard, Annie, 82
discernment
    action and, 8, 24–25, 27, 29, 33, 40–41, 183
    awareness and, 25
    careful process of, 15–17, 19, 22–26, 40–42
    clarity and, 9, 90–91
    compassion and, 15–16, 33
    control and, 240–241, 248
    defined, 15–16
    fear and, 15–16, 27
    listening and, 9, 40–44
    for meaningful life, 246
    mindfulness and, 7
    overview of, 229–230
    perseverance and patience, 29–32
    positive psychology and, 22–26, 242
    self-questioning and, 2, 27–29, 33–35,
        184–185
    spiritual, 184–185, 188

with trauma, 223
unlearning and, 15–16
discouragement, 10, 30, 68, 83–85, 96,
    113–114, 137–138, 154–155, 198, 230
Dostoevsky, Fyodor, 97–98
du Boulay, Shirley, 87
Durkheim, Émile, 221

Edison, Thomas Alva, 44
Emerson, Ralph Waldo, 97–98
emotional reasoning, 198
energy release, 142–143
Epston, Dave, 111
Evans, Ian, 44, 67
examination process, 2, 76, 168, 205, 241–242
The Excellent Mind (King), 196
external change, 1–2, 31, 56, 65, 88, 184, 246,
    249–250
extra-ordinariness, 17–22

failure
    awareness and, 179, 184–185
    Buddhism and, 53, 230–231
    compassion and, 173–175, 177–178
    creativity and, 186–187
    critical thinking and, 186–187
    dealing with, 165–180
    fear and, 168–170, 179, 181–182
    friendship and, 50
    intrigue and, 170–171, 187, 189–191
    introduction to, 165
    knowledge and, 11
    motivation and, 18, 171–173, 183
    perspectives on, 182–185
    possibility of, 167–169, 174, 183, 185
    resilience and, 18, 167, 173–174, 179, 189
    self-questioning and, 188–191
    talent and, 177, 183
    uncertainty and, 185–187, 191, 195,
        238–239
fear
    Buddhism and, 239
    clarity and, 195
    discernment and, 15–16, 27
    encountering, 239–241
    failure and, 168–170, 179, 181–182
    friendships and, 40, 45–47, 53
    of letting go, 3
    mindfulness and, 127, 130–131, 150, 156
    of possibility, 98–99, 115, 117
    resistance to change, 64, 67, 68, 77, 90, 94
    of unknown, 127, 205

unnecessary, 15–16, 19, 27, 45–46, 230
    worry and, 200
Feeling Good (Burns), 198
Fogel, Robert, 240
France, Peter, 128
Frank, Anne, 214
Frankl, Victor, 10, 56–59, 145, 218, 229–230
friendship
    awareness of, 39–40, 44
    change in life and, 46–47
    the cheerleader in, 47–50
    compassion and, 46, 49, 56–59
    decision-making and, 41–43
    examples of, 39–41
    fear and, 40, 45–47, 53
    the harasser in, 50–52
    importance of, 43–46
    inspiration from, 52
    mentors and, 52–56
    overview of, 230–233
    persons of possibility, 56–59
    the prophet in, 46–47
    resilience and, 233
    self-awareness and, 51, 55
    self-questioning of, 247
    social connectedness and, 42, 44–45
    talent and, 37–39

Gallagher, Winnifred, 31
Gandhi, Mohandas, 46
Gardner, Daniel, 181–182, 240
Georgiou, Steve, 55
Germer, Chris, 139–140
gift-giving, 8
Godfred, Melody, 165
Goodhill, Ruth Marcus, 107
Gosetti-Ferencei, Jennifer Anna, 153, 196
Grant, Adam, 9, 52–53, 182–183
Grumbach, Doris, 130
guilt, 20, 70–71, 78, 82, 113–114, 198, 212,
    215, 222

Happiness (Ricard), 11, 57–59, 230–231
the harasser in friendship, 50–52
Harvey, Andrew, 54
Haydn, Franz Joseph, 152–153
Healing and Wholeness (Sanford), 20
Hebbel, Christian, 10
helplessness, 11, 70–71, 103, 113, 137–138,
    212, 216
Heschel, Abraham Joshua, 107–108

Hidden Potential: The Science of Achieving Great Things (Grant), 182–183
Hidden Potential (Grant), 9, 52–53
Hope in the Dark (Solnit), 185
hopelessness, 70–71, 82, 96
Horowitz, Vladimir, 54
Housden, Roger, 71, 73
How and Why People Change (Evans), 44, 67
humility
    being wrong and, 168–169
    clarity and, 186, 196, 197
    De Botton on, 241–242
    as element of wisdom, 11, 92, 108, 189, 197, 202, 205
    King on, 196–197
    knowledge and, 7–8, 201–202
    lack of, 37
    letting go and, 234–235
    mentor and, 53, 58–59
    mindfulness and, 58, 156, 160
    ordinariness and, 17
    resilience and, 26
    Rilke on, 237
    talent and, 17

If Only . . . Finding Freedom from Regret (Leahy), 118
ignorance, 21, 25–26, 66, 78–79, 138–139, 230, 245
In A Path with Heart (Kornfield), 143
inner freedom
    friendship and, 58
    possibility and, 99–101, 103–106, 108–110
    resistance to change, 74, 87–88, 94
inner transitions, 1–3, 31, 184, 234, 241–242, 249–250
innovation, 19, 92, 130, 136, 189, 230, 232–233, 244
In Pursuit of Silence: Listening for Meaning in a World of Noise (Prochnik), 146
intrigue
    change in life, 4–5
    clarity and, 201–202
    failure and, 170–171, 187, 189–191
    meaning-making and, 230
    mindfulness and, 141, 156–160
    ordinariness and, 19–20
    overview of, 78–79
    positive psychology and, 23
    post-traumatic growth and, 215, 222
    self-questioning and, 92, 95–96
    talent and, 230

Jackson, Maggie, 185–186, 196
James, Erwin, 128–129
James, William, 72
John XXIII, Pope, 170
Journey in Ladakh (Harvey), 54
Joyce, James, 123
Jung, Carl, 32, 47, 63, 67, 123, 168

kenosis, 11, 99–101, 114–115
Kierkegaard, Søren, 153
King, Martin Luther, Jr., 46
King, Nathan, 196–197
Kipling, Joseph Rudyard, 15, 132–133
knowledge
    failure and, 11
    humility and, 7–8, 201–202
    meaningful life and, 1
    possibility and, 103
koans (life puzzles), 156, 223
Koellhoffer, Christopher, 8
Kornfield, Jack, 84, 109–110, 132, 143, 148
Kottler, Jeffrey, 66, 175
Krishnamurti, Jiddu, 2, 67, 193
Kübler-Ross, Elizabeth, 10

Lamotte, Anne, 2–3
Lao Tzu, 98, 100
Lawrence, D. H., 3–4
Lax, Robert, 55
Leahy, Robert, 118
"Learning to Fail" (Bennett), 178
Le Guin, Ursula, 244
Letters to a Young Poet (Rilke), 31, 199, 237
letting go
    fear of, 3
    humility and, 234–235
    introduction to, 3–4, 9, 11
    mindful reflection and, 234–238
    possibility and, 99–103, 106–110
Lincoln, Abraham, 44
love in resistance to change, 79–81

Madigan, Stephen, 112–113
Maitland, Sara, 126–127, 131, 143–144
Making Meaning of Difficult Experiences (Rauch and Rothbaum), 221
Mandela, Nelson, 12
Man's Search for Meaning (Frankl), 10, 56–59, 145, 218, 229–230
Marley, Bob, 6
Maslow, Abraham Harold, 220
Matlock, Erin, 38

Matthiessen, Peter, 114, 124
McClain, Paula, 173
Mead, Margaret, 104
meaningful life
    compassion and, 10–11
    discernment for, 246
    Frankl on, 10, 56–59, 145, 218, 229–230
    knowledge and, 1
    leading of, 10–12
    search for, 10–11, 56, 116, 145, 201–202,
        218, 229–230
meaning-making, 28, 193, 212, 216, 218–223,
    234–235
Meaning of Difficult Experiences (Rauch and
    Rothbaum), 42
mental filter, 198
mentors/mentorship
    friendship and, 52–56
    humility and, 53, 58–59
    resistance to change, 79
Merton, Thomas, 19–20, 39, 50, 63, 114, 135,
    167, 178, 182
Millman, Lawrence, 129, 149
Milne, A. A., 1
mindfulness
    action and, 6, 139, 140
    alone time and, 128–139
    in Buddhism, 124, 128, 130–131, 138–139,
        145
    clarity and, 193
    compassion and, 126, 134, 140, 152,
        160–163, 229, 236–237
    complete practice of, 148–149
    discernment and, 7
    experiences of, 156
    fear and, 127, 130–131, 150, 156
    healthy perspective on, 160
    intrigue and, 141, 156–160
    introduction to, 123–128
    letting go and, 234–238
    meditation approaches, 147–148
    positive movements in, 160
    red flags of, 158
    releasing energy, 142–143
    resilience and, 134, 137
    retreats for, 149–151
    silence and, 132–135, 152–155, 236–237
    solitude and, 132–135, 140–146, 149–151,
        236–237
    talent and, 136
    time and space for, 146–147
    true awareness and, 139–140
    willingness and, 123, 127, 132, 141, 156
The Mindful Path to Self-Compassion
    (Germer), 140
mindful reflection, 234–238
mindlessness, 125–126, 140–141, 154–155,
    158, 222
Monet, Claude, 152–153
The Monk Who Sold His Ferrari (Sharma), 28
motivation
    clarity and, 195–196, 198–199, 201, 202
    failure and, 18, 171–173, 183
    friends and, 16–17
    introduction to, 8
    love and, 48
    mindfulness and, 146
    positive psychology and, 230–231, 242
    resistance to change, 63–64, 75, 77
My Reading Life (Conroy), 52

narrative therapy, 111–113, 121
negative emotions, 40, 75–76, 91, 100, 172,
    195–196, 198, 201–202, 204, 212–213, 221
negative thinking, 198–199, 241
new experiences, 3–4, 90, 105, 229
Niebuhr, Reinhold, 54, 178
Nietzsche, Friedrich, 53, 214–215
Night Bloomers (Werdel), 243
Nine-Headed Dragon River
    (Matthiessen), 114, 124
Norris, Kathleen, 165–166
not knowing, 2–3, 193
Nouwen, Henri, 43, 126, 133–134

On Being and Becoming
    (Gosetti-Ferencei), 153, 196
One Minute Wisdom (DeMello), 44, 64, 110
On the Brink of Everything (Palmer), 27
openness
    to change, 4–7, 111–113
    to gift-giving, 8
    possibility and, 111–113
    post-traumatic growth and, 207, 209,
        212–215, 217–220, 222–223
    in resistance to change, 63, 65, 67–69,
        71–80, 84, 85–86, 88, 90, 94
    talent and, 37–38
    willingness to meet, 4–6
ordinariness
    exploration of, 21
    extra-ordinariness and, 17–22
    humility and, 17

ordinary self/ordinary selves, 20–21, 54,
   126–127, 130, 131, 156, 180–181, 239
overgeneralization, 198

Palmer, Parker, 27, 111
*The Paradox of Trauma and Growth in Pastoral
   and Spiritual Care* (Werdel), 207
Pasteur, Louis, 98
A Path with Heart (Kornfield), 109, 148
patience. *see* perseverance and patience
Patience: Taking Time in an Age of Acceleration
   (Busch), 30
Patmos: A Place of Healing (France), 128
Patterson, James, 8
Percy, Walker, 126
perseverance and patience, 29–32, 215–216
personal growth, 28, 51–52, 78
personalization, 8, 177, 198
Petterson, Robert, 11, 229
The Piano Player (Vonnegut), 27
pilgrimage, 98–101, 103–104
positive change, 66, 215
positive experiences, 198
positive psychology
   clarity and, 241–242
   defined, 21
   discernment and, 22–26, 242
   intrigue and, 23
   overview of, 22–26, 242–243
   resilience and, 25–26
possibility
   action and, 8, 47
   awareness of, 80–81, 103, 105, 167–169, 173
   Buddhism and, 98–100, 106, 116
   clarity and, 103, 113, 115, 118
   compassion and, 102, 104, 118
   emotional darkness and, 113–115
   of failure, 167–169, 174, 183, 185
   fear of, 98–99, 115, 117
   field notes and, 103–106
   friendship in, 117
   grieving and, 115–118
   habits and, 99–102, 116
   honesty and, 101–103
   inner freedom and, 99–101, 103–106,
      108–110
   introduction to, 8, 97–99
   kenosis and, 11, 99–101, 114–115
   knowledge and, 103
   letting go and, 99–103, 106–110
   memory of self, 109–113
   narrative therapy and, 111–113, 121

openness to change, 111–113
   overview of, 245–246
   pilgrimage and, 98–101, 103–104
   psychological seeds of, 8
   resilience and, 56
   resistance to change, 63–67, 71–74, 80, 81,
      86, 88–89
   Ricard on, 57–59
   self-questioning and, 102
   transitions and, 118–120
   welcoming change, 101–104
   willingness in, 97–101, 106, 108–109, 117
post-traumatic growth (PTG)
   anomie and, 221–223
   awareness and, 213, 217–218, 222
   compassion and, 213–214, 220, 222–223
   healthy perspective on, 227
   intrigue and, 215, 222
   introduction to, 207–212
   meaning-making and, 212, 216, 218–223
   new perspective on, 216–218
   openness and, 207, 209, 212–215, 217–220,
      222–223
   overview of, 212–215
   patience, timing, and
      perseverance, 215–216
   principles of, 243–245
   resilience and, 214–218, 220, 243
   self-questioning and, 223
Pound, Ezra, 126–127
The Power of Pause (Hershey), 110
Prather, Hugh, 144
Prochnik, George, 146
progress, 3, 9, 64, 69–70, 81, 94, 96, 183, 186,
   240, 242
the prophet in friendship, 46–47

Rapt: Attention and the Focused Life
   (Gallagher), 31
Rauch, Sheila A. M., 42, 221
resilience
   clarity and, 92
   decision-making and, 41
   failure and, 18, 167, 173–174, 179, 189
   friendship and, 233
   humility and, 26
   mindfulness and, 134, 137
   positive psychology and, 25–26
   possibility and, 56
   post-traumatic growth and, 214–218, 220,
      243
   resistance to change, 25–26

resistance to change
    action and, 64, 67–70, 72–73, 80–81
    arrogance and ignorance, 78–79
    awareness and, 130
    being fed up, 76–77
    blame and, 64, 67–68, 71, 77–81, 83–84, 92, 94
    clarity and, 79–81, 90–93
    compassion and, 81–82, 85
    defensiveness and, 64, 71, 74–75, 77–78, 80–81
    fear and, 64, 67, 68, 77, 90, 94
    inner freedom and, 74, 87–88, 94
    introduction to, 7, 11, 63–64
    love and, 79–81
    openness in, 63, 65, 67–69, 71–80, 84, 85–86, 88, 90, 94
    overcoming, 233–234
    overview of, 65–76, 229, 233–234, 248
    possibility in, 63–67, 71–74, 80, 81, 86, 88–89
    psychology of, 88–89
    resilience and, 25–26
    role models and, 86–88
    self-awareness, 64, 74–76, 80–81
    self-questioning and, 67, 74–75, 90–96
    structured reflection, 82–85
    unwillingness, 66
    willingness, 69–71, 74–76, 80, 81, 84, 85, 95
Ricard, Matthieu, 11, 57–59, 127, 230–231
Rilke, Rainer Maria, 31, 151, 184, 199, 237
Ritter, Christine, 129, 149
role models in resistance to change, 86–88
Romero, Oscar, 207
Rothbaum, Barbara Olasov, 42, 221
Rumi, 25, 39–40, 232

Saint-Exupéry, Antoine de, 165, 217
Sanford, John, 20
Schneerson, Rebbe Menachem, 55–56
Schneider, Pat, 20
Schoemaker, Paul J. H., 165, 168–169
The Science of Fear (Gardner), 240
search for meaning, 10–11, 56, 116, 145, 201–202, 218, 229–230
secondary stress, 25, 177–178, 208, 209–210, 231
self-awareness
    friendship and, 51, 55
    resistance to change, 64, 74–76, 80–81
    talent and, 19–20, 22, 234–235
self-blame, 71, 78

self-care, 25, 39, 41–42, 50–51, 137, 195
self-change, 76
self-condemnation, 42, 78, 80, 141, 168, 180, 238
self-doubt, 15–16, 27, 246
self-esteem, 41
self-examination, 76, 168
self-interest, 15–16, 25–26, 58, 69–70, 92, 189, 202, 244
self-protection, 244
self-questioning
    of awareness, 23, 93, 94
    clarity and, 204–205
    critical thinking and, 203
    discernment and, 2, 27–29, 33–35, 184–185
    failure and, 188–191
    friendship, 247
    possibility and, 102
    post-traumatic growth and, 223
    resistance to change, 67, 74–75, 90–96
    sense of self and, 21
    talent and, 34
self-talk, 91, 121, 160, 188, 197–199, 204
self-understanding, 41, 51–52, 54, 75–76, 104–105, 152, 199
Seligman, Martin, 21
sense of self, 4–5, 19–22, 53, 102, 104–105, 111, 166–167, 172–173, 236–237
The Seven Storey Mountain (Merton), 19, 63
Sewall, Richard, 166
Sharma, Robin, 28
Sheng Yen, 70
shortcomings, 17–18, 34, 52, 180, 238–239
"should" statements, 198
silence, 132–135, 152–155, 236–237. *see also* solitude
social connectedness, 42, 44–45
solitude, 132–135, 140–146, 149–155, 236–237. *see also* silence
Solnit, Rebecca, 185
spiritual wisdom, 7, 43, 76
stage of life, 22–23, 27, 30, 37–38, 113, 179
Stokes, Gillian, 145
Storr, Edwin, 129–130, 135–136
structured reflection, 82–85
Sudhakar, Shiv, 186
Suzuki, Shunryu, 53, 63, 127

talent
    awareness of, 22
    challenges to, 37–38, 172–173
    clarity and, 201–202

talent (*Continued*)
    concern and, 201
    critical thinking and, 195–196
    failure and, 177, 183
    feedback on, 95
    friendship and, 37–39
    humility and, 17
    intrigue and, 230
    introduction to, 8
    mentoring and, 37
    mindfulness and, 136
    narrative therapy and, 121
    positive psychology and, 22–23
    role models and, 87
    self-awareness and, 19–20, 22, 234–235
    self-questioning and, 34
10 Poems to Change Your Life (Housden), 71
A Therapeutic Journey (De Botton), 241
The Science of Fear (Gardner), 181
Thich Nhat Hanh, 154–155, 236–237
Thoreau, Henry David, 46, 144, 149, 220
tolerance, 19, 21, 66, 168–169, 183, 186–187,
    230, 249–250
Tolle, Eckhart, 193
The Top Five Regrets of the Dying (Ware), 28
toughness/tough times, 10, 20, 39, 80, 81,
    177–178, 207, 214–215, 223
Transitions (Bridges), 65–66, 119, 234
true awareness, 139–140
Tubman, Harriet, 114
Turnbull, Colin, 104
Tutu, Desmond, 17, 28
Twain, Mark, 199

Ullman, Liv, 111
Uncertain (Jackson), 185–186
uncertainty
    Alter on, 183
    coping with, 233, 239
    failure and, 185–187, 191, 195, 238–239
    healthy perspective on, 93, 246, 249–250
    introduction to, 4–7, 9, 11
    Jackson on, 185–186, 196
    Lao Tzu on, 98
    mindfulness and, 237
    new experiences and, 229, 244
    Ricard on, 57
    self-questions about, 2, 191, 204, 212
    will to meaning, 56
unexpected experiences, 3, 92, 119, 132, 158,
    186–189, 205, 215, 218–219, 223
unlearning
    discernment and, 15–16
    introduction to, 4–7, 9, 11
    pilgrimage attitude and, 99
    resistance to, 89, 196
    self-awareness and, 74, 249–250
    willingness to, 1, 3, 108, 123, 141, 156, 203,
        223
unnecessary fears, 15–16, 19, 27, 45–46, 230

Vaughn, Lewis, 196
Vonnegut, Kurt, 27, 50
A Vow of Conversation (Merton), 20, 135
vulnerability, 17, 37–38, 56, 76, 116, 172, 222,
    232

Ware, Bonnie, 28
The Way of Chuang Tzu (Merton), 167
The Way of the Dreamcatcher (Georgiou), 55
The Way of the Heart (Nouwen), 134
Ways of Seeing (Berger), 107
Weiss, Andrew, 132
Weller, Francis, 116–117
Werdel, Mary Beth, 207, 214, 243
When Things Fall Apart (Chödrön), 239
White, Michael, 111
Why Are You Worrying (Ciarrocchi), 200
Wiesel, Elie, 55–56
Wilde, Oscar, 207
Williams, Redford, 43
willingness
    clarity and, 195–196, 203
    mindfulness and, 123, 127, 132, 141, 156
    openness, 4–6
    in possibility, 97–101, 106, 108–109, 117
    resistance to change, 69–71, 74–76, 80, 81,
        84, 85, 95
    in unlearning, 1, 3, 108, 123, 141, 156, 203,
        223
Winfrey, Oprah, 233
Winnicott, Donald, 129–130, 135–136
wisdom
    humility as element, 11, 92, 108, 189, 197,
        202, 205
    post-traumatic growth and, 207–216, 223
    spiritual, 7, 43, 76
The Wisdom of Heschel (Goodhill), 107
A Woman in the Polar Night (Ritter), 129, 149
Woolf, Virginia, 123, 144, 246
Writing Alone and With Others (Schneider), 20
The Writing Life (Dillard), 82

Yasutani-Roshi, 124
Yes to Life (Frankl), 56